The Ministry of Guidance Invites You to Not Stay

The Ministry of Guidance Invites You to Not Stay

An American Family in Iran

HOOMAN MAJD

ALLEN LANE
an imprint of
PENGUIN BOOKS

ALLEN LANE

Published by the Penguin Group
Penguin Books Ltd, 80 Strand, London WC2R ORL, England
Penguin Group (USA) Inc., 375 Hudson Street, New York, New York 10014, USA
Penguin Group (Canada), 90 Eglinton Avenue East, Suite 700, Toronto, Ontario, Canada M4P 2Y3
(a division of Pearson Penguin Canada Inc.)
Penguin Ireland, 25 St Stephen's Green, Dublin 2, Ireland
(a division of Penguin Books Ltd)
Penguin Group (Australia), 707 Collins Street, Melbourne, Victoria 3008, Australia
(a division of Pearson Australia Group Pty Ltd)
Penguin Books India Pvt Ltd, 11 Community Centre,
Panchsheel Park, New Delhi – 110 017, India
Penguin Group (NZ), 67 Apollo Drive, Rosedale, Auckland 0632, New Zealand
(a division of Pearson New Zealand Ltd)
Penguin Books (South Africa) (Pty) Ltd, Block D, Rosebank Office Park, 181 Jan Smuts Avenue,
Parktown North, Gauteng 2193, South Africa

Penguin Books Ltd, Registered Offices: 80 Strand, London WC2R ORL, England

www.penguin.com

First published in the United States of America by Doubleday,
a division of Random House, Inc. 2013
First published in Great Britain by Allen Lane 2013
001

Copyright © Hooman Majd, 2013

Printed in Great Britain by Clays Ltd, St Ives plc

A CIP catalogue record for this book is available from the British Library

ISBN: 978–1–846–14490–5

www.greenpenguin.co.uk

MIX
Paper from
responsible sources
FSC
www.fsc.org   FSC™ C018179

Penguin Books is committed to a sustainable
future for our business, our readers and our planet.
This book is made from Forest Stewardship
Council™ certified paper.

For Khashayar

In memoriam Nasser Majd
(1928–2012)

The inhabitants of Tehran are invited to keep quiet.

—ATTRIBUTED TO SHAH REZA KHAN PAHLAVI

If I sit in silence, I have sinned.

—MOHAMMAD MOSSADEQ

CONTENTS

PROLOGUE

"Hello?" I didn't recognize the number of the incoming call on my cell phone, but it was from Washington, D.C., so I answered, standing on a deserted stretch of the waterfront in Greenpoint, Brooklyn, on a September day in 2010.

"*Agha-ye Majd?*"

"*Baleh?*" I answered, yes—in Farsi, since the caller was obviously Persian.

"I'm calling from the Iranian consulate, and I have a question about your applications for your wife and child."

"Yes?" I said.

"You were married, it seems, after your child was born," the lady said. My longtime girlfriend and I had had a son a few months prior, and we had finally gotten married in a civil ceremony a month before he was born. Realizing that in order to get them Iranian citizenship and passports, we had to be married in an Islamic ceremony—even before the Islamic Revolution, the only marriage Iran recognized was a religiously sanctioned one—we had done exactly that, three months later, at the Islamic Institute of New York, which shares a building with the Razi School ("Academic Excellence in a Distinctive Islamic Environment"!) in Queens. My wife was instantly converted to Islam, Shia Islam, as required. The mullah had patiently explained then, in Farsi while begging me to translate, that converting didn't mean rejecting Christianity or Jesus Christ; it only meant that my wife was accepting Mohammad as the last in line of the holy Abrahamic prophets.

Yeah, whatever, let's do this. That was what my wife's expression had communicated from under a hastily improvised head scarf consisting of our son's monkey-print blanket. I hadn't realized that scarves were mandatory, although I should have checked the Razi School Web site, where the uniform for girls is listed as "navy overcoat, white scarf." Meanwhile, our son, now deprived of his blanket, screamed and farted in what sounded to me like pretty good harmony. "How about Buddha?" my wife wondered. She told me to tell the mullah she accepted *him*, too. I nodded and ignored her request.

The lady calling me now was from the Iranian Interests Section at the Embassy of Pakistan in Washington, D.C., the office that handles the consular affairs of Iranians in the United States in the absence of diplomatic relations between the two countries. She was technically incorrect in identifying herself as "from the consulate," since there is actually no such thing as an Iranian embassy or consulate on American soil, but it was a minor technicality; the Interests Section was authorized to issue citizenship papers for Iranians born in the United States and to issue passports to American wives of Iranian citizens—but not to American husbands of Iranian wives, or to children of those unions, who are not considered Iranian by virtue of marriage or birth to an Iranian woman.

"Well," I said, "we were married before my son's birth, but if you mean our Islamic marriage—"

"No," she interrupted me, "it's no problem really, but it seems you were married in 2010, and that was after—"

"No," I said, my turn to interrupt. "We were married a month *before* he was born."

"It's no problem," she repeated, "but I mean, umm, you were married *after* he was, umm, conceived." She sounded embarrassed. "Was he adopted?"

"No!" I replied, taken aback by the question. "If he was adopted, we wouldn't have been identified as his birth parents on his birth certificate, would we?" What I wanted to say to her was that it *is*, perhaps contrary to her beliefs, actually possible for a man and woman to have a child out of wedlock, that conception doesn't happen only if the man and woman are married, but I bit my tongue. I knew that in the Islamic Republic authorities have to maintain the appearance, at least, that men and women do not—perhaps even *cannot*—have sex before marriage. Just the appearance, mind you, for no one is that naïve in Iran, not even employees of the Islamic state.

"Well," she said, "it *is* possible to have you listed as the father if you adopted, but it's no problem. We just ask you to fax us a letter saying that your son is not adopted, and Tehran will be able to issue his birth certificate, and then we can issue a passport." It seems she still didn't believe that I was the biological father, perhaps not just because of the premarital sex that may have offended her sensibilities, but also because of my age, which she must have thought far too old. Iranians my age tend to be grandfathers. But there was another element at play, too: this passive-aggressive (and very Persian) behavior in social intercourse really meant that she wanted me to agree and declare, to her and the Iranian bureaucratic world, that my son was conceived out of wedlock. *Gotcha!*

Getting citizenship papers for my family was actually much easier while we were still in the United States (or anywhere else outside Iran) than it would have been in Iran, and it had been something I was eager to do, since I was confident that a time would come when I would want to visit Iran with my wife and son. My wife had expressed her desire to travel to Iran with me in the past, when it was a practical impossibility, but now that we were married, her having an Iranian passport meant there would be no obstacles to her accompanying me on one of my trips, with our son if we wanted, even a trip that came up at the very last minute, as had often happened for me before. Appearances aside, paperwork is something the Iranian bureaucracy, the single largest employer of Iranians, excels in, even in the age of paperless communication and record keeping. "You know," one Iranian official at the Interests Section, a longtime resident of Washington, mentioned to me when I told him I was sending in my applications, "Tehran won't return the original American birth certificates of your son or your wife." When I expressed surprise and was a little hesitant to just hand over these precious documents to the Iranian government, never to be recovered, he said, "Well, America is not like Iran, is it? It's not like you have to jump through hoops to get a replacement birth certificate—you just ask for one in any U.S. state, and they'll send it to you!"

I hadn't thought of it, but of course he was right. It's not that hard to get a birth certificate, a driver's license, or even a passport in America or Europe. It's not that hard to open a bank account, rent an apartment, register a child for school, or get a doctor's appointment if you can afford it or have insurance. I may be Iranian by birth, and I may have traveled there often enough, and I may have friends and relatives and connections there across the political spectrum, but I hadn't lived there as an adult, and only barely as a child. I was aware, at second hand, of what living in Tehran entails and understood Iranian bureaucracy, but if I ever wanted to live there myself, with a family no less, it was going to be another thing altogether. Doing anything concerning Iran is generally impossible, as a bureaucrat usually explains with a regretful shaking of the head, and the occasional tut-tut. But with passports in hand, I realized, if we ever decided we *did* want to live there, whatever the reason, it would be a simple matter of buying airplane tickets.

My wife, who comes from a small farming town in rural Wisconsin, was as eager to become an Iranian citizen (and secure her son's dual citizenship) as I was, which was why she had readily converted to Islam. Before we had a child, she had expressed interest in traveling with me to my country of birth, mainly out of curiosity, I thought, but also because, she told me, she worried that if I ever got into trouble in Iran—and she had read reports of Americans and Iranian Americans who had been arrested there—she wanted to be able to get on the first plane to Tehran as easily as an Iranian could.

We had met years ago, and I would talk to her about Iran, well before I visited the country for the first time in adulthood, and she continually urged me to go there, to not let anything stand in the way of my reconnecting to the land of my birth. "You need to go home!" she once said, after I described my grandfather's house to her. "You'll never be happy with your life until you do." She was right, I realized after I finally set foot in Iran. That was reason enough for me to want to take her there, too—to let her actually see why she was right. When it came to converting to Islam, she also understood well that for Iranians, the appearance of belief is paramount, not belief itself, so she humored the mullah who married us, and he seemingly understood the same, given his relaxed attitude, humor, and the almost dismissive manner in which he converted Karri to submission to Allah.

For years it has been extremely difficult for Americans to travel to Iran as tourists, obtaining a visa being the single biggest obstacle, but Karri, to my surprise, was keen on spending an extended period of time there—well, perhaps a month or two. In a way, it shouldn't have been surprising, given what I knew about her. She wanted our son to see, feel, smell, and touch where her family had lived since the eighteenth century from an early age. We had taken him to Wisconsin and the family farm as an infant, and her sense of fair play, and her insistence that we all have a sense of our roots, made her want him to experience his father's birthplace, too. It was her willingness, even eagerness, to travel to Iran, as well as the newly minted Iranian passports that showed up via FedEx not long after I sent in the applications, that persuaded me to look at the idea of actually moving to Iran for a year, more or less, to give me an opportunity to properly reconnect with my history, and to give Karri and our young son a proper introduction to my culture, but also to chronicle our lives as insider/outsiders in a land so few know very much about.

I imagined my story as one that could illustrate and illuminate the larger culture, not so much in the "gee whiz isn't this fascinating" way that often prevails among memoirs of expatriates living abroad, or in the politicized form that most writing, even travel writing, on Iran has taken, but more as an account of what is to *be* an Iranian in Iran. Of course, an Iranian who is also fully American, or at least that's how I, and my friends, imagine me to be. My wife warmed to the idea, even if it meant leaving her family, friends, and work behind, and she understood that the opportunity might never present itself again, especially now that we had a child who would, before we knew it, be in school and have a life that would be difficult to interrupt for any long period of time. Karri, who had over the years spent months alone in India on intensive yoga programs (and had lived alone in Italy, modeling and studying Italian after college), was still adventurous and even fearless, and a year, she reasoned, was not very long in the scheme of things. Our son would, if we went to Iran, be about the same age as I had been when I left it, less than a year old (I had accompanied my diplomatic family on my father's first posting abroad, to London), and he would spend his first birthday in the country of his father's birth. That probably mattered mostly to me, certainly not to him and by nature less to my wife, but I was happy that she was as keen on exposing our son to the culture of his father and his father's father, even if he didn't quite understand yet, early in his life. That Karri would finally see what she had heard about for so many years, and that I could show her something of my country of birth that might explain me better, was equally, if not more, appealing.

Like most Americans and Europeans, my wife had an image of Iran (and of Iranians) that was shaped by the headlines, and the headlines have not been kind to Iran or Iranians for over thirty years. Unlike most non-Iranians, however, her life was intertwined with that of an Iranian; and Persian culture, even Islamic Persian culture, to which she had been exposed through meeting the religious members of my family and which she recognized was quite different from Arab culture, was not completely unfamiliar to her. It is a culture that has been described to Westerners mostly by Iranians, but it is still very much hidden behind veils of modesty, furtiveness, and suspicion. We have an idea of what it is to be French or Italian, or to live in Paris or in Florence, based on a certain familiarity with those cultures and the writings of English-speakers who've lived there, but we have little idea of what it is to be Persian or what Iranian society is really like. The idea of trying to discover that, both for myself and for potential readers, began to hold greater and greater appeal.

"You don't know, you don't know, how life can be *shameful*." Those are lyrics from a song, a piece of music in the classical Iranian form, written by playwright Bijan Mofid in the early 1970s and recorded by many different artists over the years. The song, "Dota cheshm-e seeyah daree" ("You Have Two Black Eyes"), can be searched today on Google, in Finglish, the term Iranians use to signify Farsi words written in the Latin alphabet, and an important tool in the days before most computers came with Arabic fonts installed. I often think of the song when I'm thinking of Iran and Iranians, of what defines our behavior and our view of life. (Unlike Western classical music, Iranian classical music coexists—and is equally popular among all age groups—with contemporary pop.) I think of the song because it had struck a chord with Iranians well before the revolution—when I was a teenager, my father would listen to it while drinking his whiskey—and it continues to be relevant to Iranians today.

But life is *shameful*? Yes. The idea that life in this world can be (or even is) shameful resonates with Iranians, a Shia people who, regardless of their piety or lack of it, are culturally programmed to imagine human behavior as ignoble: as ignoble as the prophet's successors' murder of his offspring, and as ignoble as the tyranny that they suffer no matter what leaders rule them. There's certainly an element of self-loathing to it, although not quite the self-loathing that Western psychology analyzes. The pizza deliveryman in Tehran believes it, as does the pizza restaurant owner, and so does the customer ordering from the comfort of his high-rise apartment, worth millions of dollars (yes, dollars). The Iranian government officials who wanted to know if my son was adopted believe it, as does the mullah who married my wife and me in New York while sheepishly acknowledging the greatness, but not the divinity, of Jesus Christ. Living in Iran, I knew, would mean confronting that concept head-on, something few non-Iranians have done in recent times, and writing about Iranians and Iranian culture, even if only about one's own experiences, would mean understanding it. In Iran, life isn't necessarily ugly or difficult, but regardless of one's standing—whether one is rich or poor, a success or a failure in love—the idea that life is somehow shameful is powerful and one that I wanted to explore.

Iran, the country once known to Westerners as Persia, its name evoking exotic images of *A Thousand and One Nights* and bejeweled kings ruling over adoring masses, fully burst into the American consciousness in 1979 with the Islamic Revolution essentially reversing the image we had, if we had any at all, of the country that American politicians had usually described as our "staunchest ally in the Middle East." After Israel, of course, which happened to be an ally of Iran then, too, albeit unofficially. Naturally, as long as Iran was America's "staunchest ally," ordinary Western folk had little interest in the country beyond the occasional news item related to oil or concerning some intriguing event in the royal family, say a marriage, a divorce, or a coronation. Iran was a curiosity at best, and although there were at one time some forty thousand Americans living there, most were expats in what we now think of as a colonial sense: they lived insulated and isolated from the native population, attended their own schools and clubs, and undertook tourist jaunts to famous sites while rarely experiencing the culture of the land. Practically no Americans or Europeans moved to Iran simply to experience the Persian life. Although the shah once proclaimed, in his vainglory years, that Tehran would soon become the "Paris of the Middle East," Tehran of the 1970s was certainly not Paris of the 1920s, and Iran held no attraction for artists and intellectuals looking for inspiration away from home. That was equally true for Iranian artists, most of whom, including one of my uncles who ran away from home to become a painter in Paris, at that time looked for inspiration in the cities of Europe.

The modernizing and Francophile shah of Iran (or as some Americans occasionally mistakenly wrote, the "Shaw of Iran," unintentionally ascribing to him perhaps the one talent, playwright, that he *didn't* claim) seemed to symbolize Iran, at least until the day he unceremoniously departed Tehran, and throngs of bearded men and chador-clad women flocked to the streets to celebrate his departure, along with whatever dreams he had of a Westernized Iran. When the revolution took hold and Ayatollah Khomeini became Iran's new de facto "shaw"—unlike the shah, he actually did compose, in his case poetry—Americans moved on: How interesting could Iran be, now that its rulers wore robes and turbans, sat on the floor, and ate dates and yogurt for lunch? As long as the oil flowed, another backward country regressing even further wasn't going to hold anyone's attention for very long, and the culture was seemingly irrelevant to Western civilization in the twentieth century.

Indeed, interest in Iran faded until the new Persian royalty and the masses of angry Iranians who worshipped them stormed the U.S. embassy and took American diplomats hostage, in contravention of international law and all notions of international relations, to say nothing of civilized behavior or common decency. Iran was not only no longer the charmingly exotic East we once imagined it to be; it was an implacable enemy forever at odds with not just us but the community of nations at large. Iran, Khomeini proclaimed, needn't recognize international law since she hadn't been consulted on its various aspects. The impudence of the world's nations! Not only that, his declaration that "America cannot do a damn thing" about its hostages was proven true in the end, much to Americans' dismay, and the revolutionary government extended that ideal to *anything* America wanted to do vis-à-vis Iran—Khomeini's slogan is still emblazoned on the walls of the former U.S. embassy in Tehran, more than thirty years later. If the nuclear issue and Iran's growing influence and power in the region (in Iraq and Afghanistan, for example, or even in Gaza) and beyond (in Africa and South America) are any indicators, Khomeini's wish is still coming true, much to the chagrin of President Obama—the sixth American president to have to deal with a worrisome Iran.

Thirty-plus years. Years marked by indifference, enmity, accusations, and recriminations, occasional flare-ups, and for the past few, deep disagreements over a nuclear program that appears to be leading inexorably to a nuclear-capable Iran at best and a nuclear-armed Iran at worst. What's been happening in Iran in our absence? The population has more than tripled, and industry has grown to the point where Iran can be virtually self-sufficient in many ways, including militarily (albeit on a crude and somewhat outdated level), partly because unilateral (U.S.) and multilateral (UN) sanctions have *forced* Iranian industry to adapt in order to survive with little, if any, outside help. Superhighways crisscross the country, dotted with technical schools and universities, and Iranians have the greatest rate of higher education as well as Internet penetration in the region. Iranian artists sell their works at European and Persian Gulf cities' auctions for millions of dollars, Iranian cinema *is* the nouvelle vague, and Iranian literature is slowly being recognized outside Farsi-speaking countries. Iranian cuisine is even making inroads in Western countries. "What's the best Persian rice cooker?" a WASPy American customer asked the clerk at an international food store on Lexington Avenue in New York, not long after my experience with the Iranian Interests Section. I nosily volunteered a brand I own, whereupon he asked me, "Does it make good *tahdig* [crisped rice]?"

We're certainly much more aware of Iran today than ever before, I've discovered. Just about every American and European can identify the country on a map, even if they cannot identify their own neighboring states and countries or principalities, and as awareness has increased, so, for many, has curiosity. Iran's cultural influence— political and otherwise—seems to be on the rise, certainly in places we worry about, such as Lebanon, Iraq, and Afghanistan; but can Iran, like China and to some degree India, become an influential economic and military power? One whose culture, from food to literature, from art to spiritual values, permeates Western civilization the way Chinese and Indian culture do? Today there are over one million Iranian Americans, and hundreds of thousands of Iranians in Europe and all over the Western world, and their influence (good and bad, admittedly) is already being felt. Iran hawks, both in the United States and Europe, as well as in Israel, certainly believe Iran can become a power to be reckoned with and advocate confronting Iranian ambitions before it's too late; others claim that Iran's power and influence, even its nuclear capability, are greatly exaggerated. But if Iran does achieve what it seems to be striving for—a reborn empire of sorts—and if it remains an independent Islamic force allied with "neither West nor East," as it declares on the walls of its Foreign Ministry, what will that mean?

Almost certainly Iran, regardless of whether its future government is fairly elected or otherwise, will continue along the path it forged in the early days of the Islamic Revolution. That path, one of modernity fused with religion—with very mixed results—is unique in the world today, but in the minds of the country's leadership and of

Iranians who believe at least half of its story, this path is the only one that can guarantee progress for Iranians. The Islamic Republic has raised the literacy rate to over 90 percent, educates far more women than men in its universities, and has made great strides in medicine, science, and the arts, all while insisting on a veneer of Shia Islam. A veneer? Yes, but not always a false front. Former president Mohammad Khatami, who served two terms, from 1997 to 2005, once said in a speech—at a time when he was under fire from progressives for not bringing about "change" fast enough; President Obama might relate—that in Iran, democracy would come about only if it were Islamic; otherwise, the country would be a dictatorship much like its neighbors. Perhaps he was right, or maybe over time Iran will become a democracy stripped of its religious veneer. Either way, Iran today is still mostly in the dark, much as China was until the 1990s, both in terms of opening up to the West and in terms of Western understanding of its culture. But Iranians are prepared to turn the lights back on at a moment's notice. Until then, I hope that this book, born in Iran, might cast some light on their still-clouded story.

A TASTE OF THINGS
TO COME

At a few minutes before midnight on January 13, 2011, I strolled off a Lufthansa plane and into the one terminal of Tehran's Imam Khomeini International Airport. The place was familiar enough to me, since it had finally opened to European airlines in 2008, after years of delays—at one point it had been shut down and then taken over by the Revolutionary Guards, the military force answerable exclusively to the Supreme Leader, Ayatollah Ali Khamenei, the ultimate authority in Iran. I was accompanying correspondent Richard Engel and an NBC News crew, who had short-term entry visas to interview Iran's chief nuclear negotiator, Saied Jalili, the following morning. Or, this being Iran, the day after that, or whatever day his office decided would be appropriate. I had been to Iran many times in the previous few years; as a journalist on assignment for U.S. magazines, as a writer researching for my books, and as a consultant to, and sometime interviewee on, various NBC News programs. As the next morning was a Friday, the Muslim Sabbath, I had told Richard to expect at least a one-day postponement.

Richard, his two cameramen, and I stood in line at immigration: the Americans in the foreigners' line, and I, with my Iranian passport, in the much longer line for nationals. Iran is probably the only country in the world where the lines at immigration are much longer for citizens than for foreigners; just as airplanes flying to Tehran, no matter their place of origin, are mostly filled with Iranians who are less put off by the thought of traveling to the strict Islamic Republic than most Westerners are. As expected, the NBC crew were whisked off for further processing (all Americans are subject to fingerprint-ing, in the same way Iranians are at American ports of entry), and I expected to have a long wait at baggage claim while my colleagues were being slowly and methodically—in a purposefully drawn-out procedure—checked over. Even when Iranian immigration officials have nothing further to do, after they've done every procedure and cleared Americans to enter, they seem to hold them back a little lon-ger, making me wonder if they are basing the timing on the latest information about how long it takes Iranian citizens to get through U.S. immigration at busy airports.

When it was my turn to approach the immigration officer, I handed my passport to him; he nonchalantly scanned and closed it, then got up from his chair and told me to wait one minute. A sud-den fear came over me, the fear all Iranians who suspect that they are disliked (or worse) by the authorities in the Islamic Republic feel whenever they cross the border. I had reported enthusiastically on the Green Movement and the antigovernment protests in 2009 for a number of publications, including the *Los Angeles Times,* the *Financial Times,* and *The New Republic,* but after a year's absence had returned to Iran in May 2010 for a short visit without any problems. In the interval, however, I had a published a book that was critical of the hard-liners in Tehran who had brutally crushed dissent, and sup-portive of reformist, even liberal presidential candidates Mir Hossein Mousavi and Mehdi Karroubi, who were now under virtual house arrest. (They subsequently were put under official house arrest.) I was still, as the authorities well knew, related to former president Khatami, who had been under surveillance and barred from travel since the presidential election of 2009. But I was traveling with an NBC News crew, and the Iranian mission to the UN had secured their visas and the interview with one of Iran's top leaders (Jalili was also the secretary of the Supreme National Security Council, the powerful body reporting to the Supreme Leader), so the government was aware of my work with NBC on what was intended to be a short trip. Clearly, the government had been looking for me at the airport. I was perplexed: had there been any issues with my welcome in Tehran, surely the UN mission would have told me before I boarded my flight. It was the first time I hadn't breezed through immigration in Tehran, and thoughts of arrest and interrogation, as had happened to other Iranians, swam through my head. *This is a good start,* I thought, *to moving to Iran with my family in a few weeks.*

The immigration official returned after a few minutes and told me to sit down in an area off to the side, in full view of the passengers making their way through passport control and who, being Iranians, couldn't help but stare at me, either in pity or perhaps in fear that but for the grace of Allah, they too would be subject to uneasy detention at their country's border. I waited for what seemed a long time, but checking my watch as a tall, bearded man walked purposefully toward me, I realized that less than ten minutes had passed. The man was wearing light gray pants and a nubby gray sweater, and as he approached, his shoes, the hard plastic sandals many Iranians wear at home, clip-clopped loudly on the marble floor. I was certain he enjoyed making the sound, and equally certain that he enjoyed looking like a disheveled working-class stiff—in contrast to the well-manicured and well-coiffed ladies in their designer head scarves and the men in the latest Western fashions who were still waiting to pass through immigration—and although he didn't look around, I could sense his smugness at the enormous power he wielded over these "westoxified" Iranians who only hours before had surely been cavorting in a Western capital. *Not here,* I imagined him thinking. *No, you're in my country now, the country of the* mostazafin, *the oppressed.*

"Hooman Majd?" he asked as he stood over me, my passport open to the photograph.

"Yes." I stood up.

"Follow me," he said sternly. Holding my passport in one hand, he led me down a long corridor. He turned at one point and said, rather than asked, "You're a journalist."

"Yes," I said, "but I'm not here to work as a journalist."

"You're a journalist," he repeated, saying the words as an accusation rather than a statement of fact.

We reached an area of the airport I'd not seen in previous visits, a corridor with a number of offices with the doors open and white plastic chairs lined up outside.

"Sit here," he commanded, pointing to a chair, and disappeared into one of the offices and closed the door.

I sat down and wondered how long I would be held up, or if I would be sent to a different place, perhaps even a prison, for interrogation. What would NBC do? Would they wait for me until they realized I had disappeared and then try to find out what had happened to me? Or would they carry on with their assignment? They had only forty-eight-hour visas, after all, so maybe they'd just carry on. It wasn't as if I was their employee, I reasoned, just a consultant. And I was their consultant in part because of my access to Iranian officialdom—to Khatami, naturally, but even to the administration of Mahmoud Ahmadinejad, whom I had met a number of times and with whose Foreign Ministry I had cordial relations. If, with my access, I got into trouble, how could I expect NBC to think it might help?

I didn't have long to ponder my fate, though, as the man soon came out of the office and approached me, still holding my passport. "You are to report to the Ministry of Culture and Islamic Guidance on Saturday at nine a.m. At the foreign journalists' division. Do you know where that is?"

"Yes," I said, standing up, familiar with the Orwellian-sounding ministry that is responsible for culture but also the kind of "guidance" that most journalists, Iranians and foreign, and artists seeking permission to film, exhibit their art, record or play music, or put on a play, abhor. "But who do I ask for?"

"They're expecting you," he replied with a smirk.

"Just the accreditation department?"

"Yes. Be sure to be there, or else you'll have a problem leaving the country," he said, a little menacingly. "Let's go."

I followed him as he shuffled back along the corridor, his sandals as loud as before, maybe louder, on the marble floor. At passport control, he handed my passport to a bored official who stamped it, and as he turned to leave, he said, "Don't miss the appointment."

I still got out of the airport before Richard and the NBC crew did, and found the waiting van hired by NBC. Suddenly my plan to move to Iran with my wife and son, and to spend a year living among my countrymen, seemed rather too optimistic, if not downright stupid. I was certain I wouldn't be jailed on Saturday—surely if they wanted to imprison me, they would have led me out of the airport in handcuffs—but the Ministry of Intelligence might not look as kindly on my next trip. I felt an antipathy for the man who had seemingly derived pleasure from making me sweat. If living among my countrymen meant living among the likes of him, I thought, then perhaps I wouldn't, after all, want to expose my family to my people.

As I waited for Richard and his crew to clear customs, I contemplated the irony of having to confront simultaneously the two fears I have harbored since the Islamic Revolution toppled my father's employer from power and drove my family into exile: that I would never again see the country of my birth, and that if I did, I would never be allowed to leave. Even after I started to travel to Iran regularly, these fears never completely left me: from the moment I stood in line to board a flight to Tehran from the safety of a foreign airport, to the moment I'd hand over my passport at immigration, to the hours I'd spend at Tehran's airport waiting to leave, I never quite felt safe, for I knew (and my father and other family members constantly reminded me) that Iranian administrations—indeed, the country's entire political climate—could be capricious no matter who, king or cleric, was in charge. Yes, the fear had subsided over the years, as I made numerous uneventful trips back and forth, but I now realized that whatever allowances the bureaucracy made for West-based Iranians (including for a son born out of wedlock), they did not extend to writers who might publish something the state viewed as not just uncomplimentary but actually treasonous. Not in post–2009 elections Iran. I had already decided not to tell any intelligence officers, or officials of the Ministry of Culture and Islamic Guidance, that my extended stay in Iran might involve writing a book on my experiences. Although such a plan was not technically illegal or even a reason to secure advance permission, I knew that telling them about it might cause them to monitor my activities with greater zeal than they might otherwise have done.

My traveling companions finally made it to the van, and as we rode into town, I reflected on what I would say to my interrogators when I met with them in less than forty-eight hours. The signs weren't good for a friendly meeting over a cup of tea: NBC in Tehran (the only U.S.

network with a full-time bureau in the Islamic Republic) informed
me that the hotel we were booked at, the Laleh, had refused to take
my reservation at first, under orders from the ministry, and had finally
relented only after back-and-forth phone calls and discussions.

Signs that my appearance in Tehran was more than a little unwelcome grew the next morning. The Laleh, like Soviet-era Mos-
cow hotels, was essentially a spying apparatus for the state, but I
had failed to realize before (perhaps because of the relative ease with
which I had traveled to and from Iran) just how good that apparatus
actually could be. I was sitting in the lobby lounge having coffee
with the American news crew and discussing the best tack to ensure
a productive interview, as well as how to get Dr. Jalili to agree to let
NBC into a nuclear facility, when one of the doormen (who had not
been present when we checked in) approached us. "Mr. Majd," he
said, "may I have a word?"

I rose from my chair and followed him a short distance, out of
earshot of the rest of the party, wondering how he knew my name.
Could it be that the hotel's shabbiness masked a level of customer
service more common at Claridge's or the Ritz? Certainly not. So
what could he possibly want?

"Mr. Majd," the doorman repeated. "I advise you not to hang
around the Americans very much."

I was a little shocked, immediately realizing that he was an
informer, presumably for the Ministry of Intelligence but perhaps
for one of the other intelligence services. "Well, I'm here with them,
working. I can't exactly avoid them."

"I'm just saying, it's better that you don't associate with them."

"That's not possible—we're traveling together," I repeated, "and
I'm here to work with them."

"Friendly advice, that's all." He nodded, then turned away. Friendly
advice indeed, from a Tehran hotel doorman, no less.

"I'll try," I said to his back, "but I wonder if you could answer a
question no one else at the hotel seems to be able to."

"What is it?" he said, stopping.

"Why are all the electrical outlets in the hotel British-style ones?" I asked. "I mean, no traveler brings British plugs to Iran. *British* plugs."

"We have converters."

"I know, but why are the outlets three-pronged to begin with?" I couldn't resist making the dig, partly because of my anger and frustration with the authorities but also because I wanted to throw something at them that they couldn't defend. Iranians in general and the revolutionaries in particular hate the British government more than any other.

He shook his head and returned to his station at the door, probably aware that I was needling him but refusing to acknowledge it.

It was Friday, the Sabbath, and my meeting with my interrogators was still a full day away. I wondered what I should do, knowing that I was being watched in the hotel, and that my movements outside would probably also be monitored. Since the NBC crew were allowed only to conduct the interview with Jalili—which had by now been rescheduled for Saturday morning—and had no authority to work anywhere else in the city, they were going to stay at the hotel all day. I decided to go out and visit friends.

Getting around sprawling and densely populated Tehran, with its paralyzing traffic and lack of order, is a feat even on daytime Fridays, and I spent much of the day, and into the evening, in taxis. Pollution, which only goes from bad to worse in Tehran, was headache-inducing that winter, due to an inversion layer common in cities surrounded by mountains, but was the throbbing in my temples due solely to the fumes and caustic air, or was the prospect of an interrogation by infamously ill-tempered intelligence officials the following morning causing my brain to object? That morning I had spoken to Ali Khatami, former president Mohammad Khatami's brother and chief of staff, and I planned to meet him and our mutual friend Sadegh Kharrazi, another former official, later in the evening. That visit, I was sure, would be duly recorded as a mark against me by the intelligence community—Ali and Sadegh were notoriously liberal reformists. But Ali was also a relative, I reasoned, so they couldn't possibly be too disturbed by my seeing him and Sadegh, who was untouchable due to his incongruously close relationship, familial and otherwise, with the Supreme Leader.

When I told them that I had been summoned, Sadegh gave me a knowing smile. "Welcome to Iran," he said. "This isn't Switzerland." *No kidding,* I thought. Ali wanted me to call him as soon as my interrogation was over, to be sure that everything was okay, and I told him I would. I also told him I didn't think, under the circumstances, that it would be wise for me to pay ex-president Khatami a visit on this short trip, either for him or for me. Ali agreed, and I wondered whether he was more worried about me or his brother. I suspect it was both.

The Ministry of Culture and Islamic Guidance, the overseer of all cultural activities in the Islamic Republic (and always known to Iranians simply as Ershad, or "guidance"), including news media activities, keeps its foreign media offices on Eighth Street and Ghaem Magham, across from the Tehran Clinic, a famous hospital in central Tehran. I had made many visits to Ershad in the past, but today for the first time the Tehran Clinic's proximity struck me as convenient in case of a serious medical emergency following a summons to the ministry. From the taxi window I looked out at the bustle of the city, wondering how ordinary Tehranis could appear to be so completely unconcerned with what Iran had become since the elections of 2009: a police state behind a veneer of freedom—"Islamic" freedom, that is—that the regime claimed to offer its citizens. A police state had long existed in Iran, of course, but now it had taken on a malicious and bellicose form unseen or felt since the early 1990s.

I arrived a few minutes before nine, and I was indeed expected. The guards in the lobby took my Iranian national ID card and told me to go upstairs to the journalists' office. So even the guards—who normally would ask with suspicion what I was there for and whom I wanted to see—knew I had been summoned. Were they intelligence ministry informers, too? I took the stairs to the second floor and stepped into the office I had visited on previous trips to obtain my press passes. The young male secretary was also expecting me, it seemed, and politely asked me to take a seat. Tea arrived out of nowhere.

After about half an hour, the deputy head of the foreign reporters' bureau, the gentle and ever polite Mohammad Shiravi, walked in and said hello. Holding a glass of tea himself and wearing an Ahmadinejad-style windbreaker, he wandered in and out of the reception area looking a bit uncomfortable, then finally told me that I should wait in his office. I had known Shiravi to be a liberal—by Islamic Republic standards—and I wondered if his choice of jacket had shielded him from the purges at the ministry after the 2009 elections and the appointment of the president's arch-conservative ally Mohammad Hosseini to the post of minister. (Mohammad Javad Aghajari, Shiravi's immediate boss and the man ultimately responsible for foreign correspondent activity in Iran, was a reliable conservative with no suspicious liberal leanings.)

I followed Shiravi into his office and sat down on a sofa. He left, closing the door firmly behind him. Again, a glass of tea appeared, this time with a plate of biscuits. He was not going to be the one to interview me, and whoever was had to be important enough in the intelligence services to kick him out of his own office. I waited another fifteen or twenty minutes, staring at the large jug of ice water on the coffee table before me: large drops formed on its outside surface in the overheated room, trickled slowly down the side, and plunged into the saucer under the jug. Sweat.

The door opened and two men walked in, an older one with a full beard and a younger one almost clean-shaven, both wearing badly mismatched gray jackets and trousers that seemed to be the uniform of choice for government employees below the rank of minister (and sometimes minister, too, depending on how much he wanted to associate himself with the downtrodden of society). I rose to shake their hands and noticed the younger one had a deformity on one hand. Injured in the Iran-Iraq War? I wondered automatically. Nah—he was too young to have fought. They sat down in armchairs across from me without introducing themselves, not even with a fake name like Mohammadi or some other commonplace but very Islamic name of the sort that intelligence officers seem to favor. Both held thick files in their laps.

"You wrote this article," the younger man said, opening his file and looking over some pages, "and you didn't have a press pass."

"What article?" I asked.

"About your trip here eight months ago. The nuclear conference." He sucked air audibly, biting the tip of his tongue with his front teeth at the end of every sentence—an annoying tic. The article he was referring to was one I had written for *Foreign Policy* magazine, on an international "nuclear conference" that the government had held the prior year to trumpet nuclear advances and to reaffirm that those advances were for peaceful purposes. The conference had been boring, a show of propaganda, and very little of my long article was about the conference itself.

"I did have a press pass," I said. "The Foreign Ministry issued it to me at the conference, and I was with the media in the press box."

"The Foreign Ministry does not issue press passes," he snarled. "You know that." Hiss.

"I don't," I said. "The Iranian mission to the UN told me that I could pick up my press pass at the conference, and I did, the morning I arrived."

"I just told you the Foreign Ministry has nothing to do with press credentials." Again, hiss.

"Well, that's not my fault—I live in New York, and I have to go through them to get credentials."

"Just because you have an Iranian passport doesn't mean you can come here and write whatever you want when you leave—"

The older man gestured for him to stop and picked up a paper from his own file. "Listen," he said, "here you refer to the president as being a part of a 'circus.' Why do you make fun of the president of the country? And you even once translated for him at the UN!" He sounded almost hurt. I had indeed translated for Ahmadinejad at the UN, but I wondered if my interrogator understood that it was for a cover story for *The New York Observer* in 2006, complete with unflattering caricatures of the easily caricatured president, and not an expression of admiration or support for the president. This interrogator was softer-spoken, clearly the "good cop" to the other's "bad cop," but in truth it was really more a case of "bad cop, worse cop," and like much else in Iran, the concept had lost something in translation.

He was referring to a piece I had written a few months before, about Ahmadinejad's 2010 trip to attend the UN General Assembly, in which I had called the yearly presence of the Iranian president in New York, along with the attendant publicity, the "Ahmadinejad circus." Since exile Iranians sometimes likened Ahmadinejad to a chimp, and since cartoons on opposition Web sites lampooned him as such, I could see why the Intelligence Ministry was sensitive to the word *circus*. I patiently explained that it wasn't a reference to the president himself, and that in English it wasn't necessarily pejorative. He seemed unconvinced.

"Here in your second book," said the worse cop, "you insult the president again." He read aloud a paragraph in Farsi.

"That's not my translation," I said. "I don't read or write Farsi well enough to write in the language. My book is in English."

"That what I expected you to say," he snorted. "Typical response—avoid responsibility by saying you wrote in English, or it wasn't you, that it was your editor who made you write it."

"It wasn't my editor," I said, "but it's true that I wrote the book in English. Do you have the English copy?"

He clearly didn't, but instead of saying so, he sucked air rapidly through his teeth and shifted his weight.

The bad cop took over. For the next three hours we went back and forth, as the bad cop and the worse cop accused me of "unpatriotic" writing at best and seditious acts at worst. Almost everything I had written in the past seemed to be at their fingertips; each would pull a sheet out of his file and wave it in the air as if it were a piece of evidence being presented to a judge. I kept glancing at the sweating jug of water, wanting to pour some for myself but refraining from doing so, not wanting the two men to think I was nervous. In my mind, I praised the power of American antiperspirants.

"You Iranians who live abroad think you can say anything, unconcerned with our national security, don't you?" the worse cop said toward the end. "Have you changed your mind now?"

"About what?" I asked, careful to say it politely.

"About your writing!" He was almost shouting.

"Well, um," I replied, "I change my mind frequently about things as I learn something new, yes. But I'm not sure what you mean."

"Oh, so a 'journalist' can change his mind? Really?" He said the word *journalist* mockingly, as if he really wanted to say *spy*.

"Well, yes," I said.

He merely grunted, unconvinced.

When they finally closed their files, I knew we were almost at the end of the interrogation, and besides, it was past lunchtime and no one in Iran, not even secret policemen on a mission, will miss their lunch.

"Who have you seen while you've been here?" asked the worse cop, leaning back and hissing through his teeth again.

"My friends Khosro Etemadi [an old college friend whom I often stay with in Iran] and Mr. Kharrazi [a former diplomat and powerful, albeit reformist, political figure]." I don't know why I didn't mention Ali Khatami—I suppose I thought the name Khatami might send them into convulsions—and I was a little surprised that they didn't bring it up themselves.

"Which Mr. Kharrazi?"

"Sadegh."

He curled his lips, but didn't say anything. He wasn't going to disparage a man close to the Supreme Leader, no matter what his opinion of him was. "And when are you leaving?"

"Tonight. Actually, the flight leaves after midnight, so technically tomorrow."

"Don't miss your flight," he said firmly.

"So this NBC crew you came with," said the bad cop. "They are interviewing Dr. Jalili?"

"Yes, and hoping that they can visit the Tehran nuclear reactor."

"And you want to go with them?"

"Yes, I do, but if it's not possible, then I won't. I'll just see friends and family."

"No, it's okay," he said. "You can go with them." The worse cop, the younger man, was turning into a veritable good cop now.

"Really?"

"Yes, why not?" He squinted at me as if he were sizing me up before a boxing match.

"Okay." I stood up as they did and shook their reluctant hands. "One other thing," I said. "I won't have any trouble at the airport—leaving, I mean—will I?"

"No," they both said, shaking their heads. "It'll be taken care of," added the now-good cop.

"I'm coming back in a few weeks, with my American wife and child, for an extended stay," I said. "I won't have trouble at the airport then, or will I?"

"Why should you have trouble?" asked the worse cop, with a sneer. "What are you coming for? To cause trouble? Or maybe to gather information?"

"To spend time here with my family," I said. "Not as a reporter."

"Then you won't have any trouble," he said. "Now, you won't write about our little meeting here, will you? As a journalist?" he added. It wasn't a question. "You won't, because you want to come back with your wife and child." He stared straight into my eyes.

"No, I won't write about it," I lied.

They left the room and closed the door, and for a moment I wasn't sure what to do. My session had been remarkably mild, I thought, compared to what others had gone through, especially the political prisoners who had been interrogated at Evin, the notorious prison, in the aftermath of the 2009 elections. But the meeting still spoke to the extreme paranoia the regime felt since those elections. That paranoia brought it a big step closer from being an authoritarian state that made a good pretense of allowing some political discourse to being a complete dictatorship that brooked no dissent whatsoever. I walked out the door, said goodbye to Shiravi—who looked extremely uncomfortable standing outside his door, glass of tea still in his hand—and left the building.

I walked for a while, still wondering if coming back to Iran—with my family—would be a good idea. I believed the intelligence officers when they said it wouldn't be a problem, but they were warning me, too: if I overstepped my bounds—and who knew exactly what those bounds were?—I would be in trouble. Yet this was Iran, thirty-two

years after a successful revolution and two years after an arguably
unsuccessful one, and not much was new in terms of the ambigui-
ties, the unknowns, and the maddeningly contradictory behavior of
government officials. It was still an Iran I could recognize. I believed,
as I had for many years, that despite the brutality, the arrests, and
the crackdown on civil liberties as well as the press, powerful figures within Iran were working to advance a more democratic future.
Perhaps naïvely, I wanted to be hopeful, rather than—like many of
my compatriots who had become apathetic after the Green Movement, even toward the Arab Spring evolving in their own backyard—
resigned to the fact that Iran's destiny was to forever be in the grip of
tyranny. I was coming back, even if it could end up being my last trip.

The NBC crew was interviewing Jalili, so I was in no hurry to get
back to the hotel. But since I had been given permission to visit the
Tehran reactor, I did need to contact them and find out if and when
they were going. No sooner had I gotten into a taxi than my phone
rang. It was NBC's Tehran bureau chief, telling me they had finished
their interview and were to go to the reactor the next morning. That
meant we'd have to change flights. I said I had been told I could go
with them and would see them later at the hotel.

Fifteen minutes later I received a call from an "unknown" caller,
who had to be a government official, as no one else is allowed to
block his or her number from caller ID recognition in Iran. "Mr.
Majd?"

"Yes?" The caller did not introduce himself.

"You are not permitted to visit the Tehran nuclear reactor."

"But I was just told I could," I protested.

"No, you may not."

"If you say so," I said, "but the gentlemen I spoke to this morning
specifically said it would be all right—"

THE MINISTRY OF GUIDANCE INVITES YOU TO NOT STAY

"I just told you no," said the man, sounding a little angry. "Just go and visit friends and family, and then go home. Why not just have a good time in Tehran?"

I shook my head as I hung up. What kind of country was this, where you couldn't even trust the intelligence officers interrogating you to say what is permitted and what is not? Had they intentionally been fucking with my mind, or had they been overruled afterward? Did someone really suspect that I might be a spy, and that the nuclear reactor—built in the 1970s by Americans, actually—was just too sensitive a location to allow me a peek? *Gee,* I thought, *when did I become so damn important?*

There was no question of my staying an extra day now, nor even of spending much time with NBC, so I had the afternoon and early evening to visit a friend or two and then head to the airport for the long trip back to New York. If I couldn't trust the intelligence officers on the subject of the reactor visit, I wondered, could I trust that I'd be allowed to board my flight in the wee hours of the morning? But they had admonished me to not miss my flight, so after saying my goodbyes at the hotel later that day, I went to visit a friend before heading to the airport.

Snow began falling as dusk arrived, and by the time I was driven to the airport, it had turned into a veritable blizzard. Cars and buses made no allowance for slippery surfaces or poor visibility and sped along, defying traffic regulations and on occasion ending up in a ditch by the side of the unforgiving road or stranded after a pile-up. Just my luck, I thought—the Intelligence Ministry will blame me, and not the storm, if my flight is canceled and I have to return to the hotel. Almost all the international flights that night were indeed canceled, except for two: mine to Frankfurt and one to Amsterdam. When the plane took off, two hours late and after a thorough de-icing of the wings, I felt genuine relief: not only had I made it through passport control, but during the three hours that I had waited in the airport before boarding, no one had changed his mind about letting me out of the country. Furthermore, once I was seated, no one had come to drag me off the flight, as had happened to other Iranians on hit lists maintained by the competing security services. As soon as the plane leveled off, still in Iranian airspace, I ordered a scotch. A double.

What is it about Iran and authoritarianism? Why, after so many attempts in the last hundred years or so to advance democratic rule, has Iran always reneged on the promises of people's revolutions and reverted to dictatorship? Perhaps my optimism about the future, my belief that the country is on a circuitous path to an inevitable true democracy, was unfounded after all; perhaps we Iranians will forever simply replace one dictatorship with another; perhaps our very DNA condemns us to living in a society in which the absolute power of the state is accepted as a fact. I thought about it on the long flight from Tehran to New York via Frankfurt. Maybe I was more concerned now because I was about to subject my wife and child to living in an authoritarian state. Given my profession, it would be impossible for me not to be subjected to government scrutiny and perhaps constant observation.

How utterly selfish of me! I had been privileged to live in liberal democracies all my life, first far away from the shah's secret police, who had interrogated some of my student friends, and then far from the Islamic Revolution's "guidance"—which was much more about dictate than about suggestion. In my reporting and research trips to Iran prior to the elections of 2009, I had been aware that since I didn't have to live there, whatever discomfort I might feel would always be temporary. I had my escape, my foreign passport and my foreign home, and my stays in Iran were excursions, not a way of life. Although my family and I would still have that escape hatch after moving to Tehran, we would also be living as Iranians in a country whose appeal was, admittedly, more romantic than anything else. I knew people who had been caught up in the security apparatus of the state; I had friends and family members who had been arrested and had even endured long stretches of solitary confinement at Evin prison. Iran, I knew, was not quite the dystopia that Westerners sometimes imagine it to be—it could never be compared to Saddam Hussein's Iraq or the Kims' North Korea—but it was also unpredictable in terms of its politics and civil rights. My interrogators in Tehran, Mr. Bad and Mr. Worse, merely represented the long Persian tradition of absolute monarchy, of state or aristocratic control over its citizens; if the shah were still in power, they would have been SAVAK, or *his* secret policemen. And despite the mildness, the near placidity, of my experience compared to the horrors others had gone through, I again wondered if there was something innate in our culture that consistently produced men and women who happily worked to subdue free thought and opposition to their sociopolitical system, or in feudal times, opposition to what was essentially serfdom.

During those hundred years of the nation trying to free itself from despots and despotism, each time, from 1906 onward, Iran's citizens' efforts were foiled by the machinations of either foreign powers or native despots, often disguised as liberators of the Persian people. Ingeniously, the Islamic Republic's peculiar form of democracy has not only subverted traditional notions of dictatorship (there are still, even after the 2009 elections, few absolutes in Iran, as my own experience showed), it has also endowed its supporters with a sort of moral righteousness that makes them truly believe they are not just doing God's work but serving the cause of justice and doing *right*,

much as other ideologues, such as communists, have believed elsewhere. Perhaps that is the reason for the republic's longevity, despite
its vulnerability to an educated and intellectual class's demands for
change. That same class, arguably smaller then than it is today, supported the revolution against the shah, and while it is generally not
looking to overthrow the current Iranian system by force, at least not
yet, it continues to struggle against the authoritarian state it helped
to usher in. (The irony of the Persian Islamic system—rule by clerics
with unquestioned authority—is that Shia Islam, the sect to which
90 percent of Iranians adhere but a minority sect worldwide, was
founded in *response* to the tyranny of Sunni caliphs.) I wondered as
I left Tehran—my mind swimming, trying to reconcile my run-in
with the Intelligence Ministry with my decision to move to Tehran—
whether, given my fear of a flaw in our national character, if today's
Iranians ever succeed in bringing true change to their country and
making Iran a democracy with freedoms unheard of, Mr. Bad and
Mr. Worse will simply find themselves with a new master to serve.

2

TOUCHDOWN

—

Flying from the United States to Iran is taxing under the best of circumstances, but when flying with an eight-month-old baby, it is an altogether different experience. Especially if one is traveling with enough suitcases for an extended stay, a Cadillac-size stroller, and a Barcalounger-size baby car seat; and especially if that baby is accustomed to organic and natural foods that must be transported in bulk to one's destination, for god forbid that he consume what other babies do; and especially if his mother insists on bringing the water filter, weighing some pounds, along with its multiple cartridges, from our home in New York, where the quality of the tap water, just like Tehran's, is boasted about by its residents (but not this mother, who believes that fluoride is a poison, even if only applied to the skin). I was, in the past, accustomed to the mild culture shock of boarding a KLM or Lufthansa flight to Tehran in Amsterdam or Frankfurt—it's as if one were already in Tehran, okay, a *nice* part of Tehran—but my wife, Karri, wasn't. She was nervous as we waited in line at Schiphol airport to board our flight to my hometown, surrounded by Iranians, the Farsi language, and women in various states of Islamic-friendly dress, from head scarves already firmly in place to shawls draped over the shoulder, ready to be summoned for duty sometime before landing. Besides the suitcases we'd checked, we had the stroller, a baby in arms, and as much hand luggage as would ordinarily serve my baggage purposes for a four-week solo trip. Karri asked me if breast-feeding in public was taboo in Iran or among Iranians abroad, for she would be feeding our son on the flight, and I had to confess that I didn't know.

A short while before embarking on our trip, we had attended a friend's birthday party at a New York restaurant. As soon as everyone was seated, he had announced, only half-jokingly, that the party was in fact not in celebration of his advancing age but an intervention designed to persuade us to refrain from moving to Tehran for a year. He had insisted that it was too dangerous an endeavor for me, let alone with an American wife and child in tow. I had laughed it off, but now I wondered if his words had had any effect on Karri. To be fair, she mostly kept her apprehension hidden from me and anyone else who wondered about her wisdom in acquiescing to my crazy plans. Her family was certainly nervous and had made their concerns known, but they hadn't told her to refuse to go to Iran under the threat of divorce. My own father, better equipped to understand Iran, implored me to reconsider. I hadn't even told Karri or my father about being stopped at Tehran's airport the last time I flew there, for I was almost certain that if I had, Karri would have refused to go and would insist that I never set foot there again, and my father would have threatened to disown me. So here we were, six or so hours away from Tehran, and Karri and I were equally nervous, for different reasons. I was uncertain whether going through passport control would be the promised breeze: perhaps the Intelligence Ministry officers had been lying, or perhaps someone higher up would decide to detain me anyway. Although I was not particularly frightened of another round of questioning, Karri would in all probability—how to put it—*freak out* if her first experience of the Islamic Republic was her husband being carted off for questioning while she tried to soothe a crying baby in a country where she didn't speak the language, didn't have a phone, and hardly knew a soul to call anyway.

A typical flight to Iran is loaded with expats going home for vacations or to visit family, along with a smattering of actual residents of Iran returning from trips abroad and perhaps two or three non-Iranian businessmen, always in business class. Once on board, Karri checked to see who was drinking alcohol and who was looking at her, an obvious Westerner sitting in coach with an obviously Western baby, occasionally breast-feeding him. She, along with quite a few of our traveling companions, had wine with dinner.

When we landed, she adjusted the scarf she had worn around her neck to cover her head, just as most of the other women did. We followed the other passengers into the arrivals hall without speaking to each other, preoccupied with our thoughts and with keeping our son, who had been awakened at an ungodly hour for him, as quiet as possible. At passport control, when it was our turn, I handed over our Iranian passports—mine a few years old, and Karri's and our baby's brand-new.

The officer, to my relief, seemed as bored as they usually are and smiled when he looked first at the baby's picture and then at him, in my arms, with a just-woken-up sulking expression on his face.

"His name is Khashayar?" he said, mildly surprised. "And he's *American?*"

"Yes," I replied. "We call him Khash, too." (*Khash*, at least in the Yazdi idiom, means "happy" or "pleasant.")

"What a fantastic name! It's a real man's name, not like what they name their kids these days," the immigration officer said disapprovingly, referring to a recent trend among middle- and upper-class Iranians—ones he encounters at the international airport—to pick made-up or non-Iranian words as names for their children. "Can't even tell from the name if it's a boy or a girl!" He stamped our passports without another word, and we were officially in Iran.

My heart had raced when he had scanned my passport, but now
I felt relief—*no instructions to report to a ministry, no questioning, and no wor-
ries,* I thought, *at least probably not, until we're ready to leave Iran.* As we got
on the escalator to descend to baggage claim, I could see my friend
Khosro and my cousin's husband Ali Khatami through the glass par-
tition, and as soon as Khash's stroller came through on the conveyor
belt, I told Karri to take him outside, past customs, to wait with our
welcoming party while I collected the rest of our luggage. I watched
them greet one another through the soundproof and presumably bul-
letproof glass, a little horrified as Karri not only shook hands with
them but also kissed both men, and Ali's daughter, on both cheeks.
Head scarf: check. Modest clothing and the obligatory manteau (a
coat, of any fabric, that covers a woman's behind and extends to the
knees): check. Not shaking hands with and not embracing men (one
of them a former president's brother and someone who is carefully
watched and monitored) in public: definitely *no* check. It would take
time, I knew, for Karri to remember all the rules, and I suspected that
she would never quite adjust.

As I slowly put each heavy bag on a cart, two extra-large carts actually,
and made my way to customs, I started to worry anew. Each bag had
to be unloaded and pass through an X-ray machine—the equivalent
of a lie detector for one's luggage—and as I received the assistance
of a young man whose sole job is to help with the oversize and overweight bags Iranians always seem to travel with, I watched my wife
and son with my friends and family and wondered if this had been a
big mistake. Was I incredibly irresponsible, as my friend Glenn had
suggested, or was I just selfish? I was a new father at an advanced age;
had I given enough thought to the well-being of my child? What if
his mother got herself arrested by the morality squad tomorrow for
some unintended infraction? What if I got myself arrested for saying

something not to the liking of one of the many authorities in charge of the national security of the Islamic Republic? Looking at Khash through the glass made me panic for a moment. Had my years of being childless made me completely ill suited to fatherhood?

I had spent the first half century of my life—I'm not suggesting there will be a second half century—childless. It's not that I was against having a child or children, although I did spend part of my youth clinging to the tired cliché that bringing yet another life into this shameful and overcrowded world was an act of supreme vanity at best and completely irresponsible at worst; it's just that I never gave it too much thought. My friends had kids, some while in their thirties, others later; my siblings and cousins had children of their own, and I loved them all. I always enjoyed seeing them—really I did—and I could recognize the joy they brought to their parents' lives. But somehow I didn't see myself as someone who needed to experience that particular kind of joy. Having a baby is an act of selfishness, I thought when I wanted to rationalize my hesitancy, but of course it is simultaneously an act of supreme selflessness. I recognized that, too, but the idea of selflessness wasn't enough to make me want to be a father. You can be selfless in other ways, perhaps even by contributing in some way to the part of mankind that's already been born. Plus, as a perpetual worrier, I knew that worrying about mankind in general was probably a little easier on the nerves, having practiced it from an early age, than worrying about my very own little mankind.

Once we had our son, all those ideas went out the window, and worrying about my child didn't seem a big deal anymore; it was simply no longer something to actively contemplate. The worry is just there, accepted, a new constant, like breathing, involuntary and not worthy of thought, for the rest of one's life. But here I was consciously worrying about my son, Khashayar, the guy with the cool name, according to one government official, who like all infants was just happy he had woken up to his parents still being around, and who seemed to also be happy with the attention my friend and family were paying him, but who had no inkling of what his father might be subjecting him to. The idea of selfishness and selflessness crisscrossed my mind, and I was suddenly sure I'd be condemning myself later for depositing my family in a strange country where the rules of the West did not all apply.

The water filters in our luggage, along with the baby food, the diapers, the medicines, and all the other personal belongings, passed the X-ray test with flying colors. The machine operator looked bored as he glanced at the see-through bags on his screen, and I wondered what he was looking for, if not strange-shaped charcoal filters and plastic packages filled with gooey substances. Alcohol? Subversive literature? I had magazines, as I always do, in my carry-on, along with my laptop, and Karri's Kindle had books loaded on it, so that couldn't be it. Alcohol, although banned in Iran, is readily available everywhere, so I couldn't imagine anyone bothering to smuggle in a few bottles of booze. It remained a mystery to me what exactly would trigger suspicion at customs—except for weapons, of course—if not a solo man with six heavy suitcases and three carry-ons.

It was fortunate, in the end, that both Khosro and Ali Khatami had come to the airport. I had known Khosro was coming (we were going to be staying with him at his house until we found our own apartment), since he had insisted that with all our luggage we'd need the use of his truck. But not even his vintage Nissan Patrol could accommodate everything, so we split our belongings between his truck and Ali's SUV and headed to town. I sat in the passenger seat of Ali's car, with Khash, Karri, and Ali's daughter Nasseem in the back, while Khosro and his sometime employee Ali *Amreekayee* (Ali the American, known for his love of all things United States) rode in Khosro's truck with most of our luggage.

We approached the city on a clear moonlit spring night, speeding through empty streets, passing through tunnels, on and off overpasses and the highways that ringed and bisected Tehran. Garish neon lights everywhere illuminated fluttering flags on every bridge.

With twinkling lights extending as far as the eye could see, I turned to ask Karri how she felt, now that she was finally in the country she had heard and read so much about. "I feel like I'm in a cartoon," she said. A cartoon? It was alien, yes, with the fancifully colored lights, the flags, the strange writing everywhere, and that's what Karri, ever the visually oriented person, meant. But Iran, the country I was born in, a country I always thought of as sophisticated, cultured, and my home, reduced to a cartoon on first impression? *Yes,* I thought, *but that won't last very long.*

International flights from Europe arrive in Iran in the early hours of the morning, usually between midnight and six, ostensibly for security reasons, but I've always thought it was to spare poor travelers from having to spend as long in Tehran daytime traffic as they did on the flight over. We breezed into town in the middle of the night, and perhaps what made the place seem cartoonish, beyond the goofy and garish neon colors or the alien alphabet on the billboards, was the speed with which we made turns, crossing one highway after the next and ending up on a narrow street in the middle of the city.

We were at Khosro's house a good fifteen minutes before he made it back, his vintage Nissan no match for Ali's late-model Toyota SUV. I had a key, and we went into the house, slowly carrying each overweight suitcase up a flight of stairs to the private apartment Khosro had set aside for us. Karri seemed relieved that we were in a comfortable home, but at the same time she was looking around for every possible danger to Khash—first the stairs, then the wall sockets, and finally every piece of furniture, especially the glass-topped tables. But it was time to put Khash, whose sleep had been interrupted by our arrival at the airport, to bed, so I left Karri to that thankless task and went downstairs to chat with Ali and Khosro, who had just arrived.

"So," both of them said, almost simultaneously, "you're here!"

Yes, we were in Iran, and while they expressed it in a happy, pleasant, and welcoming way, I panicked for a moment. Now what? I wondered. How would I even begin to organize our life in Tehran? On my previous trips, sitting with Khosro in his living room after I had arrived from the airport had been an exciting moment—I would enjoy myself, knowing that I'd have no responsibility for others' well-being and happiness, and that I'd probably be leaving just as I was getting homesick. But this time, and for the first time for me in Iran, I had no idea what to expect, and no idea how my wife and child would cope.

The panic subsided quickly, though, and all I could think, as I went upstairs to get ready to go to bed, was that we had done it. We were here, safe, and it would all be okay. It was Iran, after all, my country and my people. I was going to let nothing faze me.

3

WE LOVE YOU
(US EITHER)

Waking up the first day in Tehran has always been for me an extraordinary feeling. I don't feel the pollution in the air, and I don't really hear the incessant traffic noise; I only feel a comfortable sense of home. Waking up with my wife and son the first day of our stay in Iran was different. Apart from the fact that Khash wanted to explore the house where we were staying by crawling everywhere on the hard, slippery marble floors, floors that led to hard marble stairs, and apart from the fact that I had yet to persuade Karri that the water from the tap was quite drinkable, I had a to-do list that I had no idea how to fulfill. Sheep's milk yogurt? American-style diapers? Nontoxic baby wipes? Organic nuts and raisins? I had to quickly figure out how to replenish our stock, and I wanted to get an early start, before Karri sank into depression about leaving behind a perfectly good life to live in an alien country, all for her husband's vanity and his incomprehensible yearning for a motherland.

Khosro lives in the house where he was born, an early-twentieth-century traditional Persian house, surrounded by high mud walls that hide it from Safi Alishah, a street in downtown Tehran, just south of the former U.S. embassy, in a neighborhood that was once upper class but is now middle to lower and very religious. Motorcycles zoom up the one-way street and occasionally down, identical cheap 1960s-era Chinese 125cc bikes assembled in Iran and sold under so many different brand names—Tondar, Rayka, Behrun, Shayda, Parvaz, Pishro, Tondro, and many, many others—that I lost track ages ago. They sound like 1960s-era bikes, too, and belch fumes like vintage vehicles begging for service or an engine overhaul. Bought new, these bikes cost less than a thousand dollars, with drum brakes, kick starter, and all; used, they can be had for the price of dinner for two at one of the fancier Tehran restaurants; and *very* used, for the price of a couple of kebabs. As such, they are ubiquitous, but nowhere does one feel their presence more than downtown Tehran, in the business districts, where they are used in lieu of trucks. They carry impossible loads through impossibly narrow streets and alleys that were never designed for anything but the horses and donkeys that were present even in my young days and omnipresent when my mother grew up not too far from where we were staying. In the poorer residential parts of town, a motorbike might be a family's sole mode of transportation, and sometimes entire families ride on one, making for a visual spectacle as women balance their children and clutch their chadors simultaneously, and a horrifying sight on the highways.

One can understand why the government makes available a vehicle that almost everyone can afford, yet it's incomprehensible that a government so proud of its technological abilities and accomplishments persists in allowing vehicles on the road that don't meet the very safety and pollution standards that officials themselves insist are important in tackling Tehran's air quality issues and reducing its unenviable accident rate. Anyone wondering whether Iran's trumpeted scientific progress is bluster or fact has to think the former, as I do, based solely on the motorbikes it manufactures. *How hard can it be,* I wondered, more annoyed this time than on previous trips, *to build a cheap but modern scooter?*

Karri remarked on the cacophony the moment we woke up.

"What's with all the motorbikes? It's worse than in India." She had spent months at a time in Mysore studying Ashtanga yoga, which she teaches in New York while also designing and manufacturing her own active-wear clothing line. In fact, she always rented a scooter herself in India as her sole means of transportation. "It's only like this in this neighborhood," I assured her, "and we'll find an apartment where you won't hear a single bike." But it was the pollution that seemed to affect her most. Her throat was already itchy, she complained, and it was only her first day. Khash, in his new pajamas, was black from the soot that settles on the floors within minutes of mopping them. And Khosro obsessively mops every day, sometimes twice. I hadn't noticed that in my previous trips, having not ever gotten down on all fours, and it suddenly gave me a new appreciation for the plastic slippers that Iranians wear indoors. Karri was terrified by the amount of dust and soot Khash was collecting—just as much was entering his lungs, she said—and by his cheerful attempts to pull at every electrical cord and glass object on any table within his tiny grasp.

"My throat is swelled up," Karri announced for the second time, as we drank Nescafé, the coffee of choice in Iranian households, where tea is taken far more seriously. Even top hotels in Iran proudly serve Nescafé, I had warned Karri—almost certainly a remnant of the days when instant coffee was viewed as a miracle of modern science—but we'd be able to get good coffee at the numerous coffee shops that have sprung up around the capital in recent years, like the Starbucks knockoff Raees Coffee, which has a litigation-worthy logo and actually serves Starbucks coffee beans imported by individuals in suitcases (as do other coffee shops).

"Your throat?" I asked. "Do you think you caught a bug on the plane?"

"No!" she cried. "It's all the pollution."

"And this is the good time of year," I said. "Just wait until winter. But we'll be in a part of the city that's less polluted, I promise."

The noise from the traffic outside was now compounded by the screams and cries of hundreds of little boys playing in the courtyard of the kindergarten and elementary school, Payam Ghadir, across the street, waiting for class to begin. Payam Ghadir is a highly regarded and expensive institution, academically rigorous, but because of its religious leanings and its location, it mostly serves the sons of the wealthy religious classes, including a good number of mullahs, some of whom drop their kids off and collect them personally, highly conspicuous in their priestly garb to any Westerner and an exotic first sight for Karri. Incessant traffic noise, screaming schoolchildren, pollution, and dust, dust everywhere: this is the bristling metropolis on any given day, and it's a less-than-pleasant welcome for visitors from afar.

On that very first morning in Tehran, and well before we had become accustomed to the vagaries of Iranian traffic, Karri decided we needed to get a car to take us to a market she had found on the Web, a market that supposedly carried organic products, which she was desperate to prove existed in Iran. "Organic?" Khosro had said questioningly. "Everything is organic here. Nobody wants to spend the money on pesticides or stuff like that! It's cheaper to let half the crop go bad than to spray it with chemicals." He was half right— some produce, particularly from smaller farms, is indeed "organic," or close enough. But Iranian farmers do also use pesticides, probably some that are banned in the West.

The efficient local car service, Safi Cars, sent a car around right away, a small Iranian-made Kia Pride, and I noticed the dismay on the driver's face when I walked out of the house carrying a car seat, an object I now despised even more than I had in New York for having lugged it across continents. He opened the back door, and I set it down on the seat, realizing then that there were no seat belts in the back to secure it.

"Passengers don't like the seat belts," he explained, as Karri looked on with a horrified expression to which I was soon to be accustomed. "The clips dig into their backsides, so we stuff them under the seats."

I looked at Karri imploringly, but her expression was firm. *It's our first day,* I thought, *and I'm not going to disappoint her.* "Yeah," I said, "but we need them for the child seat."

He shrugged and opened the trunk, dug around for a few minutes under the backseat for the belts, and finally pulled them through the seat from inside the passenger compartment, sweating profusely and looking a bit unhappy. Seat belts are mandatory for front seat passengers in Iran, and most people wear them (I even got ticketed once for not wearing one), but the idea that one would fasten a seat belt in the back is completely alien, even if a baby is involved. In fact, although car seats are readily available in the shops—at twice the price of the same ones in Europe or America, too expensive for most Iranian families—I realized that I had never actually seen one in a car, and I also soon realized that Iranians carry their babies in their laps. The way everybody in the world did when I was growing up.

"That's not going to happen," said Karri firmly, when I opined that car seats were impractical in Iran, unless we owned our own car, and that we might want to leave ours at home. I knew better than to argue, but I was also confident that after this first experience, Khash would be riding in our laps. And I was right. Iran is like that. It makes you adjust, quickly, no matter your life philosophy.

The organic market turned out to be a complete bust, a small store that carried very little of anything, let alone anything genuinely organic, but after some prodding from Karri, I asked the driver if he knew where we could get sheep's milk yogurt. I had promised her that all Iranians ate sheep's milk cheese and yogurt, which by definition would be less hormone- and antibiotic-laden than cow's milk equivalents, but having never before shopped for groceries in Iran, I had been wrong. Iranians *used* to eat sheep's milk dairy products, but times had changed, and the bovine dairy industry had effectively promoted its products as safer, more sanitary, and "better" than the traditional ones. Even the famous Iranian feta cheese, a staple for many families, was now mostly hermetically packaged in plastic tubs and made from pasteurized cow's milk rather than raw sheep's milk.

The driver, though, knew of a *labaneeyat*, a dairy shop, nearby, where sheep's milk products might be available in season (which we discovered later is rather short and depends on the sheep's natural cycles rather than on the demand of the market). Iran, despite its modern supermarkets and grocery stores, still has traditional shops such as butchers, dairy markets, and bakeries in every neighborhood, although they are rapidly decreasing in number. But the idea that we could get fresh yogurt from a specialty store appealed to Karri. Early spring is when the sheep-milking season begins (another fact I was previously ignorant of), so I was ecstatic to discover that indeed, large buckets of locally made sheep's yogurt were available at the shop, and at a decent price, too.

The yellow-tinged rim of fat on the lip made me hesitate for a moment, and I asked the shopkeeper if the yogurt was pasteurized. Laughing, he replied, "Yogurt is by definition pasteurized, or at least free of harmful bacteria. That's the whole point of yogurt, isn't it? It's safe." Of course, I thought, somewhat embarrassed. When we arrived home from our last trip in a taxi with a car seat, we all ate the yogurt except for Khosro, who refused to have anything to do with something as backward and potentially dangerous as yogurt made locally by who knows whom.

We hadn't been in Tehran long before I was reminded that children in Iran, boys and girls equally, are considered precious, conspicuously so. Too precious at times, it seems to me: mothers refer to their sons as *doodool talah*—golden penis—which has only resulted in millions of Iranian men the world over truly believing that their manhood is gold, to be treasured by every woman they meet and even those they don't. My own rather Westernized parents never took expressions of filial affection to that extreme, so I never imagined quite how Iranian society treats children until I had one of my own and walked the streets of Tehran with him.

In our first few days on Safi Alishah, we had ruled out using our stroller in the neighborhood: not only was it rather cumbersome and heavy to maneuver on the tapering or nonexistent sidewalks of downtown Tehran—never mind getting across the *joobs*, the narrow canals that line Tehran streets and that once used to channel water from the mountains north of the city to residents in the flats and beyond—but it would be impossible to go into even a deli with the damn thing, given that entrances to stores were barely negotiable by single adults. No, children too small to walk are carried by Iranians, and strollers are an extremely expensive proposition in Iran anyway, purchased and used only by upscale Persians farther north in the city. Although we were proud, like all new parents, of our son's percentile ranking in weight and height, it ruled out actually carrying him even a few blocks, so the BabyBjörn sling became Khash's mode of transport for a short while. We didn't know, of course, that baby slings don't exist in Iran, or that even if they did, no self-respecting man would strap his son to his chest rather than just carry him, like a *real* man.

The looks I received from women, but mostly men, were disapproving to say the least. Unlike Westerners, Iranians are entirely comfortable expressing their thoughts on children and child care to complete strangers. I caught on fast that walking down the street with a baby against my chest seemed unmanly to passersby, but there was apparently another concern on the minds of some. "Don't carry your son like that!" one elderly man admonished me. "He'll get a hernia." *Huh?* My quizzical look encouraged him to explain. "His legs are spread too far apart, and you're bouncing him up and down."

"Thanks," I replied, walking away. "He'll be all right." Like staring, which is also perfectly normal and acceptable among Iranians, nosiness, or *foozooli*, is a Persian trait one simply has to adjust to if one lives in Iran. And other complete strangers, if not worried about our son's well-being, felt free to marvel, quite sincerely, at his beauty, or to comment on how fortunate we were to have been bestowed this gift from god, some expressing their undying love for him and even begging for a kiss or a hug.

Iranians' solicitude toward children and their well-being is annoying and touching at the same time, but it doesn't extend to two particular circumstances: while driving in traffic and in crowded situations, such as in the bazaar, where people jostle one another trying to move forward, backward, and into the merchants' stalls. Karri refused to return to the Tehran Grand Bazaar after our visit the first week to buy some washcloths and to look for manteaus for her: she walked with both hands protecting Khash from the elbows and shoves of shoppers, and in the Friday Bazaar, Tehran's main flea and antique market, which I ordinarily like but which Karri also refused to ever set foot in again, she faced not only rude and aggressive behavior, despite the baby strapped to her, but the admonitions of a young woman who chased us down an aisle in the searing heat and repeatedly told us, in English, that the bazaar was no place to bring a child. "Mind your own business!" I finally yelled, not for the last time on our visit.

But of course she was right. Here it was, the unique beauty of con-

tradictory Iranian behavior: simultaneous extreme concern and complete disregard. My friend Khosro, cynic that he is, recognizes the
contradictions inherent in Iranian culture and in societal norms, but
he was convinced that the only reason that woman chased us down
was to practice, or to show off, her English, as loudly as she could.
And that, sadly, was probably partially true, because for an Iranian
there is almost no greater contribution to a sense of self-importance
and vanity than to be seen in public comfortably conversing with a
foreigner in his or her language, English ranking highest. Oddly for
an Islamic country, it's usually women who insist on striking up a
conversation with *farangis* (foreigners, from the root word *farang*, which
once meant "France" but now denotes "anywhere not Iran"), even
when it's just to berate them.

The combination of traffic and children is a whole other story, perhaps the single most disturbing aspect of Tehran, to any foreign
mother and probably to some Iranian ones, too. I had experienced,
naturally, the city's horrific traffic and, more important, the aggressive driving that makes it a requirement for any pedestrian to undergo
a course on how to cross a street, but I hadn't imagined that Tehran's
drivers—men, women, and in some cases children, yes, children sitting in their fathers' laps and actually driving; one time we saw one
as young as Khash doing so, with a wide grin matching his father's—
would not only be discourteous to someone crossing the street with
a baby stroller but would actually in some cases accelerate, as if the
child were an obstacle to be avoided at top speed or run down if
collision was unavoidable. By the end of our stay, after almost a year
of crossing streets at clearly marked crosswalks, often while a traffic policeman viewed the parade of cars refusing to slow down for
anyone unless they flung themselves into traffic (as I had been taught

to do by Khosro years earlier), it was still unclear to me whether the drivers thought more points were to be gained in that unique Tehran derby by avoiding a baby or by slamming into him.

Karri, needless to say, was purely horrified. How, she wondered, could a people so polite, so gracious, and so orderly in normal life turn into Nightriders of *Mad Max* fame and transform Tehran, with its utter ordinariness and occasional beauty, into a dystopian nightmare of homicidal drivers and impotent cops? After a while, she developed her own method of crossing the street with Khash, a peculiarly New York method that involved raising her hand palm outward, as if she had the full authority to halt traffic, and yelling at the top of her voice, in English, as she made her way across. Always her screams would involve profanities, of the "What the fuck!!" and "Shit!!" and just plain "Fuck!" type, reminding me of Ratso Rizzo in *Midnight Cowboy* and his contretemps with a Manhattan cabbie: "Hey, I'm walking here! I'm walking here!" If only Tehran could be as civilized as New York—in the driving habits of its citizens, I mean.

It soon became routine: me trying to use my "pedestrian ed"—far more important in Iran, it seems, than "drivers' ed"—and gingerly cross, holding my hands down low and waving to indicate to the drivers aiming for me what my next move would be; Karri insisting, with raised arms, on her right to cross; and Khash, after numerous experiences, thinking that yelling at the top of one's voice was just something one did when one crossed the street, a habit he kept up long after we returned to New York. Fortunately he was too young to understand his mother's cursing, but on the occasion now when he says something that sounds terribly like "fuck," and we wonder where he could have possibly heard such an utterance, I can't help but think he's retrieved a distant memory of crossing the streets of Tehran in his stroller—and not from the drivers. In Iran, as in New York,

I occasionally would get into a screaming match with a driver if he or she actually slowed down enough to hear me. Sometimes my pushing Khash along forced a car to come to a complete stop, and I was often taken aback by women drivers' vehement insistence that it was me and my baby who were the inconvenience, and not them and their cars accelerating through the crosswalk—they would even curse me as they drove by. Karri came to believe that women drivers, socially oppressed in many ways, act out their frustrations when they are behind the wheel, exercising one of the few powers they have in Iran. I tend to think of the behavior less in feminist terms; loving children and running them down in the street is just one of those Persian contradictions that is probably impossible to understand or explain.

One time, near our own apartment when we first moved there, a taxi with four women passengers was moving slowly, very slowly, out of a parking spot. Karri held up her hand as usual and continued to walk in front of it. The taxi didn't stop. "Hey, hey, hey!" she shouted, as it almost hit her and Khash's stroller.

"'Hey, hey'?" the driver mocked at my wife through his open window. "What do you mean 'hey, hey'?" he sneered.

"She means 'stop,' you *ablah*," I said, using a word that emphatically denotes an idiot. "It's people like you who make foreigners think we're a bunch of savages."

That set the man off. He stopped the car and got out, ready to fight, an occurrence unfortunately far too common on the streets of Tehran, where tempers flare at the slightest perceived insult. "Come back here if you're a man!" he shouted, as the women in the car remained silent. "They *think* we're savages?" he cried. "We *are* savages! Don't you know that?"

I kept walking, now pushing the stroller, as he continued his rant, insisting that yes, we Iranians are savages, and how could I think otherwise? "Yes, we *are* savages!" he yelled, again and again, his voice fading as I climbed the hill to our apartment, wondering when he'd give up or when the women in his car would finally insist he drive them to their destination rather than engage in verbal battle with someone who had married a *farangi* and had been foolish enough to bring her to Iran.

"Savages" is exactly how Khosro often describes his fellow residents of the city of his birth. He bemoans the loss of Persian *farhang*, the culture he claims we once had, lost forever in this impossibly over-crowded and chaotic, haphazardly expanding capital of a rapidly developing country. He still loves his hometown, more as a concept—the romanticized quiet and beautiful place he grew up in—than as a functioning, modern city whose more than twelve million residents all fight for a small piece of whatever it can offer. But unlike Khosro, I have little nostalgia for the city of my birth, and once established there, I began to feel that his sense of the place and the culture was not unlike my own (and other New Yorkers') sense of New York, a sense that the changes we witness over the years are not happy ones, that a once-livable city is no longer so, and that new generations of residents have little in common with us, the long-term and older citizens. Tehran has changed dramatically in a short period of time, and the sense of loss for people like Khosro, and even the taxi driver who wouldn't stop yelling at me, is palpable. Traffic, or dodging it and its attendant clamor, is only one element of Tehran that is disturbing to its residents and visitors alike; the city is also an architectural disaster: a hodgepodge of the monstrously ugly new and the gracious but deteriorating old—like Khosro's house—lends the city an unfinished quality, mirroring the revolution itself.

The newly constructed high-rise apartments and office buildings—none designed to reflect anything other than the enormous sums of money spent—add to the feeling that the city makes no sense. It doesn't, but nonetheless it functions. From the millions of automobiles that pour into the ill-suited streets and alleys and somehow make it to their destinations, to the lush parks that the city has built and maintained and that my family and I took full advantage of every day, to the oddly clean streets and pristine water supply, it all does work. And the culture—a mash-up of self-deprecation, prescribed and proscribed behavior, a superiority-inferiority complex, and a Shia sense of martyrdom, prompting Tehranis to proclaim their fellow citizens, and even themselves, savages—endures just fine. It's a culture not particular to Iran's biggest, most chaotic city but applies to all Persians. Still, the paradoxes of Iranian life are on extreme display in Tehran, visible to everyone—especially to a couple with an infant in tow.

For instance, the cultural penchants for exaggeration and exaggerated behavior, the inappropriate-to-Western-ears expressions of love and devotion for a complete stranger, and the obsequiousness toward foreigners were quickly evident. We experienced them all from the doormen in our apartment building, who couldn't let Khash walk by without picking him up for a hug. (One said, when he first met him, "*Ghorbooneh esmesh beram, khoda hefzesh koneh,*" which means literally "May I be sacrificed for his name, god protect him.") The doorman of the *next* building down the block would run out of the building and grab him, lift him in the air, and give him a hug every time he spied us walking by. So did the shopkeepers whose stores we'd frequent daily, the people in the parks we'd take him to play with, and the patrons, waiters, and waitresses in our favorite restaurants and cafés.

At one of the very few vegetarian cafés in downtown Tehran, which had a hip, artsy clientele—women in tight manteaus and haphazardly worn scarves, men and women almost all in jeans and printed T-shirts—an older man seated at the next table with two young girls couldn't stop talking to Khash, telling him how much he loved him and also how he wanted to hold him. "Can I borrow your

jeegar?" he asked. *Jeegar* means "liver" in Farsi and for some unfathomable reason also means "beloved." It was hard to translate for Karri,
but she understood. I told her I know Persians like their barbecued
chicken livers, a favorite street food, but no one has ever been able
to tell me why or how *liver* and *love* became linguistically intertwined,
foie gras notwithstanding.

Another time, outside the same café, near Khosro's house and
a regular stop for us, a young woman dropped to her knees, made
a ring out of paper, and proposed to a curious Khash. He happily
accepted the ring, but marriage was out of his league, I explained to
her, and would be out of hers when it was in his. Another woman, no
older than twenty, made us promise we'd bring him back in twenty
years so she could date him, while a young man in a different park,
who sat watching him with a notebook in hand, occasionally writing, finally mustered the courage to approach me and ask if it was
okay for him to give me a poem he'd just written about my son. "I
was depressed," he said, "until I saw your son. What's his name?" I
told him; he scribbled a few more words on the paper, then tore some
pages from the notebook.

I took the pages and tried to make out what he had written, slowly,
since my Farsi reading skills still left much to be desired. "Thanks
very much."

"No, no, really," he replied. "I've been depressed for a long time,
really depressed. It's hard, this life in Iran. But your son awakened
something in me. I must thank you." He left me to decipher his
poem, waving farewell to Khash, who was busy stuffing grass into
his mouth and was by now hardly surprised by all the attention he
received the moment he left the house.

"Hands and knees on the ground," it read,

Curious of everything,
Smiling lips,
Golden hair and hanging cheeks,

Without a care for the miseries of life,
What a pure, delicate creature is a child!
Full of movement, full of happiness,
A child of humankind, I know
Maybe you'll be the start of a new world . . .

Okay, it's not Milton, at least not in my translation, but his gesture was sweet and, more important, genuine. I felt bad for him, a young man, like many Iranian youth, sitting on a park bench on a weekday afternoon contemplating life. Unemployment is staggeringly high here—government figures in the low double digits are widely believed to be supremely optimistic—especially for the millions of university graduates, and with all the social restrictions in place under the Islamic system, such as the prohibition on the mingling of unmarried men and women and the absence of any bars, there's very little hope for them to have any real pleasure in life. Other than sitting on a park bench, of course, occasionally inspired by a young child, or by the couples who do manage to find love and sit together, furtively holding hands and stealing a kiss now and then, away from the morality police, who patrol everywhere except, it seemed, this one park that we frequented almost every day.

I struggled to read the rest of the poem. At the end the man had penned a little note, and signed his name. "I was sad," it read, "so I came to the park. The smiling Khashayar's playing around and his happiness brought a smile to my lips. Wishing everyone happiness, freedom, and love." Indeed. Love to all. That was my Iran, and my Tehran—its warts receded just a little in the shadow of humanity.

Much later in our stay, the overly fulsome greetings Khash received led to a more ominous encounter at a rest stop on the highway connecting Tehran with Qom, the religious center of power in Iran, a couple of hours south. (The road is well traveled by devout Tehranis who escape the havoc of the city more often for pilgrimage reasons than for any other.) As we were walking from the parking lot to the building, Khash and Karri hand in hand, a large, rotund, bearded man in his forties with his black chador–clad wife—signaling a religious family—a few paces behind, suddenly rushed over to Khash, bent down, and said a few words in Farsi. Karri shook her head, but he tried to force a kiss on Khash's cheek, managing to get a peck in.

From a few yards away, I yelled at him, "Stop! No, you cannot kiss my son! Go away!"

He gave me a dirty look. "I was doing it out of kindness," he snarled, "and I asked permission."

"You can see that my wife is foreign, that she's not Iranian and doesn't understand Farsi. Can't you see that a stranger rushing up to her child will freak her out?" I said angrily, then grabbed Khash and walked away.

I was furious, but also a little concerned. Getting into a fight with a religious man just outside Qom was not a good idea, not while our taxi driver was busy praying inside the building. As we approached the doors to the building, a family that had been watching glared at me. "It's disconcerting to have strangers grab and kiss your child," I said to the husband, a man in his thirties with jet-black hair, a finely trimmed thick beard, and a windbreaker, who looked very much like the Revolutionary Guards and the Basij—the volunteer ultrareligious militia, originally formed during the Iran-Iraq War, who in recent years have been employed by the Guards to crack down on protesters—who all seem to trim their hair and beards in the exact same style. His wife, under a black chador, pulled their two children close to her, as if it might be me who was the menace, and not the middle-aged man who grabbed my son and kissed him.

"He was just doing it out of *kindness*," he admonished, emphasizing the word as he put his hands in his pockets and paced slowly. He shook his head as I walked away, but I wondered if he, and perhaps his zealot buddies, would be waiting for us when we came back out of the coffee shop, to teach me and my wife a lesson in *mohabat*, or kindness, that he thought I didn't comprehend.

The fact that everybody—even strangers on the street—would give advice on what our son should and shouldn't be doing initially annoyed Karri, but ultimately it proved a comfort. It reinforced the idea that Iranians are obsessive about health and well-being. I've always maintained that Iranians are the world's biggest hypochondriacs—after the French, perhaps, and Karri—and that they take not just love, but self-love and vanity, to extremes. Yes, life may be shameful; yes, we may not be able to do anything about the environment and the noxious fumes from our cars, bikes, and furnaces; those are realities that we refuse to take responsibility for, but why not be healthy, and look good, in one's shame? There is almost nothing an Iranian won't go to the doctor for, no fever that isn't debilitating and in need of antibiotics, no pain that doesn't require an X-ray, if not an MRI, and no pill that they won't take if told it is good, and it doesn't matter what *for*.

Pharmacies, all spotless and modern, stand on every corner in Tehran exactly as in France, and twenty-four-hour drugstores dot the city, for that emergency dose of whatever medicine one might need, plus every imaginable cosmetic ointment, cream, or makeup item, domestic and imported, required for primping and youth maintenance. Viagra and Cialis may be two of the most popular drugs in the wee hours of the morning, for they are sold without prescription and advertised prominently in every pharmacy, usually next to the huge display of condoms near the front door. Their presence came as a shock to Karri, who had not imagined open condom sales in a country that essentially forbids sensuality and in a culture that frowns on explicit mentions of sex. (Self-diagnosis is another common trait of Iranians, and perhaps of other hypochondriacs, and few would think that they needed a doctor to write a prescription for erectile dysfunction.) The sheer number of pharmacies, and the astounding number of doctors, as evidenced by the numerous medical buildings in every neighborhood, sometimes whole blocks of them, advertising their practitioners' specialties on signs outside, gave peace of mind to Karri early on, as did the fact that in my family we have doctors and pharmacists who obtained their advanced degrees in Europe.

That said, Karri also took to carrying an amulet to ward off the evil eye, as instructed by countless strangers every day—who would exclaim upon sight of Khash, "*Khoda hefzesh koneh!*" ("May god protect him!," among the first words in Farsi that Karri learned and understood). Merchants gave them to her to pin on Khash, even as they implored us also to burn *espand*, a wild rue, to protect him (presumably in case god forgot, or was too busy that day). Later on, when we were well established as residents of Tehran, my optician, an Esfahani, actually bought some *espand* for us, perhaps not believing we ever would, and gave us precise instructions for its use, which I tried to follow at Karri's insistence. Pre-Islamic Iranian superstition, as well as Islam's acceptance of the notion of the evil eye, makes every Iranian bazaar or trinket shop into talisman and *espand* central, and they, along with the thousands of pharmacies, clinics, doctors' offices, and medicinal herb stores, make Tehran a hypochondriac's delight.

Our first days passed in a tumult of errands and outings and welcome parties, but most afternoons found me standing peacefully in the gated courtyard of Khosro's house, sometimes holding Khash in my arms while watching the school across the road as classes let out. The racket of the morning was repeated then, and traffic would come to a grinding halt as taxis, buses, and private cars arrived on the narrow street to retrieve the boys, all seemingly desperate to exercise their lungs with the most polluted air of one of the most polluted cities on earth, exactly at the moment when the idling vehicles pumped even more toxins into their little bodies. But in a remarkable display of street theater, the traffic jam is sorted out every afternoon by a man whose only job seemingly is to ensure that every boy is united with his proper car, and that the various vehicles then extricate themselves from the bottleneck at the school gates and go on their way.

A big, burly man in his late thirties, always dressed in a pair of gray slacks and a white or blue dress shirt with the sleeves tightly buttoned at the wrist, no matter the weather, also usually clad in plastic slippers or occasionally a pair of sneakers, he resembles an orchestra conductor waving and pointing an imaginary baton, then a baritone opera singer as he bellows instructions to the drivers and the boys. They mock but don't taunt him and curiously seem to need no help in finding the right taxi to get into. Curious because the taxis are almost all the same, pale orange or green domestic models, such as the Saipa Saba (based on the Kia Pride, a car outdated even before its introduction in Iran), the IK Peugeot 405 in various guises (a 1980s-era vehicle still inexplicably produced in Iran), the Paykan (Iran's original domestically produced car, a deathtrap that was finally mercifully killed off in the twenty-first century), and the IK Samand, a newer Iranian car that is often equipped to run on natural gas, alleviating only slightly the pollution crisis in the city.

Despite the similarities of the vehicles and their random placement in the queue, which could not possibly be the same as it was when they dropped off the boys in the morning, the children fly out of the yard and rush to their cars blindly, the conductor only making sure that motorcycles snaking their way through the traffic don't run them over, and pile into the taxis that are often shared by three or four families—without a glance at the drivers, who all look the same anyway in their short Ahmadinejad haircuts, three-day-old beard growth, and short-sleeved dress shirts. Within fifteen minutes the school is quiet; the conductor, his surprisingly gentle manner with the unruly boys no longer on display, is on his own motorbike,

looking like a giant on a toy tricycle, and is heading home; and the
street is back to its normal, relatively calm state of a constant stream
of cars and motorbikes zooming by the house.

The noise from the school, early in the morning and louder in
midafternoon, didn't particularly bother me or Karri, perhaps because
our own son now provides plenty of immature vocal accompaniment
to our daily auditory experience. But the charm of the scene, which
so vividly illustrates the ability of Tehranis to make order out of
chaos, has eluded childless Khosro, whose life is still centered on
the street of his childhood, and who forever has to put up with the
din of traffic that barely existed even in his recent memory. He complained about it all the time, and even more about those infernal
two-wheeled machines called *motor* in Iran, and still more about what
the country, and his city, had come to. It was an early taste for Karri
of the ever-griping Iranian, who incongruously laments change while
rejecting traditions he or she views as backward (sheep's milk yogurt,
just for one example) and while deploring the persistence of the class
structure that was the norm in Khosro's childhood. "No one would
ride a *motor* when I was young," Khosro told Karri haughtily, "for
doing so was awfully lower class." Savagery and charm are in the eye
of the beholder on this once-elegant street of mansions and homes
and once-peaceful gardens, behind now mostly crumbling walls.

4

THE BIG SULK

—

Ghahr. Ghahr, ghahr, ta roozeh ghiamat, ghahr. "Sulk, sulk, until the day of reckoning, sulk." And boy, do Iranians know how to sulk. Sulking is a high art among them, and they do not limit it to personal relationships or dysfunctional families, as much of the world came to understand in the spring of 2011, when the president, Mahmoud Ahmadinejad, the bête noir of Western leaders, went on a public sulk for eleven days. He did so soon after we arrived for our stay in Iran, and naturally it was the only talk of the town, in a society as obsessed with the dynamics of its internal politics as it is with enforcing social behavior. Ahmadinejad, like virtually every Iranian politician before him, had indulged in minor sulks before, but this time he went all out, in a power play that he must have known he was destined to lose. But then, Iranian sulking isn't always about seeking immediate rewards, as we Iranians knew. And Ahmadinejad, the loser in this very Persian game of sulking, may have ultimately gotten what he really wanted out of his little episode.

What transpired to bring about the sulk was this: sometime in early 2011 (at the start of the Persian year), Ahmadinejad's chief of staff, Esfandiar Rahim Mashaie—the bête noir (everybody in Iran seems to be a bête noir of sorts, whether to a domestic audience or an international one) of other conservatives for his unorthodox views on Islam, social attitudes, and Iran-centric nationalistic sentiments—discovered that the Intelligence Ministry had been bugging his office. (Why was that a big surprise to him? many Iranians wondered. What did he think had been going on in the last thirty years of the paranoid, sometimes schizophrenic, Islamic Republic?) The deputy minister who informed him of this was an Ahmadinejad loyalist, while the intelligence minister, Heydar Moslehi, was a cleric, in effect appointed by the Supreme Leader and therefore loyal to no one but him. As the *vali-e-faqih*, or supreme jurisprudent, the Supreme Leader's title leaves no room for interpretation, even by a rascally president. So when Moslehi discovered that a deputy had been giving information to the Ahmadinejad camp, he fired him. Mashaie, incensed, called Moslehi and told him that he could not fire the deputy and in fact should himself resign immediately, per the president's order.

Here is where it got complicated. Under the Iranian constitution, the president is in charge of the cabinet, which includes the intelligence minister. But this is the Islamic Republic and not Switzerland, as I have been reminded, and when it comes to the Intelligence, Interior, and Foreign Ministries, he is only nominally in charge. Ahmadinejad had already infuriated the Supreme Leader, Ali Khamenei, by firing the foreign minister without permission a few months prior—presenting it as a fait accompli that the Supreme Leader had no choice but to go along with, given that he had so forcefully backed Ahmadinejad in the disputed 2009 elections and couldn't really be seen to publicly disagree with the man whose election he had deemed a "divine" decision. This time, however—perhaps because enough time had passed since the elections and the wave of protests that followed, or perhaps because Khamenei felt he had to put the president in his place, if only to avoid setting a dangerous precedent where a president might presume he really is in charge—the Supreme Leader reinstated Moslehi as intelligence minister, telling him to continue to work as if nothing had transpired.

An uncomfortable situation for all concerned, to say the least: *ghahr, ghahr, ta roozeh ghiamat, ghahr.* Ahmadinejad then did what any self-respecting Iranian would do when given offense: he sulked. He had no choice, really. He couldn't disobey the Supreme Leader, who isn't called Supreme for nothing. He also couldn't bow down and admit he'd been wrong, which would mean weakening himself in the eyes of his supporters as well as the general public, whom he had been desperate to woo since the Green Movement protests of 2009 showed how unpopular he was among a segment of society— upper-middle-class Iranians—with powerful economic interests and matching bank accounts. So he retreated to his home, refused to go to work or to attend cabinet meetings, and declined to comment or to talk to anyone about the affair. Sort of like the "I want to spend more time with my family" line that Western politicians peddle when they're retiring, or being forced to retire, from public life— which Ahmadinejad also claimed later, along with exhaustion, as his excuse. Except Ahmadinejad did talk to Ayatollah Jannati, the hard-line octogenarian mullah, a close confidant of the Supreme Leader and someone whom the Iranian secular class mocks not only for his too-often-preposterous views on everything from true Islamic values to the healthy state of democracy in Iran, but also for his capacity to have looked the same age for some thirty years now. Jannati, a one-time supporter of the president, was undoubtedly hoping to remind Ahmadinejad that he held a subservient role in Iranian politics, and Ahmadinejad was undoubtedly hoping to persuade, or threaten, the clerical leadership that he was not to be messed with. According to sources close to Jannati, and to text messages subsequently leaked to the cell phones of Iran's inquiring minds (in Iran every tidbit of polit-ical intrigue somehow makes the round of cell phones, forwarded and reforwarded by everyone almost as fast as a tweet in the West), Ahmadinejad had whined in his meeting, complaining that he should be allowed to have his say over the Supreme Leader because in the 2009 elections he would have received 35 million votes instead of

25 million if it hadn't been for the Supreme Leader's support, which he claimed *degraded* his standing among voters. Voters in Iran famously ignored the Supreme Leader's wishes in the elections of 1997 and 2001, which former president Khatami won in landslides, but no one had up until now suggested that one could win in a landslide if *not* for the Leader's support. But this was Ahmadinejad, who is either as delusional as some people believe, or a cunning operator who knows how to cajole, needle, and threaten his opponents into submission. Telling Jannati (which was the same as telling Khamenei) that the Supreme Leader of the Islamic Revolution *cost* him votes was about as big a *fuck you* to him—the Supreme Leader, that is—as anyone has dared to utter in the entire history of the republic. This fact was not lost on the population: Ahmadinejad's popularity actually grew because of his sulk and the insults, spoken and unspoken, that he had hurled at the Supreme Leader. The *nezam*, the system or regime, then came down harshly on Ahmadinejad through the state-controlled media, and even some reformists or people who had joined or sympathized with the Green Movement expressed to me a certain satisfaction that the pugnacious little president had challenged the emperor, not on the fact that he had no clothes, but on the notion of what exactly their so-called democracy was supposed to be. Okay, *also* on the fact that that the emperor had no clothes, or that his clothes were getting a little musty.

Mahmoud Ahmadinejad knew, of course, that he wouldn't win in an outright battle with the Supreme Leader and the old men who wielded real power in Iran. Despite having its first lay president in a generation, Iran was still controlled by the mosque, and its byzantine and even Orwellian political structure that laid ultimate authority at the feet of one ayatollah remained unchanged. Yes, that system's separation of powers in theory means that the judiciary, the execu-

tive, and the legislative branches are independent, and Islamic Iran
has other layers too—importantly, the Guardian Council, a body
consisting of six clerics directly appointed by the Supreme Leader
and six jurists charged with interpreting the constitution, who have
the power to veto any legislation passed by the parliament, or Majles.
There are also two other bodies: the Expediency Discernment Council, an assembly appointed by the Supreme Leader that is charged
with settling disputes between the Majles and the Guardian Council,
and the Assembly of Experts, a directly elected body of senior clerics, mostly in their old age, who are charged with choosing Supreme
Leaders and monitoring their performance—a Shia politburo, if you
will, but one that has always remained loyal to the Supreme Leader
and endorsed his policies.

So Ahmadinejad wouldn't be able to fire the minister of intelligence if the Supreme Leader decided it was against "expediency"—
the exact word used by hard-line conservatives to defend the Leader's
blatant, direct, and public interference in the affairs of an administration that in the past had only ever been subtle, indirect, and
private with the full and confidential compliance of the presidents.
But Ahmadinejad was going to gain something from the sulk, for as
much as Khamenei was unwilling to tolerate a president going rogue,
Ahmadinejad knew that he also couldn't tolerate another political
upheaval, which would likely come to pass if the sulk turned into a
resignation or if Parliament impeached him as a result of his challenge to the Leader. Impeachment—which Sadegh Kharrazi, a close
associate of the Supreme Leader, related by marriage even, who is
also a staunch reformist (the Supreme Leader has never completely
disassociated himself from reformists), once told me would occur if
Ahmadinejad won the 2009 elections and strayed one inch from his
designated operating sphere—was essentially out of the picture if the
president came out of his sulk.

More important, his most trusted aide, the spied-upon Mashaie, whom he had been prevented from appointing vice president

in 2009 by Khamenei and who after two years of withering attacks against him was now in danger of being arrested for, among other things, sorcery and leading a "deviant" current in Iranian politics, would gain a certain immunity from actual prosecution whenever Ahmadinejad deigned to return to work. Ahmadinejad had planned his sulk and knew the cards he was holding. Many observers, both in Iran and in the West, thought that Mashaie, whose daughter is married to Ahmadinejad's son, wouldn't survive and that Ahmadinejad, even if he survived himself, would have to sacrifice his in-law to remain in his post. But as in almost every media analysis of Iranian politics, either Ahmadinejad's wile was underestimated or Iran was simply misread.

While there was no question that the Iranian president had been weakened by losing the support of many hard-line politicians and clerics, he crucially had strengthened himself against what Kharrazi had once predicted, and he had saved his most trusted aide from the ignominy of sharing a prison compound with Iranian reformists and even ordinary civil protesters—people he had, indirectly at a minimum, helped put in shackles over the last two years.

The big sulk was big news all over the world, which continued to take a keen interest in anything Iran-related, nuclear or otherwise. Iranians in Tehran had mixed reactions, ranging from schadenfreude (on the part of those who despised Ahmadinejad and who reveled now as the cocky president seemed to be on the slope to political irrelevance or worse) to sudden support (on the part of those who hated the man he challenged even more than they hated him). But life in Iran went on as usual: despite Iranians' preoccupation with politics, as entertaining as they can often be in Tehran, the episode brought neither the government nor the people to a halt. Not even a pause. As Khosro likes to remark whenever a scandal, an uprising (as in the Green Movement), a putsch, or anything else excites the media: "Absolutely nothing will happen." And he's often right.

Karri's immediate concern during the big sulk was finding an apartment for us to move into, in a neighborhood that had a better supply of oxygen, and perhaps a more constant supply of natural, if not organic, foods. But as we focused on our future, I was also pulled into the past, reminded of the sulk that my own father had employed years ago as a foreign service officer, when I was a freshman in college.

My father was a career diplomat, having joined the Foreign Ministry with a law degree before I was born, at a time when it had only a few hundred employees, few of them actually fluent in foreign languages, and not many embassies abroad. In the early 1970s, he was assigned as DCM, deputy chief of mission, to Washington, D.C., to work under the ambassador, Ardeshir Zahedi, who was a close confidant of the shah. (Zahedi was once married to the shah's daughter and fathered the king's only grandchild while the shah was alive. He was the son of a general who had been instrumental in returning the shah to his throne in the CIA-sponsored 1953 coup against Prime Minister Mohammad Mossadeq.) It was a prestige post, to be sure, but my father probably didn't know what he was getting himself into, or didn't imagine the complications that would arise from working with both Zahedi and the foreign minister, Abbas-Ali Khalatbari. The two men didn't speak to each other—their own form of sulking. Zahedi had been the foreign minister prior to Khalatbari's appointment, at a time when he famously didn't speak to the prime minister, Abbas Hoveyda, either.

Zahedi's close relationship to the shah meant that he could get away with his silent treatment of those he deemed either rivals or beneath him, but my father was a friend of Khalatbari's, the embassy in Washington was Iran's most important, and the lack of dialogue between the ambassador and the foreign minister meant a highly stressful work environment for anyone trying to actually work. Sulks all around, but they didn't matter, for the shah was the only person who counted back then, especially when it came to U.S.-Iran relations. Zahedi spoke regularly with the shah—he may in fact have been the only Iranian who could reliably get the monarch on the phone at will—and was a popular figure in Washington society for the lavish caviar-fueled parties he threw and for his own oozing charm, which snared the likes of Elizabeth Taylor into a short-lived tryst and attracted other Hollywood types, who my father cared little for, to the embassy on Massachusetts Avenue.

For a serious political officer like my father (who nonetheless enjoyed a good party as much as the next Iranian, and boy do we like our parties), working under such conditions at the Imperial Embassy in Washington, which I thought enormously fun and perfectly reasonable—in fact, a good reason to join the foreign service myself—soon became intolerable. His requests for relief, a transfer perhaps, were not taken seriously by the ministry, nor was his frustration appreciated much by Zahedi, who was far too busy socially and in frequent conversations with more important people, like the shah, for example. Zahedi had always been a virtuoso at romancing U.S. congressmen and Hollywood stars, all in the name of promoting Iran as the next best thing to '53 Dom Perignon, Havana cigars, and the finest Iranian Beluga, which he generously served at his mansion on embassy row in truly obscene amounts (and I mean kilos).

So my father did what only an Iranian with supreme confidence in his indispensable talents would do: he requested retirement. Mind you, he wasn't even fifty yet, although he was eligible for retirement according to Foreign Ministry regulations. He made a convincing case to my mother and myself that he would indeed be happy as a retiree, but I think we both knew that he wouldn't, and that his "retirement," more precisely his sulk, would last only a short while.

Khalatbari, over the objections of Zahedi (who probably thought my father had taken leave of his senses, as my mother and I did—in the booming Iran of the 1970s no one voluntarily left a senior government job), agreed to let my father take a leave of absence in London, after it became clear that he wouldn't take no for an answer unless something better than retirement was on offer. The foreign minister essentially agreed to a sulk for a time, away from Tehran, until a final determination could be made on whether to call my father's bluff or to fold. Iranians don't claim to have invented poker, unlike almost everything else good or interesting, but they do bet, call, bluff, and fold in their everyday lives. Every day.

My father's sulk lasted less than a year. In a sign to his bosses in Tehran that his sulk was serious, he grew a beard—a big no-no in the government of the shah, who hated facial hair more than he hated monogamy. (The Islamic government to come would hate the lack of a beard more than it hated the shah. If Ahmadinejad had *shaved* during his eleven-day sulk, he might have been taken more seriously than he was, and he would have gained even more supporters among the secular elite, but it probably never crossed his mind.) In the end, Khalatbari lured my father back to Tehran with a senior post at the ministry, meant as a temporary sojourn before he would be named ambassador somewhere, but somewhere good, *dammit*, or another sulk. My mother and much younger sister didn't even go to Tehran, thinking his appointment there would be very short-lived, or else he would return to London to sulk. My father spent his time between the ministry and a hotel, then was offered the ambassadorship to Tokyo, a prestigious post for Iranians if only because the shah rather fancied and placed great importance on countries that also had emperors whose subjects thought of them as gods. His four-year posting to Japan, which was interrupted by the Islamic Revolution two years later, however, may have contributed to his being deemed either persona non grata or persona-in-Evin-prison for a few years after the revolution.

He did eventually return to Islamic Iran to clear his name: he had to endure a sort of trial at the Foreign Ministry, rather than in the notorious revolutionary courts, at which he was only partially successful in establishing his innocence. He was accused of serving alcohol at the embassy while he was ambassador, which he openly admitted and which he pointed out was not illegal under the shah; and he was accused of having a close relationship with the now-hated shah, which wasn't true and which he of course denied. After the revolution and the ransacking of the shah's offices, zealous revolutionaries had amassed thousands of the shah's personal papers related to affairs of state, and among them they had found handwritten notes signed by my father. He was surprised that his notes, which were addressed to his boss, the foreign minister, and not the shah, had ended up in the shah's office and personal papers, but the reason was simple: the always honorable Khalatbari, rather than present my father's opinions and positive findings to the shah as his own, something many if not most politicians would have done, had simply delivered my father's messages directly to the shah in his weekly meetings. This was beyond the comprehension of the revolutionaries. Khalatbari was a career diplomat with no strong political leanings, but much to my father's dismay and utter sadness, he had been executed days after the revolution. At the conclusion of his own trial, my father was fired, rather than retired, from the Foreign Ministry he had served and loved. And now my father could sulk again.

This time he knew the sulk could have no effect; nor would anyone else care or even be aware of it. But sometimes the sulk itself was enough. It was a peculiarly Iranian sulk in that it was performed solely for the sake of pride. He refused to appeal or challenge the verdict against him, refused to hire an attorney and press his case that he deserved his pension, if not his good name back, because pride told him he mustn't demean himself. Pride told him that somehow his inquisitors would be embarrassed by his refusal to challenge them; they would realize by his silence that they had been mistaken in their treatment of him and would eventually come around and offer their apologies along with all his back pay. Of course, that was never to happen; nor did anyone at the Foreign Ministry give a damn at the time, or even now.

But I do sometimes wonder, more than twenty years into the sulk, if my father hadn't been right all along. For every time I've had a meeting at the ministry, the older diplomats—and even some younger ones who have studied the history of Iran's diplomacy—praise my father for his impeccable reputation and even his honor. I remind them that he lives in a small flat in London and hasn't been paid in over thirty years; the only response, as is not atypical in Iran, is an awkward, even uncomfortable smile—one that would have given my father great satisfaction in his sulk, if he had ever seen it.

The various forms of sulking have always been a part of the Iranian national character. In my own family, which I've hardly ever thought of as dysfunctional, sulks have been plentiful—one or another members of my extended family, especially those in Iran, aren't speaking to some other member at any given time—and it's often hard to keep track of who is not speaking to whom, over what particular slight. But sulking is also common among friends, in business, and of course at the highest levels in politics, since way before Mahmoud Ahmadinejad's eleven-day public fit of pique.

Mohammad Mossadeq, the oil-nationalizing prime minister who was famously overthrown in a CIA-MI6 coup in 1953, was given to fits of pique, too, and was often portrayed in the West, particularly in the British papers, as an emotionally unstable person who would faint, retreat to his bed in pajamas, and generally appear to act like a stubborn child if he didn't get his way or if he wanted to make a point. *Time* magazine even said, in a report published in 1951, "Better than most modern statesmen, Iran's Premier Mohammed Mossadegh knows the value of the childlike tantrum." *Time* editors understood the value of a tantrum, or a sulk, but surely didn't understand its part in the Iranian character. Years before his tenure as prime minister and on the world stage, in 1919, he had sulked all the way to self-imposed exile in Switzerland, so offended was he that Iran had agreed to a treaty with Great Britain that gave the colonial empire control over his country's finances and armed forces. He returned home only after the Majles, the parliament, rejected the treaty, something he had worked feverishly against while abroad. But Mossadeq's behavior was never a shock to Iranians, who understand the value of a good sulk, not even to the shah, who fled to Rome before returning to reclaim his throne almost reluctantly, and whose criticisms of Mossadeq, before and after the coup, didn't include questioning his rival's proclivity to petulance.

Yes, the big sulk that attracted the world's attention in 2011 had been preceded by Iranian sulks of all kinds, but none greater than the sulk by the Islamic Revolution itself, directed at the United States. No one has really thought of it as a sulk, but the strained relationship, or lack of relationship, between the United States and Iran fits with the Iranian temperament. In a sulk, usually the sulking party wants the other to come to admit its offense, its mistakes, and to correct its behavior. By sulking, the Iranian party also presumes that the other party needs, and will miss, it more than *it* needs the other. That has been Iran's position vis-à-vis the United States ever since the hostage crisis of 1979, if not from the moment Ayatollah Khomeini set foot in Tehran nine months before.

Certainly many Iranians harbor a deep-rooted antagonism toward the United States, which they view as the successor to the British Empire in the Middle East, especially since the 1953 coup removed the democratically elected prime minister, Mossadeq, in favor of the shah, who then, with the full backing of the United States, built a security state and a secret police that tortured and jailed many of the revolutionaries in power today. But those very same revolutionaries also feel a tremendous admiration for America and American values. And I think that this admiration—this sense of desire for a relationship—is necessary to give a sulk a raison d'être. Iranians' litany of complaints against their former patron, a country whose values they admit in private that they admire, might be collected in a book entitled *Why We Sulk.* Iran has been waiting for more than thirty years to hear that America—and only America, the world's sole true superpower, matters to Iran—will respect her, that she can be an independent, sovereign state with the full ability to chart her own destiny without interference from any power, something that has not been the case for the past two hundred years.

Only when Iran is convinced that America sincerely accepts her as she is, not as what the United States wants her to be, may the thirty-plus-year sulk come to an end. Meanwhile, the sulk baffles many Westerners and makes them think the ayatollahs and revolutionaries who rule Iran are simply impossible, just as Westerners once thought Mossadeq impossible. The pain Iran has suffered—U.S. sanctions have meant, for example, that since 1979 it can't upgrade even its civilian Boeing aircraft fleet, resulting in a scandalously high airplane accident rate—has also made her strong in many ways. It has forced Iran to seek more reliable and less politically fraught—European and Asian—alternatives to U.S. technology and even to boost its indigenous industry, lending credence to the opinion that it is the United States that is losing out in its long-standing grudge match with Iran. That may be the case in some aspects of geopolitics, but from the perspective of an American family trying to live in Tehran, the Iranian sulk, and the U.S. response to it, is highly inconvenient and at times downright stupid, even as the sulk, because it is not what most Americans think—an instinctive hatred for Americans—allows for Americans to visit Iran without the real possibility that they may come to harm. *Ghahr, ghahr, ta roozeh ghiamat, ghahr.* Judgment day can't come soon enough, and certainly not for American Iranians and Iranian Americans.

5

FARDA

—

Waiting for the day that Iran normalizes its relationship with the United States and therefore with the rest of the West has become for many Iranians, real-life Estragons and Vladimirs, an absurdist play. While waiting and hoping that things will change, some sulk. Many Iranian youth have been in a sort of collective political sulk since 2009, when an intolerant regime dashed their hopes for a better future, and they have virtually withdrawn from civil society, waiting to join the millions of Iranians who have emigrated, or else retreating to their homes—often their parents' homes—waiting for an invitation to do something semiexciting in a republic where excitement, at least of the public sort, is effectively banned. Older Iranians, whether onetime revolutionaries, proponents or opponents of the *nezam*, or merely apolitical, often wait for something else, and it's usually a business deal, or a court date over some disputed property seizure, or an appeal of a court decision, or really anything that has to do with money.

Outwardly Iran is economically not very different from Europe or the United States, at least in terms of busy shops, Western and Asian consumer goods aplenty, billboards advertising the latest electronics, automobiles, and luxury items, and new construction in the capital rivaling Eurozone boom towns of the 1990s like Dublin. But a not insubstantial number of Iranians, unemployed and unemployable (there simply aren't enough jobs for the population, an issue exacerbated by the effect of years-long economic sanctions on the country), sit around and wait for deals they are working on to materialize. And an equal number of Iranians are waiting to happily assist them, or to take advantage of them, depending on one's point of view, in their business and legal ventures.

When we first arrived in Tehran and were staying at Khosro's house, a frequent visitor—actually, an almost daily one, usually at lunchtime—was Reza, a sort of business associate of his, a man with a pronounced and sometimes difficult-to-understand Rashti (from Rasht, a northern city on the Caspian Sea) accent. I had met Reza on my previous trips to Tehran; he was supposedly helping Khosro with a court case involving some land belonging to Khosro's family. In the early days of the revolution, the state had confiscated the small parcel, and the law stated that in cases of nonpolitical property seizures, the government had to reimburse the landowner. But this being Iran, years had gone by, and despite almost weekly appeals to the court, nothing had happened. Reza had promised Khosro that he would expedite the case, for he had connections at the courts, but that was a few years ago. Eight years, Khosro reminded me. *Eight* years? Karri couldn't believe it. And he still comes by every day? For what? He came for lunch, of course, which Khosro happily served him and us, but also for a little money, you know, to help continue greasing the wheels. Fifty here, Khosro told us, a hundred there (in U.S. dollars). After lunch, Khosro would mark in a ledger how much he had given Reza that day. It added up, and fast.

Reza Farda, we called him, not his real surname but one given him by Khosro, because every day Reza said he would have Khosro's favorable court decision in hand "tomorrow," *farda* in Farsi, or *fuurrd'a,* as it sounded to us in Rashti. Or actually, maybe the day after tomorrow at the latest.

A short man with a large belly that matched his appetite and thick graying hair and beard, Reza had his charms, and like all Iranians we met, he wanted to play with the baby. Every day in Khosro's small kitchen, he picked up Khash and kissed him and professed his undying love and admiration for the boy. We often tried to leave Khosro and his sometime employee Ali alone with Reza to discuss their business over the endless cups of sugared tea Iranians consume with abandon, both before and after a meal, but apparently they really had no business to discuss. Karri was bemused by the fact that she and Khash caused no interruption (or embarrassment) in the routine whereby Reza would show up, hungry and ready for a little snack or a big lunch, depending on what Khosro had on offer that day, simply to show his face and to report that he had just come from somewhere or other and to assure his client that his land, and his money, would be his within twenty-four hours. *Farda.* Khosro was in a bind, he explained to Karri, for if he stopped feeding Reza or, worse, didn't give him the money he demanded, all the money he had given him up till then would have gone to waste, and he'd be back to square one with the court. Certainly true, Karri argued, but surely Reza can't be telling the truth about the court case, that it will be resolved *tomorrow*? No, of course he isn't, but Khosro felt he had no choice but to wait it out.

Reza, whenever he sensed Khosro's frustration and sometimes his anger, would make outlandish promises beyond his usual ones. One day, in front of all of us, he not only promised that the case would be resolved by tomorrow, but he told Ali to go and pick out a new motorcycle, right away, for he was going to buy him one with the fee he was about to collect. *How's he going to get out of this one?* I wondered. "That'll be interesting" was Khosro's response, but of course after a few days there was neither money nor motorcycle to be seen, and somehow all involved knew there wouldn't be. Yet lunch was still served. *"Khejalat nemeekeshee?"*—"Aren't you embarrassed?"—Reza's wife had asked him on occasion, he admitted, probably because he never came home for lunch rather than because he was leading Khosro on, but he had no qualms about disclosing his wife's concern. No, he wasn't embarrassed, and the wife remained, as they tend to be in Iranian business relationships no matter how close, unseen. On another occasion, when Khosro was particularly frustrated with Reza (and perhaps because of Karri's incredulous questioning), he asked Reza how and what he should think of him if Reza never delivered on his promises. "*Kola-bardar*, of course," exclaimed Reza. A con man.

During the time we were at Khosro's house, and in the months that followed in our own apartment and even to this day, Reza continues to visit Khosro and collect fifty here, a hundred there, and consume a delicious lunch courtesy of Khosro's mother. She lives in the house behind Khosro's, separated by a small garden that was once lush but has since been taken over by families of stray cats that she can't help but feed. And Khosro still waits. Reza Farda's obligation to him was informal, in that any agreement had been made verbally, and there were no documents to prove bad faith on Reza's part if Khosro one day decided to give up on the game and try to recover some of his cash outlay, if not the lunches he's served.

This type of arrangement is more common in close relationships, when family members or very close friends are involved in a business transaction, than in the kind of relationship that Khosro and Reza had. But I suppose eight years of breaking bread together had created a relationship beyond business, as reluctant as Khosro might have been about it, and at any rate if Reza is unable to deliver for him, it isn't clear at all that he never intended to in the first place. In fact, Khosro is confident that Reza would love to deliver, for that way he will actually make far more money than the fifties and hundreds he pockets from time to time. His capacity for lying through his teeth about when he might deliver, a running daily joke, is mostly indicative of a comfort in Iranian society and particularly among Tehranis with lying and exaggerating, rather than any real confidence game, Khosro believes. Comfortable with lying? My people? Really?

———————

"We've become a nation of liars," the cabbie said after he felt a little more at ease with me. He had picked me up downtown, near the Foreign Ministry, and my destination was way uptown, a good forty-five-minute or hour drive away, even on the highways that bisected Tehran's clogged surface streets. "Have I met you before?" he had asked when I got in the front seat. "You look familiar. Do you live in Pasdaran?"

I was wearing a gray suit with an open-collared shirt and carrying a briefcase, and with the close-cropped graying beard, I suppose I could pass for a former Revolutionary Guard, many of whom live in that neighborhood of Tehran, named for the Guards themselves. No, I had replied, but I also hadn't offered any clues to my profession, former or current. Did he think I was lying? Perhaps.

But he had started the conversation by stating that he was a retired army officer, one who had joined the army in the shah's time, and he was in the mood, as almost every cab driver in Tehran always is, for complaining. Particularly if he thinks his passenger might be someone who will sympathize with him or, better yet, can do something about the jeremiad he is about to unleash. "The Islamic Revolution," he said, "has brought about many advances, in industry and technology and the like. But in terms of *akhlagh*, manners or character, we've regressed."

I merely nodded.

"Let me tell you a story," he continued. "A man goes to confess his sins to the prophet. He tells him he's a thief and a womanizer, constantly cheating on his wife. The prophet tells him there's only one thing he must not do anymore, and that is to lie. The man, quite pleased, goes away, but within hours he realizes that he is incapable of sinning anymore if he can't lie about it. He can't go out that night either to steal or to womanize or both, because he can't lie to his wife. You see? That's why lying is the worst sin, and why our society is crumbling."

A good story, I commented, but I was not entirely sure why he told it to me. And while I could understand that perhaps lying had become more prevalent—at least in the overcrowded and highly competitive capital, where getting ahead by any means seemed to have become accepted behavior in recent years—I still wasn't convinced that it had become a part of the Persian persona, despite the fact that time and again during our stay in Iran I heard people say that it had, and that in general the wonderful Persian manners of two millennia, which admittedly included a more refined form of not telling the absolute truth, had given way to the modern Iranian lying boor.

Life in a city like Tehran, with a population that has grown from less than three million before the revolution to over twelve million today, has certainly become more difficult than in the time of genteel manners, although Persian politesse, including the often infuriating *ta'arouf*—the back-and-forth niceties, self-deprecation, and faux-embarrassed apologies in transactions that involve money—is in abundant supply. It's in the cabbies' psyche—I have yet to have one accept payment without protesting that his service was "unworthy," even if he had been complaining of hardship on the whole ride.

Karri was aware of it too and always snickered when I'd get into an argument with a driver about paying him. But when she was riding in a cab alone, the *ta'arouf* was still there but far weaker and, she could tell, less sincere. Iranians aren't stupid, I told her. They understand that you, the blond, blue-eyed foreigner with a bad Farsi accent, might actually accept the free ride, and although they instinctively pretend they'd like to refuse payment, they'll make sure you understand that you have to pay. She actually received fairer treatment from cabbies than I did—they always seemed to quote her the correct fare, whereas I, after insisting on paying, would be quoted wildly differing rates for the same ride. If I demurred, the driver would shrug and say I could pay whatever I wanted to, always making me feel just a little guilty about paying him less than what he expected, especially if he was from a local car service and I might have to climb in behind him again the next time I called for a car.

Is it the population and education explosion, unmatched by opportunity, that makes Iranians, particularly big-city Iranians, bemoan the dog-eat-dog culture that they insist has replaced their true one? Or is it the semi-isolation from the world economy due to an anti-Western phobia on the part of the regime and an anti-Iran phobia on the part of the West? Increasingly harsh sanctions on Iran by the West, ostensibly to force the regime to give up any nuclear ambitions, have not achieved that goal but have affected ordinary Iranians in ways that the architects of the sanctions may not have intended. Small businesses that in the past relied on imports or exports have found it increasingly difficult to stay afloat, resulting in layoffs, in everything from managerial positions to janitorial staff, and complete shutdowns. Fewer and fewer international or multinational companies are willing to invest in Iran or even maintain a modest presence there, again resulting in less opportunity for ordinary workers. Most Western consumer goods are still available, smuggled in, albeit with increasing difficulty and therefore beyond the reach of many Iranians.

Inflation has always unenviably been in the double digits, but in the last two years—because of the far more restrictive sanctions that President Obama has been able to impose on Iran with the help of key allies—it has climbed to stratospheric heights, cutting the earning power of almost every Iranian, especially people on fixed incomes. (The creeping devaluation of the rial, the Iranian currency, meant that the dollars Karri and I brought were worth more almost weekly, but inflation, which could be measured just as regularly, meant that our buying power barely improved.) Beyond their economic effects on industry, sanctions have also resulted in shortages of imported medicines; even when medications are available, their prices are unaffordable, causing concern for any Iranian who does not have the ability to travel abroad for treatment, particularly for all forms of cancer. So to make ends meet—and certainly some of the difficulties have been a result of domestic economic mismanagement rather than international sanctions—Iranians at every rung of the socioeconomic ladder have resorted to practices that once would have been considered so dishonorable as to render one an outcast from society. Once a single hair of his mustache, painfully plucked by a lower-class dealmaker in the presence of a partner, would seal any agreement with far more force than the proverbial Western handshake, but today nothing so quaint suffices, and agreements are broken as often as they are signed, sealed, and delivered. Promissory notes are generally considered not worth the paper they are written on. Literally.

In earlier times, dishonor befell a debtor; today in the Islamic Republic, writing a bad check can still land you in a not-so-nice prison, lending the society an oddly Dickensian flavor. Iranians nonetheless seem to be world champions in signing worthless chits and running up debts. But while some victims of bounced checks have given up all hope of collecting their due and seek vengeance instead, others wait for the possibility that one day the debtor might make good on his promises; for if he goes to prison (and it always seems to be a "he"), the debt is wiped away. Especially among close-knit families, where the very concept of a fraud perpetrated by one against another would once have been viewed with horror, waiting seems to be the only option. My own family was no exception, in 2011.

My immediate family, meaning my parents and siblings, all live in the West, but on my paternal side I have a large extended family of first and second cousins, uncles, aunts, and their children and grandchildren. Almost all are from Ardakan, a town in the desert, but they have lived in Tehran either their entire lives or most of them. Even before she met them, Karri was aware of the fact that, their being Iranian and, worse yet, provincial in character, they would smother us with their love and attention. But I don't think she was prepared for what family means to Ardakanis or Yazdis—from the city of

Yazd, the big city to the village of Ardakan—let alone Persians. On our second night in Tehran, we were invited to one cousin's house, and upon arriving with little Khash in tow, some thirty or so family members greeted us, all desperate to play with the newest Majd and curious about the foreign woman who was his mother. "That's a big family," Karri remarked to me, a little dazed from jet lag, from being in Tehran, and from the Farsi constantly spoken around her. Yes, I told her, and this is only half of them.

My family members in Iran are engaged in different professions, from insurance and banking to politics, construction, and import-export, and there are even a couple of highly regarded doctors and surgeons. But one son-in-law of one cousin my age, who had been a teacher but had some time ago decided to become a real estate developer, perhaps to compete with other upwardly mobile Ardakanis, had been offering the family 30 percent interest on their money over the past few years, while banks in Iran were offering between 15 and 20 percent. Iran's high inflation rate is the reason rial accounts in Iran can offer such rates—those rates don't apply to the dollar- or euro-deposit accounts that have been legal for some years now. Whether out of greed or the desire to help a family member or both, many in the family handed over their savings to him, which he said was to be used for an apartment block construction project at a popular Iranian beach on the Caspian coast.

Most of them, rather than taking the monthly interest on their money, elected to leave it to compound, raising their exposure should something bad happen, say, a crash in the real estate market. The crash happened, of course, a couple of years after the U.S. crash, and although it was not as severe as in some American states, selling condos by the sea was no longer the financial slam dunk it had been when the hapless son-in-law changed professions. He never let on that trouble was brewing, naturally, perhaps because of pride and because of that "keeping up with the Majds" concern of his—until two of my cousins needed some of their cash back and asked him for it.

Wait, he told them, and you'll have it. How long? A little while.

He had also gone outside the family for money, and we discovered that he owed some five million dollars to various people, most of whom were not willing to wait very long to get it back. Between ourselves, Karri and I started referring to him as our very own Bernie Madoff, whom, to our surprise, everyone in Tehran seemed to know about. It seemed rather preposterous that someone with hardly any experience in either finance (unlike Madoff) or construction could amass that kind of debt; my cousin's son-in-law couldn't have paid what he owed even if every condo he and his partners were building sold right away, and at full price. Madoff may have figured that his scheme could last forever, barring a financial crisis, and this fellow probably thought the same, although it may have been less a scheme to embezzle than the pure folly of thinking nothing can ever go wrong when everything does, all the time.

As time went on and *farda* turned into *pass-farda*, the day after tomorrow, into next week, then the week after, I think it finally dawned on my cousins that their relative simply would not ever have the money to pay them back. Even if he did manage to come up with some cash, perhaps by selling his house or some land, he'd undoubtedly first pay outside investors, who would have no qualms about taking him to court and sending him to debtors' prison. The family would wait.

As they waited, however, relations between cousins frayed, and within a month or two some were no longer on speaking terms. The cousin whose son-in-law was the debtor was shunned by her sisters, even though she had nothing to do with the case and in fact had lost money herself, but of course she didn't want her daughter's husband, the father of her grandchildren, to go to jail. She anguished, and our visits to her house for lunch, which she insisted on when we first arrived, going so far as to cook separate vegetarian dishes for Karri, discontinued as she retreated from the family. By the end of the year, her son-in-law was in prison, courtesy of investors who were not willing to wait, were unforgiving of his bounced checks, and knew better than did his family that he would never make good on his promises.

The despair of my extended family over their own little Madoff scandal was undoubtedly shared by the many other Iranians who are caught up in scams, bad investment deals, and the struggle to get ahead in an economy that doesn't allow much room for mistakes. A big financial scandal, a $2.6 billion embezzlement case involving numerous private and state-owned banks, made news in the West while we were in Tehran—it was, not surprisingly, headline news in Iran for weeks—yet the lesser scams and financial malfeasances that are daily occurrences are not big news to anyone but those affected. The $2.6 billion case soon overshadowed everything else, even the political infighting going on at the highest levels of the Islamic Republic, to the point that it became the topic of conversation at every turn, an Islamic parable of sorts for everything wrong with Persian society.

It even seeped into ordinary day-to-day interactions, like shopping. At one's local fruit and vegetable stand, prices were rising—in the Tajrish bazaar, avocados ran to as much as fifteen dollars apiece, *apiece*, in the off season. But when customers complained, as they commonly did, the fruit seller—rather than apologize and blame everyone but himself for the sad state of inflation in the country, as he normally would—might retort that one shouldn't complain about a few pennies when people are walking off with billions. "You're from America," one of my local fruit sellers, a man I liked very much, said to me after an agonizingly long bargaining and caviling session with a woman in an elegant manteau and Hermès head scarf, a regular customer who he said lives in California half of the year. "Do they haggle as much over there?" When I responded in the negative, he merely said, "I didn't think so! And here they steal billions!"

Two point six *billion* dollars, I heard again and again. If a taxi ride cost more than one expected, the driver might tell you to not begrudge him a toman or two when others were making *billions*. It was a staggering sum, those billions of dollars, to ordinary and wealthy Iranians alike. Even the young owner of the sole Bugatti Veyron in Iran, the most expensive passenger car in the world, with a list price of over one million dollars in the United States (and quadruple that in Iran, if he is ever allowed to title and register it rather than garage it in the tony neighborhood of Velenjak, taking it out for a spin once in a while), must've been taken aback at the sum of money extracted from Iranian banks with such apparent ease by Amir Khosravi, not much older than himself, and his associates. "A.Kh.," as he was first referred to in the press, in keeping with the tradition of referring to suspected criminals only by their initials, had somehow, along with Amir Mansour Aria and, apparently, thirty other confederates, forged letters of credit that were accepted first by the nation's biggest banks (the president of Bank Melli fled to Canada before he could be arrested) and then by other smaller private banks (including the one where Karri and I had set up an account), to buy companies, including state-owned ones.

They accumulated cash on a level unimaginable to any Iranian, even to the Supreme Leader, whose own wealth probably compares favorably to the queen of England's. (Being the ultimate authority in the republic for over twenty years has meant that even without dipping into public funds, he and his family have been able to benefit from investments in any business, state-organized and private, that they have chosen to involve themselves with, and they have had access to billions of dollars in unaudited Islamic charity accounts.) The ultimate authority ultimately decided that enough was enough and that Islamic punishment was due the criminals who had made off with such a sum. Except it was unclear who in the government—and the criminals must have had government connections—was also involved, and unclear to ordinary Iranians that a scapegoat wouldn't be found to deflect attention away from the rampant corruption. Despite Ahmadinejad's campaign promises to root it out, corruption had actually increased in the years of his presidency: not only among the Revolutionary Guards, whose tentacles reached into even more of the economy than before and without whose partnership virtually no large business could exist, but in Ahmadinejad's own ministries, documented often enough but punished infrequently.

The main perpetrators of the fraud, at least those not in government, were certain to be caught and prosecuted; perhaps some would even eventually be executed by an unforgiving and highly embarrassed *nezam* whose very legitimacy rests not just on Islam but also—in keeping with the notion of justice that it promotes nationally and even internationally—on its constant and consistent defense of the *mostazafin*, the downtrodden urban poor of society, people for whom numbers in the billions are unfathomable.

In the last few years, an explosion of luxury cars on the streets of Tehran, cars that often cost far more than the homes the *mostazafin* live in, along with superluxury apartment buildings with prices matching Manhattan's or London's, has given the lie to that peculiar notion of justice; for it is impossible to accumulate that kind of wealth without strong regime connections or a strong proclivity to corruption. If a multibillion-dollar fraud was exposed in 2011, many reasoned, then what about all the frauds that hadn't been exposed in the past or wouldn't ever be in the future? They will remain a legacy of the Islamic Revolution, to be brought to light in the future either by a reformed regime or by one that replaces the current one.

The issue of *akhlagh*, the Persian character, weighed on me during our stay in Iran. If it was true, as so many people now said, that we had lost our essence—as a people who valued poetry and beauty, family and pride, charity toward the poor, and honor in business, in politics, and in social intercourse—then what emotional connection could I have any longer to the land of my birth? And why would I want my son exposed to that *akhlagh*, if it bore no relation to the *akhlagh*, perhaps one I romanticized, of his forebears?

Iranians opposed to the Islamic regime would often tell me that they were so pessimistic about the future that even if there were a revolution tomorrow to replace the system they hated, it would be of no use, since the Persian-ness that had once defined them was now lost, if not forever, then for generations. "How do you change these monsters?" a friend said to me, after a minor shouting match on the street over a perceived discourtesy, and by *monsters* he didn't just mean the stranger who was the target of his ire. "They've lived for over thirty years in a system that rewards boorishness and disciplines graciousness; there's just no hope." Those once-upper-middle-class Iranians, many of them cash-poor and possessing far less wealth than the monsters—or "savages," as Khosro described them—whom they deride, should be in the vanguard of a movement to instigate change, but they have seemingly given up on their country, even as they seem reluctant to leave it for good, as many of their contemporaries have done, often with only the clothes on their backs. The Iranian penchant for hyperbole was alive and well, I understood, and although some Iranians, older ones usually, may not be active in any meaningful way to better their country, they will still be there and will contribute to changing society—a society that has little use for them now—when and if they are asked.

My *khaleh*-Poori, for example, or Aunt Poori, as my brother and I have called her since childhood even though she is not a blood relation, has lived in Iran her entire life. She baby-sat me, even on her trips abroad, and she and her politically active husband were my parents' closest friends until, after the shah's return to power during the 1953 coup, the regime executed her husband. I try to see her every time I'm in Tehran. I was particularly eager for her to see my son during this prolonged stay—she was surprised I had one, assuming that at my advanced age I would remain childless—and to see how she would react to the child of a child she had once taken care of and loved. I've always been a little perplexed as to why she persists, a single woman living alone in Iran when she could easily emigrate, for her politics do not jibe with that of the clerics or their lay supporters, and her fluency in English and her education could long ago have provided her with opportunities and a comfortable life abroad in Europe, which she knew well and where she spent much time. I asked her, when she finally was able to come to our apartment after numerous canceled appointments and after I showed her what Skype-ing with my parents in London was like—Khash sitting on her lap and as well behaved as he could be, given that he'd starting walking recently and tore around the small apartment as if in a perpetual race—if she had ever thought of leaving Iran.

"No," she said, almost indignantly. "Why would I ever do that?"

I suggested that perhaps now, after waiting all these years for some change and after the disappointment of the post-Khatami years—particularly the failure of the Green Movement—she might want to retire somewhere she could enjoy more social freedom and escape the difficulties of living in Tehran. Poori had in fact long ago escaped the city for a village in the mountains, but she commuted to downtown Tehran every day and continued to be gainfully employed at the National Library.

She seemed genuinely taken aback by the question. "There's nothing like living in your own country," she said firmly. "This is my country—nothing else matters, does it?" She didn't say it out of some misguided nationalism, I realized, but simply out of love for what she knew, even if what she once knew, perhaps even some of that Persian *akhlagh*, had changed. Perhaps her escape from actually living in the heart of the city was a way to close her eyes to the changes, behavioral and otherwise, taking place in her country, I thought. But she didn't talk about it further, and we didn't have a political conversation, other than her asking me about former president Khatami, who had once been her boss at the library. She wanted to catch up on family news and spend time with Khash and Karri. It delighted me that she had met Khash, even if for the one and only time, and it saddened me that he wouldn't remember his father's onetime baby-sitter. But her visit confirmed to me that whatever was happening to Iran and whatever the perceived changes in the Persian *akhlagh* in Tehran,

Iran was always going to be the Iran I wanted Khash to know—frustrating, yes, but its real character wouldn't, no, *couldn't*, change. All is not well in Iran, not by a long shot, and few people I know would insist that it is, but provided the Pooris and other Iranians don't abandon her, and persist in living through these troubled times, there is hope for the Iran we love. As long as they remain in their country, Iran and the Iranian essence cannot change irrevocably.

Bringing Khash to Iran was a way to show him the sights, sounds, and smells of my country but also its character. I knew he would remember none of it, but he might not have another opportunity to visit Iran as he grew up, or as he entered adulthood, and perhaps when I was no longer around, he would at least know he had *smelled* Iran, figuratively and literally, just once. To add to my happiness in seeing Poori and to my sense of country being affirmed in some way, now that I knew Khash was in the right place, Poori, to my vainglorious delight, said she thought Khash was exactly like me, both in looks and behavior, when I was his age. But we'll see what he remembers and who he becomes, *farda*.

6

BEATING THE
SYSTEM

Renting an apartment in Tehran is no more or less difficult than renting one anywhere else. If we were to arrive in London or Paris with the intention of living there for a year, without connections, we would scan the classifieds, check Internet listings, and visit a couple of real estate agents. The same is true in Tehran; the English-language papers are filled with ads for apartments, and real estate offices dot the landscape as they do in any Western capital. Real estate offerings are less present on the Internet, where a few searches brought up sites that were inexplicably censored. Perhaps the word *bathroom* is a red flag for the filtering software Iran employs, or *six rooms* might be too close to *sex rooms*, but not many Iranians seek out rentals on the Web anyway, preferring as they do with almost everything a more personal touch.

Renting an apartment in Tehran for only a year, and a furnished one at that, leaves one to choose between living in what Iranians call "apartment hotels"—overpriced and not particularly appealing—and finding, through pure luck or an acquaintance, a decent apartment that doesn't require a huge security deposit or a longer-term commitment. One way apartments come on the market in Tehran is for the owner, who often owns the apartment purely as an investment vehicle, to demand a large sum of money, usually more than two or three years' worth of what would be the rent, up front. With that cash the owner can either take advantage of high interest rates at banks, or make other relatively safe investments, during the lease. At the end, when the tenant vacates the apartment, the owner is obliged to return the entire deposit, which sounds like a good deal except that in Iran just depositing your money in a bank can get you 20 percent interest or more, and if you are cash rich, other investments can bring returns of more than 100 percent.

Much as the idea of living essentially rent-free appealed to us, coming up with that kind of cash was out of the question, considering that we didn't have it on hand and, with international banking sanctions on Iran, it would not have been a simple matter to move funds from the United States. So we did what any sane person would do if he or she had connections in Tehran: we asked friends and family if they knew of any vacant apartments or had any friends who had apartments they might be willing to rent to us for a short period, without us digging too deep into our available funds.

We had opened a bank account within a few days of arriving in Iran, at Saman Bank, a private institution not yet subject to U.S. or international sanctions, and one that shared a name with my brother—reason enough, I thought, to choose it over all the other private banks that seem to dot the retail landscape in Iran with the same prevalence as the banks you find on virtually every corner of Manhattan. Opening an account in Iran is not unlike opening one in the United States—you have to submit every identifying document you have, and you have to be an Iranian citizen or have a residency permit. Credit cards are not accepted in Iran because of sanctions and the impossibility of paying Messrs. Visa, MasterCard, Discover, or Amex through the Iranian Central Bank, or, if there was an alternative payment channel, of them even accepting payment from, god forbid, *Iranians*. So the bank debit card is an invaluable financial tool that allows one not only to withdraw cash from ATMs everywhere but to pay for goods and services and avoid having to carry wads, and I mean literally wads, of rapidly inflating cash at all times.

The other factor making the debit card indispensable is that electrical bills, gas bills, and phone bills, and in fact almost any bill in Iran, can be paid at a bank's ATM machine: every invoice has a bar code and every ATM has a scanner that will identify it and transfer money from your account to the payee's instantly. Despite the ease with which one can pay bills, when we first arrived in the city in early 2011, Tehranis were tossing away many of them, particularly gas bills, at Ayatollah Khomeini's mausoleum on the edge of town; they were protesting the sudden massive increase in utility bills since the Ahmadinejad administration did away with (as economists had advised for years) heavy subsidies for fuel and certain food items that had been a fact of life ever since the Islamic Revolution. Tehranis realized, as their bills came in, that direct cash subsidies, provided by the government to ease the pain of moving from government-controlled prices to a free market, did not offset the rise in prices, at least not in their city.

Bills and invoices in Iran can be confusing to a non-native, and even I am at times discombobulated when dealing with the Iranian financial system, which I believe is intentionally obfuscating. It insists on having both an official currency, the rial, in which everything is priced, and an unofficial currency, the toman, which is ten times the value of a rial. When you are shopping for everything from a loaf of bread to the monthly rent for an apartment, the toman is the one you will be quoted, while price tags, if they exist, will be in rials. Karri simply never got used to it and would tell me that she paid an exorbitant price for something or another; I would assume she had been ripped off, as an obvious and clueless foreigner, until I looked at the receipt or the remaining cash in her wallet and realized she had been thinking rials instead of tomans. Or was it the other way around? Her full-mouth X-rays at a dental office, she happily announced later in our stay, had only cost $150, which Khosro quickly pronounced a blatant rip-off, but when I checked the debit card receipt, I saw they had only cost $15.

One reason so many diaspora Iranians have traveled back and forth to Iran over the years, and that flights to Tehran used to be fully booked, is medical tourism, or medical go-home-ism: not only can medical treatment be much cheaper than in the United States, but it is generally considered to be at a level comparable to First World countries, for many Iranian medical practitioners received their training in the United States or Europe. Western drugs were also affordable and plentiful, but more recently Western sanctions have increasingly made those drugs difficult or prohibitively expensive to obtain, resulting in a slowdown of medical tourism where treatment is reliant upon them.

While we were in Iran, the government actually proposed to reconfigure the currency, to lop off three zeros from the rial (not the toman, in case you were wondering) and call it something else altogether. The new official denomination would be broken down into ten units of a smaller currency, not hundredths like in Europe or the United States. Already—and to add to the confusion of foreigners—when Iranians talked about money, no one referred to the thousands unit of tomans, let alone rials: 5,000 tomans, for example, was 5 tomans. And if they were talking millions, such as the price of a car or a house, no one referred to the millions unit: a 120-million-toman Lexus cost 120 tomans. It was expected that you *knew* that a Lexus couldn't cost 10 cents, or that a bag of apples couldn't cost 4 cents, and that you knew the difference between a car and a bag of fruit, but it confused the hell out of Karri.

I wasn't sure that the government scheme would ever come about, or that it wouldn't somehow turn out to be equally confusing once Iranians created their own lingo for it. In Iran, after all, many people still use terms like *shahi, gheran* (written "kran" in English), and *hezar* (abbreviated to *zar*), currencies of the Qajar era, pre-1930s, in everyday speech. Such as "It's not worth *do-zar*," meaning it's not worth two *hezars,* a denomination no one actually knows the worth of any-more. Or, when haggling, "I won't pay a *shahi* more," meaning the same thing, but without either party knowing what a *shahi* would actually buy, although presumably it was pretty close to what a penny buys in the West today.

I didn't bother to explain this aspect of our currency dilemma to Karri, for she would not only be more confused but would certainly think we Iranians were completely mad or at least xenophobic to the extreme. Although the system is no sillier or more confusing than the old British system of pounds, shillings, and pence, and sovereigns and guineas, too, I'm convinced that the Iranian system, or systems, of currency are in keeping with the Persian character of presenting ourselves as a mystery to outsiders, particularly foreigners. It's part of our allure, you see, like the veil that hides the stunning beauty of a Persian woman, the envy of the outside world. *Right.*

Happy as Karri and I were to be armed with our very own Ira-nian debit cards, we never carried a tremendously large balance in our account. And anyone checking would have seen that our assets in Iran were extremely limited, given that we owned absolutely nothing and our credit was limited to whatever dollars we had converted to rials and deposited in Saman. My computer checking account app, though, unable to recognize rials, simply put a dollar sign in front of our available balance, making us millionaires several times over, a sure-fire way to get us investigated by the U.S. Treasury Department if the laptop ever fell into the hands of customs officials at an Ameri-can airport. It looked good to me, but the rial amount wouldn't have impressed an Iranian landlord seeking some cash to do business with.

And we needed an apartment fast. Naturally, with an extended family as big as mine, two of my cousins knew someone who had apartments for rent: the owner of a chain of boutique hotels (the best hotels in Tehran, actually, a city not known for its Michelin-starred accommodations) as well as a number of apartment hotels. Mr. Bakhtiari also conveniently owned apartments in a number of buildings (if not the entire buildings themselves) in some of the chicest neighborhoods. Soon after opening a bank account and only a short time after our arrival in Tehran, we arranged to see some of his apartments.

The third one he showed us, a stone's throw from the shah's former Saadabad Palace in Tajrish, was perfect: a small—okay, *really* small—one-bedroom in a brand-new building that he had built as an assisted living facility for seniors. But the facility had flopped: assisted living is a concept yet to take off in Iran, since the culture still demands that seniors live with their children, who should be perfectly capable of and indeed happy to assist them. So the building was now simply rental apartments. Each unit was more the size of a small hotel suite, plus a small kitchen, than that of a regular Iranian apartment, and they were probably hard to sell to Iranians who value space, but this one was okay for us. It had never been lived in, and the only drawback was that it was unfurnished.

"Not a problem," Mr. Bakhtiari said to us when we approved of the idea of living there, "I'll furnish it for you." Since he owned hotels, we didn't think that would put him, a friend of the family, out too much.

I inquired about the rent, a little afraid that it would be out of my league but that Persian manners—and the fact that he and I had been introduced by my cousin—would dictate that I take it anyway, and I was unsurprised by the response, but nervous nonetheless.

"Nothing, zero. The rent is zero," he declared, with a finality that seemed genuine.

I protested, as any Iranian would, hoping to tease out at least a range, to no avail.

"Move in first," he insisted, trying to end the conversation about something as petty as money, "and see if you like it before you worry about that."

We agreed, but I was still afraid that, weeks after we had settled into the apartment, we'd be presented with a bill, or my cousin would, that we could not afford to pay. I explained this to my cousin, and he said he'd sort it out.

We moved in and had been living in the apartment for a short while before we knew what we were paying, as my cousin had to finally threaten to personally move us out if Mr. Bakhtiari didn't accept rent. How much?

Well, he was willing to collect rent, but not to set a price. "Whatever you want to pay," he said to my cousin, "although it's absolutely not necessary." That typically Persian *ta'arouf* meant that, in our own *ta'arouf* back, so as not to appear to be taking advantage of his largesse, we should probably overpay. Based on what a nicely furnished apartment in a doorman building in the northern stretches of North Tehran would normally command for rent, my cousin decided that we should pay approximately two thousand dollars a month. I hoped his information was not wildly optimistic, but regardless, Mr. Bakhtiari finally accepted after much protestation—without ever acknowledging whether the amount was satisfactory or unfair—and said that my cousin could deposit the rent into his bank account directly on our behalf. That was easy enough to do, since the Iranian banking system is fully Internet-capable, and wire transfers from one account to another across the system are a mere click of the mouse away.

I'm still not absolutely sure if what we paid Mr. Bakhtari— through my cousin, whom I reimbursed later—was fair or if we took advantage of him, but we were probably close enough for it not to matter much. At the end of our stay, when we vacated the apartment, we said pleasant goodbyes to him on the phone, and he didn't offer us a rebate. At least he had never asked for a security deposit: such payments were an absolute given in the Tehran rental market, as they are almost everywhere, but it would have been rude for him to demand or accept one and therefore terribly gauche for us to offer one.

Once we decided on the apartment, Karri was eager to move in, not because she was particularly uncomfortable at Khosro's house, but because she wanted to leave downtown Tehran, where the persistent smog, lack of trees, and dearth of sidewalks made it difficult for her to enjoy our time in Iran. And Khash, whose commando-style crawling—using his elbows and twisting his body along—elicited laughs and shrieks of delight from my cousins and the curiosity of strangers in the park, was getting rather more aggressive, but it was inconvenient for Karri to take him out much on the busy motorcycle-clogged streets around Safi Alishah. Still, I explained to her, I couldn't very well call Mr. Bakhtiari and pester him about a move-in date when he had suggested we'd be his guests for a year, so we waited until we heard from him as to when we might be able to take possession of the apartment.

Finally, after a week or so, Mr. Bakhtiari's sister called me and said she'd be happy to show us the apartment again, fully furnished, so we could see if it was satisfactory and so he could know if we needed anything else. We were indeed satisfied and would have been no matter what the furniture—bright yellow leather as it happened, which, combined with the compact fluorescent lightbulbs that are mandated in Iran, did no wonders for our complexions but was relatively childproof—and arranged to move in the next day.

Now we had to obtain three things that every nonpious Iranian, and even some of pious ones, have to have on the home front: a good Internet connection, a steady liquor supply, and a satellite television connection. But first, even more important and on Karri's to-do list from the moment we landed in Tehran, we needed to find a pediatrician for Khash. A cousin of mine who is a well-known radiologist has a son only a few months older than ours, and Karri agreed that his pediatrician would undoubtedly be good enough for us.

We had decided to wait until we moved into our apartment—Khash had just had a check-up before we left New York—but I made an appointment to see the pediatrician as soon as soon as we had settled in, taking a taxi the following day to the midtown clinic where he kept his office. The receptionist gave us paperwork to fill out, just as we would have done back home as new patients, and I had to beg her indulgence, and her assistance, in filling it out, as my reading and writing skills in Farsi were at grade-school level at best. The other patients in the waiting room, a few cute boys and girls, and their parents stared at this obviously foreign boy among them, perhaps wondering what on earth he was doing in a doctor's office in central Tehran.

The doctor, a friend of my cousin's, spoke no English whatsoever, except for the medical terms he rattled off between sentences. He examined Khash at length, checking everything superficial from his height and weight to the circumference of his head (which I'd never seen done in New York). He checked the measurements off and gave us a sheet showing where Khash stood as measured against normal. Normal in Iran or normal in the West? we asked. In Iran, he said, or maybe Europe, excluding the head diameter. Khash was big, then, and his head growth normal by any standards.

We undressed Khash, removing his diaper, and the doctor poked and prodded. He kneaded his testicles until he cried, something I would have been concerned with back in the United States but oddly wasn't in Tehran. Then he pronounced him healthy. "Also, magnificent circumcision," he said admiringly. "Really beautiful." Karri smiled, a little embarrassed, and I told him our Chinese American, female ob-gyn had performed it in the hospital under my watchful eyes. He was surprised and probably impressed that Khash was circumcised at all, given that his mother wasn't Muslim, as far as he could tell. I explained that most boys are circumcised in the United States, to which he nodded knowingly. But these days, I added, there is somewhat of a trend not to circumcise. He looked a bit perplexed but said nothing. *Those wacky Americans*, he must've thought.

We bade him goodbye, promising to see him again in a few months, and went to pay the receptionist. I was expecting to fork over a decent sum and had my debit card ready, but when she told me it was 10,000 tomans, less than nine dollars, I paid cash, and we walked out in wonderment. Khash's visit had cost less than the taxi rides to and from the clinic. If the receptionist had said 100,000 rials to me, I would have probably mistakenly *thought* she meant tomans and been reasonably satisfied with the ninety-dollar charge.

Less than a week later Khash came down with a high fever. We called the doctor, and I described the fever. He said it was nothing to worry about, that it was in all probability a case of roseola, a virus that would show itself with a red rash on his body and face within a day or two. Karri looked it up on the Internet while I was still on the phone. "Baby Tylenol," he said, "*American* Baby Tylenol—you can get it at a good pharmacy—is all you need, and it will go away in a few days." Iranian acetaminophen was probably identical to any other, but genuine Tylenol, which gray market dealers had no problem importing into the country, conferred status, if not more confidence. But did the doctor need to see Khash? No, he told me, assuring me that my son would be fine. And sure enough, the red spots appeared and disappeared in a few days, and the fever was controlled by Tylenol. It was thankfully the only illness Khash suffered the entire time we lived in Tehran.

Those first days in our apartment, Karri depended on the Internet to ease her concerns about Khash's illness, and I was relieved that the connection I'd hastily set up had so far proven reliable. Free, and I don't mean monetarily, access to the Internet is a challenge for Iranians but one that they overcome with relative ease; for years I had availed myself of friends' WiFi connections, mostly slow but some faster, and used their PCs with their filter-busting software. Ever since President Ahmadinejad took office in 2005, censorship of sites in Iran has outpaced the growth of Web pages, and Internet connection speeds have been inversely proportional to the advancements in technology, both mobile and static. That is, true broadband is but a dream for most users. While high-speed Internet has been available in Iran for years, until relatively recently most people, even President Ahmadinejad before he took office, used dial-up connections at home. Many still do, based on the number of "Internet cards" sold at every news kiosk. These cards, in denominations of two or five dollars, have an ISP number to call and a scratch-off PIN code to enter; they buy a good number of minutes of browsing, minutes that are necessary given the speed with which pages load—if they're not blocked, that is.

Once, during his first campaign for the presidency, Ahmadinejad was asked by a television reporter if he, as a hard-line conservative, had any intentions of limiting Internet access if he was elected. He responded with his trademark smile and amused look, saying that it was a ridiculous notion, given that he hardly had use of his home phone due to the number of hours his children spent surfing the Net. Using dial-up, clearly, in 2005.

Since then, companies offering DSL connections to home users have proliferated, and blazing speeds are advertised in papers and on billboards throughout Tehran. One ad, seemingly a takeoff on the Maxell cassette tape ads of the 1970s, portrays a man literally being blown away—as if by a hurricane-strength gust—by how fast his laptop is performing. Curious, since if Internet speed in Iran were analogous to wind strength, the Iranian on the billboard might barely feel the flapping of a butterfly's wings. Perhaps it's a cynical nod to state control over Iranians' access to information, or maybe it's just the Iranian predilection for gross exaggeration, *gholov*, that's at play.

Technically, Iran could have fast Internet speeds everywhere— the various ayatollahs' offices in Qom are equipped with fiber-optic cables—but during Ahmadinejad's first term in office, somehow the decision was made that Internet speeds should be limited, for ordinary citizens, to 128K (a fraction of the capability of the network and of what Europeans, Asians, and Americans are accustomed to). Pornography is no fun at 128K; videos of fornicating couples, or of protesting citizens for that matter, are impossible to watch at that speed.

But to add insult to injury, even that maximum 128K exists at the whim of the government and seems rarely delivered to home users, no matter which ISP they contract with. However, at offices and businesses, higher speeds are available and acceptable, so one way many Iranians get around the restriction for home use is to have a letter from their employer, or a friend's employer, or anyone they know, certifying that he or she sometimes works from home; ISPs will happily accept such letters in order to provide real broadband speeds to users. Yes, beating the system is sometimes a collaborative affair. But somehow, they're still never quite real broadband speeds, no matter who you know or what your business is.

I could have asked any one of my friends or family members to provide me with a letter that would get me high-speed Internet at our apartment, which I needed not for watching porn or protests but for holding Skype video chats and staying relatively current with the news back home. Karri needed it for working on her clothing business from afar, as well as for checking every little aspect of Khash's growth progress, and potentially any maladies, against what various medical sites in the United States might say or recommend.

But instead of producing a letter for an ISP, I asked Mr. Bakhtiari, who as a hotel owner is entitled to provide his mostly foreign guests with Internet speeds that will not embarrass a regime that proclaims great scientific prowess, if his apartment building could connect to the network of one of his hotels nearby. Happy to oblige, he arranged for a wireless signal to be beamed to our router. (WiMax, a wireless broadband system, is popular in Iran, where cable lines and copper or optic fibers are rare, except in Qom.) We had thus established our apartment Internet connection easily.

But I still had to use, as most Iranians do, a VPN (virtual private network) in order to use Skype or to connect to censored sites, such as Facebook or Twitter, or even to the BBC, CNN, *The Guardian, Haaretz,* or the *New York Post.* Page Six was a daily treat Karri was unwilling to live without. In Iran, VPNs are available through various brokers whom everybody seems to know, and the rumor is that the government itself provides the service, or maybe the Revolutionary Guards—everything seems to be attributed to the Guards, but given their reach and power, it is unlikely that they are *not* involved in the VPN business. I was reluctant to use an Iranian-provided VPN, since, if the rumor is true, then the government could also potentially monitor my Internet history. Instead I used a U.S.-based service I had signed up for in New York, whereby I was connected to a server in the city, and for all intents and purposes it would appear to the gods, and to the mullahs of the ether, that I had never left Brooklyn.

This was particularly important for us, since we were trying to keep our presence in Iran unknown to the American financial institutions we used. If we checked our bank accounts back home, or tried to pay a credit card bill, online from an Iranian IP address, our accounts would be frozen until we could prove we weren't sanctions busters, something many an unwitting visitor to Iran has been accused of being. And if such a thing happened to us, it would be hard for us to make an appointment with our bank manager in New York to explain our reason for being in Iran. One time Karri, forgetting to log on with the VPN, went on her credit card Web site and typed in her user name and password, and as she hit enter, she suddenly realized she was identifiably in Tehran. Panic ensued. She closed her browser screaming, and both us of us worried for days that Chase Manhattan had discovered our presence well inside the axis of evil. Ironically, the slow speed of the Internet connection saved us, the one time we were grateful for its sedateness, as apparently she had logged off before the Web site had been able to verify her identity.

Even apart from the fact that the connection from our apartment to the hotel network seemed to fail almost as often as it worked, the Internet was a constant source of frustration for us. Despite supposedly having an exception to the 128K rule, the speed would vary wildly, and every day I imagined that someone with a big antique dial in an underground chamber somewhere in Tehran (sort of like in a scene from *Brazil*) would dial the speed up or down depending on instructions from the Ministry of Communication (a misnomer

if ever there was one) or, more likely, his own particular mood that
day. Internet variability didn't seem to bother other Iranians much;
they took it in stride, and they are at any rate refreshingly blasé about
not being permanently and inextricably wired to the world at large,
or else they are simply accustomed to not multitasking or interrupt-
ing their nonvirtual routine thousands of times a day. But for us,
and perhaps especially for Karri, not being connected to the outside
world, for hours sometimes, often made us feel isolated from reality
rather than the other way around, which is the way I suppose it really
should have been, for our reality was now our Tehran home and the
physical world right outside our door. In one sense, though, reality
in Iran *is* the Internet, for without it and bootleg satellite television,
Iranians would be isolated from real information that the censors,
often arbitrarily, decide is inappropriate for citizens to have. Which
is why VPN is an acronym that everyone in Iran understands, even if
they don't know what it stands for.

   Vee-pee-en kar nemeekoneh, "VPN isn't working," is an expression that
can strike terror in Tehran. The authorities know well that almost
everyone connected to the Net is connected via a VPN, whether it's
the government that is selling access or not, and VPNs suddenly and
inexplicably stop working on certain days. Mine, set up in the United
States, sometimes worked when Iranian ones didn't, which led me
to assume that the government could monitor theirs but not mine.
Iran's 17 million (yes, *17 million*) Facebook users, out of a total population of 70 million, are particularly incensed when they can't log on
to the social networking site; it's a useful tool in a society where public expression is virtually forbidden and a virtual friend, boy- or girl-,
is better than no friend at all. Checking out who is or isn't a *duffi*—
a "hot chick" in Iranian youth parlance and a word used by boys
and girls alike—is somewhat easier if one can see photographs of
would-be *duffis* sans hijab. And *duffis* can check out *puffis,* their male
equivalents, with anonymity. (*Fench,* a term for younger *duffis,* high
school age or younger, is sometimes used disparagingly or humor-

ously and not in a creepy way, for it is assumed that they are not yet sexually active.) That Facebook would be so widely used in Iran, particularly by the youth, was unsurprising to me, but it came as a surprise that even some conservative and older politicians, journalists, and influential figures had profiles on the site, beating their own system while they're at it. (That the Supreme Leader now has his own Twitter feed and an Instagram account, to which his office posts flattering photos of him, only demonstrates the sheer hypocrisy inherent in the system.)

The Web site *KhabarOnline* is owned by the Larijanis, the most powerful conservative family in Iran: one brother is the speaker of Parliament, another is head of the judiciary, and a third an adviser to the Supreme Leader and head of Iran's human rights commission. (Presumably he has very little to actually do, hence his active involvement in online media.) A few days after Karri and I moved into our apartment, *KhabarOnline* asked me if I would agree to be interviewed at their offices, at what they call Khabar Café. I agreed and was entertained at what turned out to be a real café, on the ground floor of their building in downtown Tehran, answering questions about America and its politics. The next day pictures of me speaking were posted to the Facebook page of the editor in chief, who tagged me. Given that VPNs had been officially declared illegal by the Ministry of Justice (what did Sadegh Larijani think of *that?*), and given that Facebook, the declared enemy of hard-line conservatives, was forbidden in Iran, it was, to say the least, a little odd.

I asked the editor, seeing as he was liberal-minded enough to venture onto Facebook, if I could meet with Mohammad Javad Larijani, his immediate boss and the human rights commissioner.

"I'm sure he'll be happy to," he replied. "I'll let you know as soon as I hear back from him." Weeks went by, and when I pressed him, the editor said he had spoken to Larijani, who had asked him if I was related to Maryam Majd. Maryam, a well-known photographer, had just been arrested on charges of "endangering national security," the

catchall phrase applied to all political prisoners. I'm not related to
her, even though one of my cousins is named Maryam Majd and is
the wife of former president Khatami's brother; but Larijani, according to the editor of *KhabarOnline,* was "afraid to meet with [me]." I
thought he should be more afraid of all the Maryam Majds who
languish in prison but will one day look to exact revenge—much
as Larijani and his ilk took revenge on former shah functionaries
in 1979—on the powerful men who have decided that any form of
dissent, even a propensity to dissent, must be snuffed out. But that
a Larijani would be afraid of me, or of what I might write, was also
tremendously gratifying to me. After all, I now lived in Tehran rather
anonymously, was not allowed to use my pen, and felt as insignificant
to the Iranian power equation as every other Iranian I crossed paths
with in my daily, often mundane routine—which included little
apart from note taking and staying abreast of the news, daily grocery
shopping, visiting friends, and taking care of a demanding infant on
the cusp of toddlerhood.

Like their American or European counterparts, Iranian youth,
flocking to Facebook and other social media, sometimes forget that
it's not only their friends and "friends" who can see their lives unfold
on their computer screens, it's everybody. Very soon after we moved
into our apartment, finding a baby-sitter for Khash became a prior-
ity. Baby-sitting is not, as in the West, a quick way for teenagers and
young women to make a buck while studying or waiting for acting
auditions. In Iran, nannies come from a somewhat professional class;
the many middle-class families who employ them expect them to
work every day and nurture a child or children all the way through
their high school years. A baby-sitter, someone who occasionally
watches a child while its parents are out for the evening, is a rarity.

But by asking around we were able to find a young woman, a
social worker in her early twenties, who also spoke good English. She
was wonderful with Khash, who seemed to like her and listened care-

fully when she spoke to him in Farsi (which we encouraged). But she often canceled on us at the last minute, usually when we most wanted to attend an event or were invited to a party we particularly looked forward to. On the days when she would show up, I would leave my computer on for her with the VPN connected, and based on the browsing history that, I'm sorry, I just had to check later, Facebook was the site she visited most often when Khash was asleep. Or maybe when he was awake, too. And she friended us both.

Usually her last-minute no-shows happened on weekends, when she, like so many other Tehranis, would escape to the mountains or the Caspian shore; she would text me or Karri to say she was stuck in horrendous traffic, which was believable enough—Iran's traffic patterns can make a one-hour trip to a mountain resort take three to four hours depending on when you leave.

One time, on a night when we were to attend a friend's fortieth birthday party—it promised to be a bacchanal unrivaled in Tehran's infamous party scene—she texted me at the last minute to say she had been in a car accident on the way back from *shomal,* the shore, and couldn't make it. That was also believable, given that the accident rate on Iran's roads is among the highest in the world. "R u ok?" I texted back. She was fine, she said, but had to work out how to get back to Tehran. Karri, who by now cried foul every time the sitter canceled, was furious. No way, she argued, had the girl been in an accident. She'd just found something better to do, like all spoiled Iranian kids.

I wanted to believe our sitter, but I thought I'd check her Facebook page to see what she had been up to over the weekend. And yes, Karri was right: less than an hour before, she had changed her status from "single" to "in a relationship." Talk about beating the Islamic system. The change in her relationship status couldn't be due to her falling into the arms of an eligible man as her car smashed into another, or an accidental brush of the lips as their faces collided when two cars did. Iran's cellular network makes updating Facebook or even accessing the Internet while in a car practically impossible, so she couldn't be stuck on the road somewhere. No, it was just a case of a Tehran *duffi* finding her *puffi*, if only temporarily, with no time for watching a baby.

While setting up an Internet connection that allows free access to information is easier than one might suspect, and easier than the U.S. administration seems to believe given that President Obama and Secretary Clinton often mentioned the "cyber curtain" that exists in Iran, obtaining a good source of liquor is easy, too. A visitor may be forgiven for thinking that everyone drinks in the Islamic Republic, since there seems to be no shortage of alcohol or of entrepreneurial suppliers, but of course it is only in the big cities, and among the more secular classes, that drinking is a regular pastime. Liquor comes into Iran via a number of sources: across the borders from Turkey, Iraqi Kurdistan, Azerbaijan, Armenia, or in small boats from the Persian Gulf countries. Iran's Christian (mostly Armenian), Zoroastrian, and Jewish minorities can legally manufacture liquor for their own use, but they are technically prohibited from selling it to their Muslim compatriots or even serving it to them. Naturally, that doesn't stop some in the community, mostly Armenians, from entering the rather lucrative and easy business of selling *aragh*, the traditional Persian vodka distilled from raisins and affectionately known as "dog sweat," and occasionally homemade red wine to customers they know, either through a personal recommendation or a genuine friendship. I needed a good supply of both foreign spirits and the Iranian one, which is far cheaper than imported bootleg whiskey or vodka and which I rather like. A year or so in Tehran, a city with no bars, meant evenings at home mostly, drink in hand.

As with almost everything illegal anywhere, one has to ask friends and acquaintances for a connection to a supplier. One friend had told me to stay away from foreign liquor—even though it looked, smelled, and sometimes tasted like the real thing, it was inevitably fake, produced in the mountains of Iraqi Kurdistan or in Turkey using "essences" of the spirit mixed with alcohol and water. "How can there be more Dewar's here than in Scotland?" he asked. "Or more Johnnie Walker? You'll get a bad hangover if you drink that shit." He himself stuck to good old Iranian dog sweat, which he happily decanted out of five-gallon drums into plastic one-liter Sprite bottles for me, and which I transported home, a little uncomfortably, in the front seat of a taxi, sweating as much as the dog in the bottle whenever we drove past leering Basij patrols under the overpasses.

But I wanted some whiskey, too, and I thought Karri would like the occasional vodka, seeing as she was unlikely to get much drinkable wine. (Beer, although available almost as widely as spirits, is not as popular in Iran, for it doesn't offer the same bang for the buck, or thwack for the toman, as spirits do, even though it is just as difficult to transport across borders. And since nonalcoholic beer is sold in every deli and supermarket in Iran, adding an ounce or two of *aragh* to the brew makes for an easy, cheap, and passable beer.)

So another friend introduced me to his dealer, a youngish man who drove up to an apartment building where we were having lunch one day and called us. We went into the busy street, where he double-parked his old Peugeot and opened the trunk. A few cases of whiskey and vodka, some open, were in view, and I asked for a couple of bottles, Dewar's and Absolut, handing over the equivalent of about fifty dollars. He removed them from the cases and put them in a black plastic bag.

That was his only nod to discretion in an otherwise blatantly illegal act that could get him years in prison and me a good lashing with a whip if a policeman, or worse, the Gasht-e Ershad, the infamous morality patrol, drove by at that moment. I had always had a drink or two, or more, when visiting Tehran over the years, courtesy of friends whose home bars seemed much better stocked than mine in New York, but the act of buying liquor myself, and the thought of making it a regular habit, was a little disconcerting. A bit thrilling, too, I'll admit—not unlike how I felt buying pot in my college days.

Karri, perhaps influenced by our friend who insisted all bootleg liquor in Iran is fake, declared my bottles to also be so after taking her first sips. And she's not even a whiskey or vodka drinker. (To be fair, however, she was, during her acting and modeling days, a bartender at a couple of New York bars, one of which is where we actually met, and she is more familiar with spirits and cocktails than I'll ever be.) Fake or not, the Scotch tasted fine to me, and the vodka no different from what I've had before, but I decided that Karri and my friend were probably right, and that drinking something that could be even more poisonous than the real stuff was probably unwise. We determined that I would only buy the real deal, if I could find it, or else we'd stick to Iranian martinis—dog sweat and whatever fresh juice was available in season. Vermouth, absent in Iran and probably considered pointless anyway, was out of the question.

A friend of mine who drinks, chain-smokes cigarettes, and uses opium with abandon told me he had a contact who could deliver genuine spirits, specializing in high-end European vodkas. (Oddly, it's almost impossible to get Russian vodka in Iran, even fake, when Iran shares a border with a number of former Soviet republics and is on friendly terms with Russia.) "They're expensive," he said, "but I promise it's the real stuff. It's the only thing I drink." I asked if I could share his contact, and he said, matter-of-factly, no. "He doesn't trust anyone and prefers to deal with as few people as possible." To me, that meant the customer had to be connected to government, but my friend said he'd be happy to order whatever I wanted. I said I'd buy whatever was genuine.

The next time I saw him, he took me into his den, opened a closet and then a huge safe inside, and said I should take whatever I wanted. He had a price list in his hand. From among the thirty or so different bottles, I chose a Scandinavian vodka—not the unexceptional Absolut that is readily available from any dealer—and paid double what it would cost outside Iran, also double what I could have paid if I had been less concerned about its provenance. Back home, Karri declared it genuine the minute she observed me unscrew the cap. "It doesn't have the shot measure pourer built in, like all the other liquor in Iran," she said. "It must be real."

As easy as buying liquor is in any big Iranian city, it's even easier to buy bootleg movies on DVD. Along with watching satellite television, watching DVDs is a favorite (illegal) pastime for many Iranians. What is legal and sold at every newsstand tends to be Iranian films that have satisfied the censors or popular television series, so for foreign films one is obliged to turn to the black market. Small shops in almost every mall carry foreign films, below or above the counter, and every day street vendors lay out their wares—the latest Hollywood hits—openly on pavements to entice passersby; if one lingers for longer than a few seconds, they'll produce stacks of DVDs from a bag or backpack.

In our neighborhood, one young man could be found outside a shoe store and near a famous ice-cream parlor and an *ash* joint (a soup restaurant not unlike the *Seinfeld* Soup Nazi's in both look and the attitudes of the servers) on the northern end of Vali Asr every day at around six in the evening. At that moment strollers out for air on the tree-lined boulevard, evening shoppers, and ice-cream or soup aficionados, depending on the season, would be out in force. Conveniently, this young man was also across the street from a small park where we would take Khash for his afternoon constitutional, and on our return home we would stop to check if he had any new films we hadn't yet seen.

The DVDs were not, naturally, originals—they were always copies made from one original smuggled into Iran, or sometimes they were downloaded from the Internet. I didn't want to buy *pardeh-ee*

films, literally "curtain-like," which were films shot in a theater with
a video camera; so the dealer, who like all Iranians was fascinated by
and taken with Khash and my American wife, would warn me off
certain titles. "These are *nines*," he'd say, taking out a stack from his
backpack, meaning they were direct digital copies of originals and
therefore watchable. I wondered why he didn't say they were tens,
but I suppose he was trying for honesty with a customer he hoped to
keep—I'd told him we'd be living in Iran for a while. He wouldn't
claim his products to be quite perfect copies, even though technically
they were.

But our man often seemed to go AWOL, not answering his cell
phone for a few days, leading us to wonder if he'd been busted. Then
I would venture farther south on Vali Asr to Vanak Square, where
another DVD seller would assure me that although his prices were
higher than others, a little over a dollar rather than a little less, he
could guarantee that all his films were nines. Not tens? No: *nines*.

I would buy as many films as possible at one time, never quite
sure if our dealers would disappear or be arrested, but they remained
a relatively regular presence—we'd usually see them on the late afternoon walk from the park to our apartment. We'd also stop for fresh
hot bread at the bakery, which Khash would get a start on nibbling,
and whatever groceries we'd missed buying earlier in the day. We
returned to the United States having seen every single film of interest
that was released in 2010 and even 2011, even a few *pardeh-ee* ones, new
releases that we just couldn't resist.

Films were an accompaniment to our satellite viewing, limited as
that was to the BBC for news, or the Fashion Channel for amusement,
since our satellite guy, who expertly connected the receiver and set
up the channels, didn't have the codes for the pay movie stations, or
so he said, and we'd have to get someone else in to unlock them. For
another hefty fee, presumably. Satellite installers are very much like
the cable guy in the United States, if not the actual character played
by Jim Carrey in *The Cable Guy*. Highly professional and technical

wizards, they can install a dish, set up a box, and show you how it all works in minutes, but of course they prefer to take hours, both to validate the amount they charge (for no Iranian would pay their rates if the job seemed a simple matter) and to pontificate on and carp about everything from the government to the state of the world.

Our cable, excuse me, *satellite* guy took an immediate liking to Khash, who played with him on the little terrace outside our living room in his brand-new *ro-ro-ak*, a child's rolling walker, while the technician smoked and tut-tutted to me about the miserable state of the economy. He'd disappear onto the roof from time to time, claiming he had to adjust the satellite dish, but I suspect he was just taking the opportunity to waste time and perhaps make a few phone calls on one of the two cell phones he carried. He was curious, though, about this family from New York who had decided to live in Iran, and his friendliness and familiarity almost made me think he'd ask to stay for dinner, although I knew an Iranian could never be so bold.

Our building, like many others in Tehran, actually already had a couple of satellite dishes on the roof, and all he had to do was connect one to our TV. But in the hours that seemed to take, he told me everything about his family, asked everything about mine, and complained about his life—the life of a tradesman whose trade is illegal. "Just on the drive here," he said, "I was stuck on Modaress [highway], and a motorcycle drove up, and the driver peered at my electronic equipment in the backseat. So he was a Basij, I figured, but what the hell is their problem? I mean, he wants to harass me? What, am I not supposed to work? Why, is it my problem that everyone wants foreign TV? Go fix Iranian TV, and then I won't be necessary!"

He went on and on about the government, about the media, and about the Gasht-e Ershad patrols, which were much more widespread in 2011 than ever before. "And they harass women for bad hijab?" he said. "Bad TV and bad hijab. Like our country doesn't have other problems. What is this place coming to? You're lucky you're only here for a while, but god knows why you're here at all, when you could be in New York of all places. *New York!*" He left a cell phone number when he finished, and I suspected he wanted me to call, but our satellite always seem to work, and I never did.

The Gasht-e Ershad he complained about, as so many other Iranians did, even very religious ones, had always been somewhat invisible to me in my previous, much shorter visits to Iran. Recognizing them by the minivans they drive and their patrol car escorts, I had seen them only occasionally, and no one I knew thought of them as much more than a minor annoyance. Their job, of course, is to stop women who are *mal*-veiled (a wonderful and purely Iranian term). They also stop men who are inappropriately dressed and groomed, but their primary targets are women. Often they will only issue a warning, but they can also haul their victims away to a police station, where the offending woman must pay a fine and promise to never dress that way ever again. Like all Iranians, I've had friends and family picked up in the past and family members stopped while driving, but the frequency of the morality squad patrols decreased significantly during President Khatami's terms in office, picked up under Ahmadinejad's first term, and then significantly increased in the past two years. While the squads—overseen by the national police—are most visible at the start of spring, when the weather turns warmer and heavier coats and scarves are shed, in 2011 the seventy thousand men and women assigned to the *gasht* were a ubiquitous presence on Tehran streets, especially in North Tehran, no matter the weather. (While we were staying downtown, we didn't see any patrols, and given that we were in a religious and conservative neighborhood, south of Vanak Square—the unofficial line dividing North Tehran from downtown and points south—the cops would have had little to do there.)

It probably didn't help that Ahmadinejad had come out publicly *against* the morality patrols, for it seemed that in his later years as president and because of his tiff with the clerical leadership—and his big sulk of 2011—everything he was against, at least from a social and religious aspect, the authorities were *for*. While we were in Tehran, he complained that the morality squads harassed the youth unnecessarily and argued that, aside from the issue of hijab, the state shouldn't care if boys and girls hung out together, something the patrols were also on the lookout for. Music to the ears of the very people who voted against him in 2009, but no one was under any illusion that he could change things. In fact, I suggested to friends, if Ahmadinejad really wanted to stop the harassment of women and the youth, he'd come out and say there wasn't *enough* of it, for if he did, the authorities would doubtless relax their efforts just to spite him. He undeniably knew that his proclamations on what is or isn't acceptable in Islam would be ignored—as they were when, after he was first elected, he pronounced female spectators at soccer stadiums to be *halal* (kosher, in Islam)—and might even promote a backlash by the clerics and a redoubled effort to remind him of his lay status.

His opinions on the morality police and the strict separation of the sexes were perhaps a cynical attempt to ingratiate himself with the more secular-minded segment of the public and future young voters who might give him, along with his base of poorer rural voters, a platform to be relevant in politics once his second and final term ended in 2013. Few were buying it. Even his publicly stated opinion that Messrs. Mousavi and Karroubi—his two challengers in the 2009 presidential poll, who were now under house arrest in Tehran—should be freed barely registered among those who despised him, perhaps because they knew that if he meant it, he could at least engage in another big sulk to try to force the issue, and maybe he'd even get away with it this time.

So the Gasht-e Ershad continued their rounds, and remarkably, Iranians continued to defy them, as they always have. They refused to adjust their attire to the preference of the state, and, as I witnessed, heatedly argued with the chador-clad policewomen who stopped them, unwilling to be intimidated. Some women even put up a fight—literally, as evidenced in the many videos posted to YouTube, which, as expected, is filtered by the Iranian ISPs. Not that that would ever stop Iranians from using it. For Iranians, after all, the autocratic system—extant from the time of shahs and viziers—is plainly there simply to be defeated.

7

A FUNNY THING HAPPENED ON THE WAY TO THE REVOLUTION

During my prior visits to the Islamic Republic, Tehran's zealous morality squad had never directly affected me, and I hadn't thought that the men in green berets and fatigues and the women in full black chadors, only their disapproving and scolding eyes visible, would be relevant even if I traveled to Iran with my wife. Despite their presence, the revolution had surely matured, and the wearing of the hijab couldn't possibly be taken quite as seriously, or literally, as it once was, could it? Karri had always said that if she ever went to Iran, she would be happy to abide by the Shia Iranian concept of sartorial decorum, but she had seen films and photographs of scantily hijab-ed women, and her idea, and mine, of what was fully acceptable was actually a little too optimistic, especially in 2011.

A few days after we moved into our apartment off Saadabad Street (renamed Ayatollah Maleki Street after the revolution but still referred to as Saadabad), we were walking on Vali Asr near Tajrish Square when we came upon the Gasht-e Ershad, their van and patrol car parked in front of Ladan, a famous patisserie. The women officers were busy pulling young women aside for questioning, but as we walked by, one of the men, a dour-looking fellow who seemed to be doing his best to appear menacing, gestured to me as he caught my eye.

I stopped and tried to act surprised, asking if it was me he wanted to talk to. I was pushing a baby stroller, after all, and Karri, Khash, and I were the most unlikely of candidates to be targeted by the morality police.

"Yes," he said firmly. "Is that your wife?"

I replied in the affirmative, adding that the baby was my son.

"Her manteau is too short," he said.

It was close to 100 degrees, and Karri, like many Iranian women, was not wearing a manteau at all, but rather a loose-fitting cotton shirt over a tank top, one that covered her posterior but not most of her thighs. Those were, however, covered by her jeans, for skirts are a big no-no in Iran unless they're long enough to cover the ankles, in which case one might as well go for the chador.

Before we left for Iran, Karri had scrutinized images of Iranian women on the Web and some days had returned home with shopping bags full of what she thought might pass for manteaus, holding them up for me and asking my opinion. They were inexpensive long cotton shirts that looked fine to me; plenty of young Iranian girls appeared to be wearing them on the streets, at least based on my own observation and the numerous photos on the Web. Since we arrived, we had seen similar ones in shops in Tehran, though not in proper manteau shops, which specialized in the heavier, more concealing tops that my cousins, but not their daughters, wore.

"I'm sorry," I said, "but she's *farangi*, a foreigner."

"It doesn't matter," he said sternly. "Tell her to cover up."

Karri's blond hair, meanwhile, was more than peeking out from under her very loosely wrapped scarf, but that didn't seem to trouble the officer, or at least he didn't mention it.

"I tell her all the time," I said, in a feeble attempt at humor, "but you know women."

"Just a warning this time," he said, unsmiling and without a hint of emotion. "Tell her to cover up."

Karri was furious. It was ridiculous, she said, that in the summer weather these men were deciding what a woman should wear—especially a Western woman who hadn't been raised in a culture where covering oneself completely was common among some women in every family, of every class. "I don't care if I get arrested," she said to me defiantly. Before we arrived, the idea of having to wear a scarf hadn't bothered her, but then she actually had to wear one every day in stifling heat and had to deal with it falling off her head every time she lifted Khash, played with him in the park, or bent down to pick something up, which happened numerous times a day.

From then on, though, we watched for the Gasht patrols, which could be spotted from a distance, and either crossed the street to avoid them or spiffed ourselves up as we walked by. (Like many of her Iranian sisters, Karri was far less intimidated by the patrols than I was.) We lived only a hundred yards or so up the hill from Tajrish Square, a busy traffic circle that seemed to be a permanent location for one or more patrols, even during winter snowstorms, and while walking down the hill, we could easily spot the green-and-white vans and patrol cars.

Karri was stopped another time, alone with Khash, as she walked through the square on her way home. Again, a male officer gestured for her to approach him, and she simply yelled, "No Farsi!," even though she understood well enough. He kept pointing to her scarf and manteau and saying something while the women officers yelled at him to give it up. *"Khareji-e!"*—"She's a foreigner!"—they shouted back at him, she told me, and *"Velesh kon!"*—"Leave her alone!" He finally did give up, throwing his arms in the air and getting into his squad car, probably more convinced than ever that foreign women were a bad influence on all the girls, not just the scofflaw *duffis* and *fenches*, of the Islamic Republic.

The days went by quickly once we had our own place and settled into our routine. We were indeed settled in Tehran, or as much as one might be, knowing that it was not a permanent condition. We had what we needed to live as middle-class or upper-middle-class Iranians do, except, in a city geographically much like Los Angeles, perhaps a car: we had satellite television, not-so-high-speed wireless Internet, a DVD supplier, a couple of good sources of liquor, a cell phone each (both with the Tehran emergency number, 115, stored in case in an actual emergency we accidentally dialed 911), bank debit cards, and an apartment that was small but comfortable.

Our building even boasted a swimming pool in the basement, which had to be reserved in advance for use, for although it was large enough to accommodate multiple families, the building owner could not risk allowing unrelated men and women to cavort there, let alone cavort together unveiled, as the sexes are not permitted to mingle on the beaches or in any public space. That is certainly why it was built in a basement in the first place—so no stray eyes could fall on it, through a window or a crack in the wall. Karri at first thought the segregated swimming hours and windowless pool amusing but annoying, yet she soon got used to having the whole pool to herself and Khash. (In the heat of the long summer, the Islamic restrictions on life in Iran were an outright nuisance, since the same pool outdoors would not only have been a luxury that made Tehran far more bearable, but would also have provided a form of relaxed entertainment where it scarcely existed.) But as the cooler months were upon us—we even had a surprise October snow—the heated pool in the basement, even without windows, became more and more attractive a proposition for wasting an afternoon.

The pool, like everything in Iran, was spotless and kept obsessively clean by the building staff. When we first arrived in Tehran, Karri had expressed relief at the city's cleanliness, despite its awful pollution, and was surprised that drinking water straight from the tap was not only okay but as commonplace as in the United States or

Europe. So was bottled water, hundreds of different brands, which she could buy at any deli or even at newsstands. Street sweepers and garbage collectors, who worked seven days a week as opposed to the twice weekly we were accustomed to in New York, were an ever-present sight, not just in the northern reaches of the city, where everything was pristine, but in the south, too, and in the midcity neighborhood where we had stayed for the first couple of weeks.

The street sweeper who covered our area was almost always there whenever we left our apartment, an older white-haired man who got to know Khash and would say hello to him every day. Khash watched his every move, gathering leaves, sweeping the dust from the pavement, and picking up stray pieces of trash. Khash was so entranced by the sweeper's twig broom that I bought a short-handled one for him, which provided hours of entertainment for him once he started walking and pure inconvenience for us, as the thin twigs would snap and make a mess in all corners of the apartment. The city's cleanliness was largely due to a concerted effort by successive mayors, strict adherents to the revolution's Islamic ideals, including the public segregation of the sexes and hijab rules, but thoroughly Persian in their zeal to provide as squeaky-clean an environment for the public as is possible in a city that has quadrupled its population in a thirty-year span.

The Islamic ideals of the revolution had once been attractive enough to the general population to induce them to support it. The ideals that were articulated, though, had nothing to do with personal freedoms, and before the revolution Khomeini had in fact denied that he would enforce the hijab. Secular women who wore chadors in street protests against the shah were doing so out of respect for Khomeini, not out of religious belief, and soon after the revolution, when the hijab and modest appearance were deemed mandatory, those same women came out in large numbers to protest the state's decision. (Few Iranian women who supported the revolution imagined that hijab would become compulsory or that swimming might effectively disappear from the list of their lives' pleasures.) Women who defied the ban on immodest clothing or appearance then were treated harshly, in some cases beaten or violently manhandled by *komiteh* members—local "committees" set up to enforce the new standards of behavior. But despite a gradual loosening of standards, particularly after Khomeini's death in 1989 and the rise of the reform movement in the mid-1990s, the concepts of the hijab and modesty endure, albeit continually challenged in different ways. Karri's hijab is a loose scarf that covers some but not all of her hair, which, according to at least one low-ranking mullah, "radiates an aura" that makes her irresistible to men; it continued to be a nuisance to her, but she did her best to stay within the boundaries of what the republic considers modest dress.

Other women, particularly younger ones, seemed oblivious both to those boundaries and to good taste, for not a day went by when Karri did not profess shock at the absolute disregard some women exhibited to the possibility of enticing men with their heavily made-up faces, bleached blond hair barely covered by a chiffon scarf, or a beehive hairdo with a piece of cloth perched perilously atop, as enticing as a virgin out of *A Thousand and One Nights,* and tight manteaus that accentuated rather than covered their sometimes-generous behinds. Heels? Yes, as high as possible, making walking the sidewalks difficult and crossing the street while dodging cars almost as dangerous as climbing Everest. Of course few of these ladies ever walked very much, alighting instead from BMWs, Benzes, Lexuses, and other late-model luxury cars, and daintily dashing, hopping almost, into coffee shops, restaurants, and the odd shopping mall, assuming the morality squad wasn't parked outside, ready to pounce.

The number of women in Tehran wearing makeup, with hair and nails done perfectly even though lipstick and nail polish are forbidden, made me wonder where all the beauty parlors were. In my male-centric experiences in Iran, I had never stopped to wonder about them and the very un-Islamic world that they represented. All my female cousins and their daughters dye their hair, some for color and others to cover gray, and most wear makeup of some sort and paint their nails; one cousin, like many older Iranian women, wears cotton gloves while driving to avoid being stopped for the offense of having manicured and polished nails.

Karri, who was less concerned with makeup or her fingernails, did want to have her hair done while in Iran, so we asked one cousin who lived nearby where she went for her hair, assuming it would be close and within walking distance of our apartment. It turns out that the salon was a stone's throw from my cousin's house in Elahieh, a chic, if not the chicest, neighborhood in Shemiran, North Tehran. I had driven past it many times but would not have known it was anything but another walled, private house on a corner of a residential street. There was no sign, and no windows, and when I dropped Karri off the first time, I waited for her to be buzzed in, still unsure whether this was what my cousin and a couple of friends had insisted was one of Tehran's most exclusive salons.

I, like other men, was not allowed inside, just as I was not allowed inside the children's playhouse a block away from the salon, where we took Khash occasionally to play with other children his age. (Mothers there wanted to be able to take their hijab off while playing with or just watching their kids, but even in hijab they weren't allowed into the exclusive and expensive health club one flight up, where they might see buffed young men sweating and in various states of undress.) In the hair salon, though, there was no activity or procedure to which the women subjected themselves that would be permissible for men to observe. The aura of their naked hair alone, washed, cut, and blow-dried might be enough to throw a mullah into paroxysms of sensual delight and was to be avoided by the pious at all costs.

Karri told me it was exactly as any upscale salon would be in New York, or in any other Western capital for that matter, with the exception of no male presence whatsoever: no hairdressers, no colorists, no assistants, and not even a tea boy, ubiquitous in every other place of business in Iran. Although one would imagine gay men to be immune to the aura emanating from women's hair, not even *they* are allowed inside, perhaps because, as President Ahmadinejad once made himself a laughingstock by suggesting, there are no gay men in Iran "like you have here" (in New York). Presumably he and his ilk imagine that Iranian homosexual men, unlike Western ones, *can* be tempted by a woman's beguilement. Perhaps *that's* what he meant by "like you have here."

One would also think that, given the phobia many Iranian men exhibit toward gays and the fact that otherwise intelligent men like Ahmadinejad think that homosexuality is a lifestyle choice made by morally corrupt Westerners, they might encourage whichever gay men they think do exist to be surrounded by hijab-less women, even naked ones, to cure them, as some mullahs believe possible, of their predilection. But no, gay and lesbian culture in Iran, like any of the mores not in strict compliance with conservative Islam, is consigned to the unseen. In a country where *lavat*, or sodomy, is punishable by death (usually for the passive partner, since the culture views only him as "truly" homosexual) but men holding hands while walking down the street are perfectly normal, the authorities may think they have been successful in driving what they don't want to see underground or behind closed doors.

But if my gaydar was as keen here as in New York, I'm certain that my own barber, his assistant, most of the employees, and some of the customers of the barbershop I frequented on Vali Asr, a ground-floor shop with expansive windows and a big sign, were gay. Not, as Jerry Seinfeld would say, that there's anything wrong with that, but Iranian gaydar must be pretty feeble (or the feminine side of straight Iranian men extra pronounced, or both), because most people who spend time in Tehran can recognize that the revolution's attempts to dispense with homosexuality have been spectacularly unsuccessful. As have the revolution's attempts to change the behavior of men and women in general to behavior that is inimical to the actual values of many of them.

At my barbershop, witnessing men getting their hair dyed was not the reason I thought some customers might be gay: Iranian men, peacocks all, have always been unashamed of primping. At a meeting with a few former senior officials of the regime, I was struck by the obviously dyed hair of one politician who spoke at length, and as I stared at his hairline for what seemed hours, it reminded me of the nouveau riche young men we'd see in cafés who were perfectly coiffed, wore the right jeans and the right watches, and conspicuously carried the right phones; many had nose jobs and depilated eyebrows. The older men, especially Islamists, are another thing altogether, as the regime once viewed paying excessive attention to grooming as un-Islamic and even derided Khatami for his elegant and too-tailored clerical garb.

But over the years, grooming seems to have become fully accepted even in the corridors of political power. The most egregious example is one Hassan Firouzabadi, or Hassan *kheeky,* as some Iranians contemptuously call him, Hassan "the fatso," for his rather corpulent figure, unusual in Iran and even more unusual among military men anywhere. The armed forces chief of staff, he has been seen variously with his hair and beard both dyed, or with one or the other dyed, or very rarely, au naturel (presumably between visits to his hair salon). An extremely powerful figure in the Iranian leadership, he is a hard-line conservative with uncompromising views, a cruel man, according to some, who wouldn't hesitate to order his troops to kill anyone who might defy the regime.

Why it is okay for a man to dye his hair while a woman isn't allowed to show even a strand, according to conservatives like Firouzabadi, is a mystery, not just to people like me and Karri, but to many Iranians. One day while I was riding a bus, a woman, conservatively dressed in full black hijab, was seated behind me—in violation of the segregation rules. She even told a man who complained to mind his own business and piss off. As a morality police van passed us, she said to her companion, "Explain to us how the hijab helps Iran, and we'll all wear it voluntarily." At the officials' meeting, as I stared at the speaker's dyed hairline, I also thought how fortunate it was that hair plugs, as an alternative to the comb-overs some older men sport, hadn't found a market in Iran. Yet.

Perhaps nowhere in Iran is the contrast between the revolutionary vision and the reality more visible than in North Tehran. We had chosen to live in the northern reaches of the city for its cool climate, trees, and parks for Khash, and in the neighborhood of Tajrish for its proximity to markets and its good public transportation, especially the rapid transit bus line that runs the entire twelve-mile length of Vali Asr; unlike most Iranians, I refuse, except under extreme circumstances, to drive in Tehran traffic. Tajrish was a onetime village in the foothills that was now upscale and modern but that still housed many religious families. Every other house or apartment building in our immediate vicinity had a Koranic inscription carved into the wall above the entrance, a sure sign of pious families within, and black chador–clad women would emerge from the doors to go about their errands, mingling as they did with their more scantily covered peers.

The diversity of the neighborhood was clearly visible at the bakery down the street, right by a mosque, where women in black, as well as girls and women with hair and heavy makeup showing, would form a line for *sangak.* The hot flat bread, sprinkled with the little stones that give it its name, was baked fresh every day by teams of sweaty men who casually threw it onto a metal grate. There customers would daintily pick up their loaf, their fingers smarting from the heat, flick the pebbles off, carry it outside, and place it on a hook while it cooled down. At the fruit and vegetable stand where I would buy our daily produce, the religious and the obviously secular mixed, often exchanging pleasantries or sharing complaints. ("Buy these," the fruit seller would say to me, picking out some less-well-formed and dull-looking fruit. "The others are to display for guests. They look good but don't have the same taste.") So did they intermingle all around Tajrish Square, a shopping mecca of sorts.

Even at the upscale Tandis mall nearby—where almost every single store (Hermès, Louis Vuitton, and so on) was either a fake outpost of a European designer or carried mostly counterfeit goods of varying quality—religious families, women in chador or full black hijab walking behind their bearded husbands, mingled freely with the younger and more daring. In the coffee shops and restaurants in the mall, older ladies often gathered for lunch, some dressed very conservatively and others, sometimes at the same table, outfitted for a bistro or trattoria in New York, Paris, or Rome. (Still, the combination of heavy and at times outlandish or even grotesque makeup, surgically altered noses, injected lips, and obvious skin treatments on some women is rarely witnessed in the United States, even on Madison Avenue or Rodeo Drive.) We wondered how these women managed to get by the morality police without being immediately arrested, but I learned from a friend that some women would specifically avoid the mall on days when the green vans were parked outside, or would cover up as much as possible as they walked through the entrance and then once inside would loosen their veils.

Not all young women, of course, push the boundaries of Islamic decency in Tajrish, or even elsewhere, particularly not the women who work as salesgirls in shops and pharmacies, tellers in banks, waitresses and hostesses in restaurants, or baristas in the numerous coffee shops that have sprung up in a city that once swilled tea almost exclusively. Every employed woman has to adhere to a quite strict dress code, for no matter what the owner of any establishment or business believes, no matter whether he or she is secular or pious, no one can risk being shut down for having created an unvirtuous environment. Every coffee shop and restaurant has a sign advising its customers to abide by Islamic dress, and while some owners might be relaxed about enforcing the rules, especially in areas less likely to be raided, others have staff who will plead with girls who've let their scarves drop to their shoulders, telling them to cover up or leave.

But many women who work still wear makeup, sometimes a lot of it, perhaps as a sign to others that they are not quite what they appear to be. The coffee shop at the bottom of the hill from our apartment, which served pretty good espresso and sold excellent South American coffee beans (not easy to come by), employed an attractive young woman with bright red lipstick who befriended Khash the first time we walked in. Whenever Karri or I strolled by the shop without intending to go in, he would point to it and inevitably insist that we do so—which kept us unnecessarily caffeinated throughout our stay in Iran. The woman would fuss over him, cooing and playing with him, and he would flirt back, smiling and laughing and generally being way more adorable than even delusional parents could believe. She always wore a green bracelet, the mark of a Green Movement supporter, and even green shoelaces in her sneakers—she clearly identified with the reformist movement that had been crushed, but not completely vanquished, two years earlier. (So did a young woman we met in a park, who also wore a green bracelet; she once tried to get Khash to make the V sign with his fingers, "like the *fetneh*," sedition, she said, laughing.) One day while we were walking home from a park we saw our barista in the street, in her trademark sneakers and green laces, and jeans; but she wore no formal manteau or hijab, just a scarf lazily thrown over her jet-black hair, the ends falling on the shoulders of a plain white shirt. She was with a boy, probably her boyfriend, judging by their body language, and she called out the minute she saw Khash in his stroller. She held him and kissed him, while the boyfriend exhibited a nonplussed expression, and I wondered about her life. In all likelihood she had protested the reelection of Ahmadinejad in 2009, she wasn't happy with the turn of events since then, and she needed to show the world she was still "green."

But was that it? Had the youth of Iran, the vanguard of the movement to bring about much-needed change, given up on their own revolution, thirty years after their fathers' and mothers' revolution? Was flashing a dash of green the most they could do? The question proved difficult to answer. Almost every time we saw the Gasht-e Ershad patrols, Karri wondered aloud why Iranian women just don't refuse to go along with state decrees on what they could and could not wear, especially after they were willing to protest an election so vehemently; if a million women removed their head scarves on a hot day, she reasoned, what could even seventy thousand cops do? I had the same thought, except that getting a million women or a million Iranians to do anything together is a monumental task under the best of circumstances; it would require a level of organization that the government could quickly uncover.

But it did seem incongruous to us that the state crackdown—on everything from *mal*-veiling to more important civil rights, such as a free press or freedom of assembly—did not fan the flames of discord, as the shah had done in 1978 and as Arab governments had in 2010 and 2011; instead it seemed to render Iranians all the less willing to challenge the state. After the massive protests of 2009, one might have expected the Arab Spring two years later to energize the Iranian opposition movement, perhaps even lead to a Persian Spring. But some Iranians bought the government line that the fall of Western-backed dictators was a blessing for the Islamic Republic; others worried that the Arabs didn't know what they were getting themselves into—an Islamist takeover of Egypt was a foregone conclusion, as far as they were concerned. And a majority simply either were not much interested or were weary of having tried and failed to challenge the authority of the Supreme Leader.

It was easy for us, a secular Iranian and his American wife, to decide what Iranians should do to confront the regime, what they should prioritize, and what kind of country they should have, and it was certainly easy for anyone living outside the country. But I always checked myself, and Karri did, too, knowing that Iranians have to come to a conclusion about what they want themselves and then act on it themselves.

I had coffee one day with a young woman who had lived in England for many years but had returned to open an art gallery. She kept adjusting her scarf as we spoke. After a while, I said it must bother her, much as it bothered Karri, but to my surprise she looked at me quizzically, then waved her hand dismissively. "Doesn't bother me at *all*," she said, and promptly changed the subject. Hijab alone was not going to be a reason for revolution, nor even for mass protest, as I already knew from past trips. Iranians had other, much bigger priorities, and their revolution, if it came, would be less specifically about dress codes than about the economy, foreign policy, and, above all, a definition of freedom. Especially as so many Iranian women, including some of my own otherwise liberal cousins, wore conservative hijab voluntarily and would continue to do so no matter the regime's opinion.

In mid-2010, when I made my first trip to Iran in the aftermath of the 2009 elections, a friend had recently been at Ayatollah Rafsanjani's office, for a gathering of young political activists either recently released from or not yet in jail. The ayatollah—a pillar of the Islamic Revolution and once the most powerful man in Iran (some thought even more powerful than the Supreme Leader, who everyone in Iran knows was actually put in the leadership role by Rafsanjani) but who had supported the Green Movement before and after the elections—was asked what was next for the movement. Rafsanjani, deprived of his soapbox as a substitute Friday prayer leader of Tehran since a controversial speech in support of the protesters immediately after the disputed presidential election, replied, "We made our revolution; now it's your turn." If that wasn't a green light, pardon the pun, for a second revolution in Iran by one of the founders of the original revolution, I'm not sure what could be, but it had no effect on the activists, or at least none that translated to Iran at large. Of course, it's hard to know exactly what Rafsanjani meant by "revolution," a word bandied about too liberally both in Iran and in the Western media to describe the Green Movement, for the movement's failure can be partially ascribed to the fact that it *wasn't* a revolution. It had started out as a protest movement, designed to force the government to reconsider its decision to let stand the suspicious tally of votes for President Ahmadinejad, and it turned into a civil rights movement when the government, contrary to the constitution, banned all protests, demonstrations, and public gatherings. But although some of its segments were radicalized, the large and disparate pro-democracy movement remained just that: pro-democracy but not pro-revolution, one that would turn the Iranian system upside down.

A number of different groups of Iranians are opposed to the current political system or the government, and certainly object to the continuing human rights abuses, but the ones looking to overthrow the regime through revolution still seem to be in the minority. Perhaps the memory of the 1979 Islamic Revolution is too strong, if not in their own young minds, then in the minds of their parents and grandparents who took part in it: for it was a revolution hijacked, a revolution that broke promises, a revolution that, even with its authoritarian and sometimes fascist impulses, has yet to provide economic security, or any other kind, for a large portion of its population. In 1979, eliminating the 2,500-year-old monarchy was supposed to usher in a democratic era, albeit with an Islamic hue; now the disappointment many Iranians feel, even pious Iranians who once believed in the revolution, is tangible and observable. Many of them seem reluctant to repeat what they believe will be another disappointment.

One day a shopkeeper in my neighborhood, with pictures of Shia saints on the wall behind him and worry beads (a sure mark of piety) in his hands, stood with me looking at a group of Basij zooming down Vali Asr on their motorcycles. "They told us that the reign of kings was bad," he said, "so why have you reigned for twenty years?"

The *you* referred to Supreme Leader Ayatollah Ali Khamenei, the undisputed lifetime leader of Iran, whose rule some Iranians believed more and more resembled that of a *shahanshah*, king of kings: the title was claimed by all Persian kings but was apt only at the height of empire millennia ago. Yes, today a kingly "priest of all priests" reigns supreme, but if he and his regime go, what will come next?

Many Iranians have simply given up on the system but are unwilling to do anything about it, fatalistically resigned to a political order they mostly cannot abide. Fatalism, a strong trait of Persians, has partially prevented them, and their many governments, from making the progress they might deserve. Our baby-sitter was one such person; young and educated, she was living at home with her parents after a stint abroad and was making the best of a life she didn't believe she had the power to change. Karri asked her one day if she wanted kids of her own, and she replied, "Not here, never in Iran. There's no life or future for them here, so only if I move abroad." The morality squads had stopped her many times, even impounding her car for a month for a skimpy-scarf-while-driving offense, but unlike some of her peers, she had never been to prison; nor did she seem eager to join in any form of activism, even on Facebook. She complained, but she showed no interest in Iranians who were still fighting the system from prison, house arrest, and occasionally in the streets. She told me she thought Iran needed sweeping change, of the kind that came with revolution, but she wasn't going to be around to see it. Many other Iranians too complain loudly but seem otherwise inactive.

The loudest complainers in public are often older Iranians. One rush-hour evening, after I'd waited at the stop for a long time, the bus pulled up, and people began boarding. When it could no longer accommodate a single additional passenger, the driver closed the doors. Suddenly, at the top of his lungs and within earshot of traffic cops—young men doing their military service—an old man who had been waiting with me yelled at the driver, "This is what happens when a two-bit mullah becomes the Supreme Leader!"

The regime is not afraid, and with good reason, of the old man who expresses his frustration in public or of our baby-sitter, who will leave Iran to the clerics and their supporters when the right opportunity presents itself or continue to live quietly, her fatalism growing stronger by the day, unable to bring herself to leave the only home she really knows and that, despite her protestations, I suspect she loves.

The Iranian sense of fatalism is often intertwined with a voracious appetite for conspiracy theories, perhaps adding to the inertia of would-be revolutionaries. The old man at the bus stop, who'd vituperated the not-so-supreme leader, took a seat with me on the next bus that would let us board, then let loose a refrain of complaints about how the very bus he was riding was part of the regime's conspiracy to control the population. I heard the same complaint time and again by people both on and off the bus.

Soon after the 2009 elections, Vali Asr, the long boulevard that the bus plied, had been turned into a one-way street with separate BRT (rapid transit) bus lanes, ostensibly to provide passengers like ourselves an efficient, fast, and cheap means of north-south transport in the otherwise traffic-clogged city. The bus-only lanes were cordoned off by concrete and metal barriers, and the traffic-free rides cost seven or eight cents (doubled to fifteen during our stay, to a chorus of rider complaints). Millions of Iranians, even those who owned cars, took advantage of this aboveground rapid transit system, so many that at rush hour buses would drive by the stops completely full.

But most people, even as they took advantage of the cheap fares and speedy rides, were having none of it. They were convinced that the regime had cordoned off the bus lanes so it could control access to a favored protest street *and* move its own government and security vehicles up and down the boulevard, in the bus lanes naturally, with ease. They made no concession to the idea that perhaps, just perhaps, the system had been put into place for their convenience and to make one of the most unlivable cities in the world (as *The Economist* had dubbed Tehran in 2011) just a tiny bit more livable. To be sure, every now and then a police car would zoom up Vali Asr in the wrong direction, lights flashing as it avoided the buses barreling down the avenue, and sometimes government cars with blacked-out windows would do the same. But many Iranians, rather than consider ease of government transport simply as one added benefit, chose to believe it was the sole reason for the changes to Vali Asr. They were certain that the bus lanes were not for the benefit of the public but rather for controlling the people. What sealed their conviction were the days when the volunteer Basij militia on their motorcycles and the black-clad government security forces would disperse, often using the bus lanes, to various points in the city where they believed a protest might erupt, especially on days like religious commemorations or, better yet, the anniversary of the 2009 presidential elections.

June 12, 2011, was such a day, the anniversary of the fateful vote two years prior that had returned Mahmoud Ahmadinejad to the presidency. On a sunny and extremely hot Tehran afternoon, the government was prepared for any outbreak, spontaneous or otherwise, of public protest or demonstration, whether directed against the entire regime or just the government of Ahmadinejad. Foreign-based Web sites had called for Iranians to come out and protest, and Facebook was filled with posts by Iranians, again mostly abroad, exhorting their fellows inside Iran to risk life and limb by marching in specific districts of Tehran, primarily Vanak Square. No one I knew was paying much attention to the calls by those in the diaspora, who, from the comfort and convenience of their Western homes and QWERTY keyboards, many felt, were encouraging what would certainly be a bloody revolution. But I planned to go to Vanak anyway, just to see if anyone showed up. Besides, I had an opium party to attend, and that wasn't getting canceled for any revolution, let alone a protest march.

At Tajrish Square, where I waited for a bus, the security forces were gathering a few hours before the protests were called for, to intimidate potential protesters and to announce their readiness for any move they might make. Motorcycle Basij and black-uniformed shock troops were stationed all the way to Vanak, a rather large contingent of them menacingly mustered under the Parkway overpass, but beyond their heavy presence, there was no sign that anything unusual was going on, not even that air of anticipation and anxiety you can almost smell in any danger zone. Certainly no one I spoke to could sense anything out of the ordinary, except the presence of the well-prepared troops, who obviously log on to the same Facebook pages and visit the same opposition Web sites as everyone else.

As the bus pulled up, I happily noted that it was an articulated and fully air-conditioned Iranian-made model, unfortunately named King Long—surely the Iranian who came up with *that* name for a bus had, unlike most Iranian men, never seen or paid attention to the clever titles of American porn films—and I dutifully boarded. It was already filled with passengers, men in the front section and women in the back, and grumbling was under way. "Look at all the Basij," one man said loudly. "What do they think they're protecting?"

A boy, probably in his late teens, got up from his seat, offering it to me. "*Befarmaeed*," he said, "Please," gesturing to the seat he had just vacated for me, the much older man. I would usually be just a little annoyed at the presumption of so many young Iranian men that I was at such an advanced age that good manners dictated that they offer their seats to me, and usually I declined, insisting that I was happy to stand, but this time I took the boy up on his insistent offer and sat down next to another man closer to my age.

He thrust his chin in the direction of the window, at the youthful security forces milling about on the sidewalk near a newsstand, walkie-talkies in hand. "They're always telling us that Islam is in danger," he whispered loudly, "but no—it's *you* who are in danger!"

I smiled and nodded.

"Islam has been fine for fourteen hundred years," he continued, "and you've been around for thirty. It's *you* who are in danger!" The *you* was obviously the state, and he was right. If it didn't sense danger, why was it mobilizing its shock troops, now and at every perceived threat? The proposed demonstrations were still hours away, but if any were to occur, they would be easily broken up by the thousands of militiamen, some of whom seemed, at least on the surface, quite sanguine at the prospect of beating their fellow citizens into submission.

I had an afternoon tea appointment near Vanak before I went to the opium party, so I got off at the Mirdamad stop, a busy intersection where grotesque cement-block high-rise apartment buildings, Eskan I, II and III, built in the latter days of the shah's rule, stood looking as if the slightest earth tremor would send them tumbling down. They anchor a once-beautiful corner of a beautiful boulevard, facing a park. The balcony of my friend's apartment afforded an unobstructed view of the square farther south and of the militiamen now milling about everywhere, their motorcycles neatly parked on the sidewalks, ready for action.

All my friend's guests dismissed the idea that anything significant would happen. "Nothing!" said my friend, no fan of the regime himself. "It's ridiculous all this talk—who's going to challenge *these* people?" I left after tea, near the appointed time of the demonstrations, and descended to the square. *Someone* was bound to show up. I continued to the home of another friend, and the opium smokers, regime haters all, were even less concerned with protest and revolution. The British were right about opium in China—it *does* keep the natives from getting restless, and I didn't expect anything different.

Later, having washed my face and eaten two or three pistachios (a Persian trick) to eliminate any residual opiate odor that might cling to my skin or my breath, I crossed Vali Asr. A stream of motorcycles was coming down slowly, as slow as bicycles, in the bus lanes. Two abreast, a passenger behind every rider, the Basij came and kept coming. Thousands, I thought, some wearing the camouflage of regular troops, others in the all black of the police special forces, some in body armor, truncheons hanging from their belts, and others in plainclothes on their private motorcycles. It was as intimidating a sight as I had ever seen in Iran, but the expressions on the faces of most of these young men were oddly peaceful, as if they expected no tension and no fight. The handful of older men among them, mostly overweight and sweating, with their small Chinese bikes straining under their weight, looked more menacing—these were the most loyal of the Basij, men whose livelihood fully depended, and always had, on the generosity of the regime.

One grunted angrily at me as I almost stepped in his way trying to cross the bus lane to the sidewalk on the other side. I stepped back just as another pair on a khaki dirt bike, young men in army fatigues without insignia, stopped in front of me. The rider edged his front wheel toward me, and I thought I might be in trouble for some unknown infraction—like stepping into a stream of Basij-laden motorcycles. But he leaned forward, arched his body, slightly raised himself off his seat, and said, "Pardon me, *haj-agha*"—imputing to me the piousness of a *haji*, someone who has made the pilgrimage to Mecca—as he gently maneuvered the bike into the traffic behind him, reversed his course, and accelerated back up the avenue. So much for trouble, but once again I was mostly annoyed that a young man would view me as old enough to have performed the hajj.

Vanak Square, on a workday, was as busy as ever with car traffic and pedestrians, and on that still bright and sunny evening, the hundreds of motorcycles and their riders, stationed all around in a sea of black, seemed like tremendous overkill. A few people, older men and women, appeared for a moment to be marching together on one side of the square, but the crowd dissipated as they passed the security forces. Another group moved past the square and toward

Gandhi Street, but it was impossible to tell if they were there to silently protest or if they were commuters who happened to be huddled close together as they made their way home. A friend who joined a group of men and women walking together—he assumed they were protesters—told me later that he was worried by the sheer numbers of Basij, so he stepped into a bakery and bought a loaf of bread; that way, in case he was stopped or harassed, he could argue that he was simply out on an errand and had nothing to do with any demonstration. An unusually large number of other pedestrians were also carrying bread under their arms, which, if anyone had realized it, could have become a sign of protest itself. But that was it, at least in Vanak, where Iranian activists outside Iran and, presumably, the security forces within had expected much more.

As I got back on a bus and headed home, I wanted to pronounce the Green Movement dead and buried—and not because of my relatively torpid state, after a puff or two (actually three or four) of select Iranian opium. Concerned about the possibility of a renewed clash between protesters and security forces, or at least about the danger of Karri and Khash being mistaken for protesters, I had insisted that they stay close to home. There they had witnessed nothing out of the ordinary, at the shops, at the Tajrish bazaar, or at the park where Karri took Khash, Basij be damned. Iranians today hold too many wildly differing views of what the country should be to form any real united opposition to the regime; even supporters of an Islamic system, who are most likely to be able to effect change, believe the regime has merely strayed from the path of Islamic democracy and needs a course correction.

The two most famous regime supporters who want change—but not outright revolution—are Mir Hossein Mousavi and Mehdi Karroubi, the 2009 presidential candidates who cried foul over the results and were under house arrest while we lived in Tehran. Karri had read and heard much about them since those elections, and she was surprised, even more than I was, that no one we came across, from die-hard regime haters to mild critics, seemed to care very much about them or their incarceration.

What had happened between the time when millions of citizens had come out onto the streets to support them, and now, when hardly any voices of protest were raised about their unjust imprisonment, let alone about the crackdown on already weak civil rights? Had security forces fired so many bullets against protesters during the Green demonstrations, had so many tanks appeared on the streets of Tehran, had the state killed so many people in suppressing dissent, that it caused the movement to crumble? Far fewer people were killed than in Egypt, as it happened, where the regime fell within weeks of the first protest in Tahrir Square. According to the government, fewer than fifty were killed in Iran, but more important, the opposition put the number at under a hundred. (Of course hundreds and then thousands were rounded up and jailed; many were released over time, but quite a few still languished in Evin while we were in Tehran.)

Arrest rather than slaughter: perhaps that was the key to the Iranian regime surviving the protests. It had had no difficulty convincing its frontline defenders, the volunteer Basij and their overseers, the Revolutionary Guards, that the protests were less about a vote than about a challenge to the very existence of the regime; but it knew it would have a much harder time convincing them to shoot or kill their fellow citizens, whom many loyalists believed to be—and the domestic media made this point—mere pawns in the Western game of destabilizing the regime. (The regime is loath to admit that millions of citizens might despise it; from a propaganda standpoint, pointing its finger only at the Green Movement "leaders" was a winning strategy, and Ahmadinejad's likening the ordinary protesters to emotional and angry fans of a losing football team effectively made them innocent of treason.)

In the revolution that toppled the shah, the army, mainly consisting of conscripts on the front lines who were reluctant to fire on protesters, declared its neutrality relatively quickly, thus cementing the shah's downfall; the revolutionaries of that time, now the leaders of the regime, were hardly going to tempt that fate for themselves by ordering their shock troops to kill their neighbors and perhaps their own family members en masse.

One of my cousins lives in an apartment building across the hall from a Basij, a family man with two small children. She told me that she couldn't reconcile the image of the man, a perfectly normal and even affable person, with that of the Robocop who every day during the 2009 protests dressed up, got on his motorcycle, and went off to corral and beat demonstrators with a stick. Would he have been able to beat, let alone shoot, his very neighbors, most of whom he knew supported the Green Movement? Once protesters were carted off to jail, they were out of sight of the militiamen, who could decline to speculate on their fate, but death and martyrdom are impossible to ignore. They have an altogether different significance in a Shia Muslim country, which is why the slow death of Neda Agha Soltan, flashed across TV screens throughout the world, had, for a moment, the potential to ignite a revolution and why the government was at pains to place the blame on foreign agitators.

The Iranians of 2009 and 2010, I knew, had been no less courageous than their Arab counterparts who were inflaming the region in 2011. But no leader inside Iran called for regime change, no one promised a rosy revolution that would bring forth democracy, and as was not the case in the Arab Spring, legions of regime supporters were willing to fight and die for the cause—defense of Islam as they saw it, and a way of life that was ensured by the preservation and perpetuation of the regime. In the midst of the Arab Spring, while some Iranians pro-

fessed to envy the success of revolutions in their immediate neighborhood, most recognized that Iran's regime still largely had faith and
Islam on its side, unlike in the Arab countries, where virtually no one,
not even in the militaries, was willing to die in support of a secular
dictator. Iranian youth who opposed the regime had no leader they
believed in, no one to rally around, and they showed as much disdain
for the leaders of the Green Movement, such as Mousavi—even if
they voted for him—as they did for any regime stalwart.

Those who opposed the regime as it was, but wary of outright
revolt against it, were still very much unsure of how they could actually effect change. The regime had effectively divided Iranian society:
one was either for or against it, with no other alternative. That was
one reason so many citizens wound up in prison during the Persian
Spring, and why so many more continued to be thrown behind bars
on national security charges while we were there, even citizens who
were apolitical or had no desire to see the regime change completely.
*You are either with us or against us, and if you have any complaints, you are against
us.* The security apparatus was watching, and one wrong move would
be enough to get you a free ticket to Evin.

It was a little disheartening and depressing, more so because we,
and I mean Karri too, cared about Iran and its future. Despite hearing
constant complaints about the system, despite the obviously heavy-
handed security crackdown, I still wasn't sure that a large majority of Iranians desired a revolution—quick and clean or long and
bloody—or even a radical change in the regime's theocratic nature. It
was easy, living in Tehran, especially in North Tehran, to be seduced,
as so many foreign journalists are, by the notion that all Iranians are
desperate for some form of regime change, but I knew that even apart
from the Basij and Revolutionary Guards, many Iranians still supported the system; and a great number of them were deeply religious
and would never abandon their beliefs that Islam must play a role in
politics and society at large, and that the Islamic system was just.

"No one stays in Evin just for thinking something," said one such young man, beard neatly trimmed, at a kebab house downtown, where communal tables allow for interaction with strangers. "Sure there have been some mistakes, but those people have always been released, and whoever is tried and convicted must have done something wrong." It was impossible to argue with anyone who still had faith in the judicial system (nor are political arguments in public particularly wise), so I rarely challenged someone I didn't know well.

Also, Iranian religious family culture, an issue that observers of Iran's political scene tend to overlook, has always played an important part in the regime's support and its longevity. A short time after we left Iran, a young woman, a recent college graduate, gave a striking interview to a foreign newspaper. The Islamic Revolution had enabled her to go to college and get an education, she said, not because of its efforts to promote university education and the attendant building of new schools, but because her father would never have allowed her to go to school in the first place if the clerics hadn't said it was okay for women to do so. Her father knew that under the regime, the Islamic atmosphere in schools—the hijab and the strict segregation of the sexes in the dormitories—would keep his daughter safe and chaste. I had heard such sentiments before, from supporters of the system and from those who believed that progress could come to the country only if Islam was a factor. Certainly some Iranians, even pious ones, have lost faith in the theocracy today, but how was one to change the beliefs, not of the young women like her, but of their fathers? Any revolution in Iran would have to account for them, even if it didn't for the Basij and the Revolutionary Guards.

8

JUDGE NOT

—

"Listen, I didn't vote, because I don't believe in it, in here [Iran]. In fact, I'm apolitical. I just wanted the whole thing to be over. I knew, unlike the kids who were dancing and singing in the streets outside my apartment during the campaign, that the freedom they had today would be gone as soon as the election was over, no matter who won. The regime has always done this: loosened the reins that suffocate before an election, only to tighten them again after."

My friend paused, lit another cigarette, and blew smoke out the window above us. "So when the election was over," he said, smoke still escaping his nostrils, "I was looking forward to the summer and maybe some better work opportunities. That evening I heard on the street that Ahmadinejad had won and was a little surprised. No one I knew had voted for him, but I shrugged it off, happy that at least the election was over now. Later that night, I was sitting in my apartment when I heard the same noise outside as I'd heard during the campaign. Cars honking, people shouting. What was going on? I wondered. Don't they know their man lost?

"I went outside to see what the fuss was all about. And I heard things I never imagined I would ever hear, not in the Islamic Republic. Things like 'Death to the dictator' and so on. I cried. My tears weren't quite tears of joy, nor were they tears of sadness. They were just tears—I'd been waiting for this for over thirty years."

I stopped the tape recorder: Karri needed help with Khash, who was wreaking havoc at a friend's house, where we had gathered for a party on a Thursday night, when parties, big, small, and even in the streets, are going on all over Tehran. I was in the kitchen with another friend, who must remain nameless, as he still lives in Iran; an artist my age, he was telling me about his arrest and experiences in Evin prison in 2009, and we were already on our second large glass of *aragh*. Quite a few people I knew, from good friends to family members, had been jailed in the aftermath of the 2009 elections, and it seemed almost a completely ordinary thing to have experienced across a wide swath of society, as if "Yeah, sure, I was thrown in jail" were no more unusual to hear than someone telling you he or she had just seen the latest blockbuster at the cinema.

My own temporary detention at the airport and subsequent interrogation in the city was nothing near the terrifying, cruel, or psychologically scarring experiences that others had had. And it was unlikely that I would ever experience prison, unless I did something egregiously wrong or pissed off the wrong person; throwing an American writer and journalist in jail for no particular reason would be too much trouble for the authorities and would bring them no particular benefit, not even as a bargaining chip in their conflict with the West over the nuclear and other issues.

While Karri, Khash, and I were in Iran, the American "hikers"— two young men and a young woman arrested for illegally crossing the border from Iraq into Iran—were still being held in Evin as spies, but their arrests and incarceration had brought Iran no advantages and were unlikely ever to do so; they were finally released toward the end of our stay with no quid pro quo from the United States. I was, however, aware that I was being monitored, certainly on the occasions when I visited a high-profile opposition figure (like former president Mohammad Khatami, who was under persistent surveillance) or attended an embassy party, where by definition every guest's attendance would be noted in a file somewhere, checked and cross-checked with other files. I also received phone calls every now and then, calls from government officials I knew, that were ambiguous but seemed designed to either draw me out and discover what I was up to in Iran, or what I thought, or simply to remind me of their presence. "*Mr.* Majd," a National Security Council staffer said, one of the times he called me, "how is this trip going for you? Are you writing at all?"

"No," I replied. "As I've said, I'm just here with my family, trying to absorb the culture."

"And are you enjoying it? If you're here as a *tourist*, I highly recommend you go on long road trips—to the sea, of course, but also to the south, with stops along the way, like in Kashan. Of course, if you're *busy* . . ."

"Yes, we'll definitely be traveling," I replied, "and no, I'm not busy with anything in particular."

"No? Okay, now of course I don't have to tell you about Yazd, but I'm sure your family will enjoy that," he said, reminding me none too subtly that they knew who I was and where I came from. "But the politics may have changed there a little," he added, referring to the change in Friday prayer leadership: to my disadvantage, he wanted to imply. I ignored the remark.

"Yazd, absolutely," I said. "We plan a long stay there."

"And when do you plan to return to New York? Will you be here for Moharram?" he asked, referring to the Shia month of mourning.

"I'm not sure, exactly," I replied. "But I'd say we'll most probably be here then."

"Well, call me and come and see us, so we can talk more." It was more than a suggestion, and I did visit the National Security Council, just to be safe, where for two hours I was politely asked my opinion on a range of subjects and given the occasional helpful hint about what I should or shouldn't write about in the future.

Karri was always a little nervous that the government hadn't bought my story—that I just wanted to spend time in my home country with my family—and might think my mission was sponsored by the CIA or some other American or foreign agency. I told her they probably *did* suspect that I was somehow passing information to the CIA, since many Iranian officials, as prone to conspiracy theories as anyone else in Iran, find it difficult to believe that any Western journalist is not somehow also tied to the Western intelligence services, especially in recent years, as cyber assaults, assassinations, and other covert operations allegedly carried out by the CIA, MI6, and Mossad burst into full view.

That's my take, anyway—for why else put such heavy restrictions on foreign journalists and writers? The authorities know that the vast majority of Iranians are unlikely to read anything written in any language other than Farsi, and that allowing journalists to freely report and move about the country would probably result in more *positive* reporting on Iran—they're "not stupid, after all," is how one government official put it to me. They seem to believe that journalists are simply not what they appear to be. But in my case, since they had no evidence that I was doing anything other than living a boring and uneventful life in Tehran—not reporting, not sending out articles, even anonymously, which I'm sure they could have traced back to me anyway—I was not overly concerned.

"You know, I've never been a religious person," my friend continued, after I returned to the kitchen and turned the tape recorder back on. "Years ago, though, after I came back from Paris, where I had been studying and learning music and art, I was taken by the voice of the narrator of a television program on the Iran-Iraq War, which was still raging. I don't know why—it was a magical voice—but I felt god had chosen him to tell the story of the war. I loved my country, and as a student of history, I knew that never before had there been a war when the entire world was gathered on one side of the conflict—all on Saddam's side against us Iranians—and yet we were not just holding our own but regaining territory we had lost in the early stages of the attack.

"The war: I was fascinated by this attack on us by the Arabs. I knew from then on that whatever regime came and went in the years, the centuries, to come, this regime and the way it had defended our nation would be forever remembered. The way Leonidas and his three hundred who fought Xerxes at Thermopylae are by the Greeks. You know, this was difficult for me, to see the brightness in what I considered a dark regime. But it was our bright moment. And I realized then, with the heroic sacrifices of our people, how our people view Ali and Hossein [Shia saints] as virtuous and heroic."

He paused again, staring into space. "But back to the elections," he suddenly continued. "People had gathered at the square by my apartment building and were shouting slogans. After shedding my few tears, I returned to my apartment, but before I could enter, three of the mothers of young men I knew, neighborhood youths, besieged me, asking if I could help find their kids. I went back out and found two of them in the square, convincing them to return home. Then the Basij came. I told the kids in my building that they shouldn't think that they'd be able to go out and demonstrate all the time—that the authorities might have been caught off guard this time, but now they knew exactly what they had to do and would extinguish all protest.

"I knew that, so you'd think I'd just sit home, wouldn't you? But for whatever reason, I was drawn, as so many others were, to the streets. By the third night—and you know, Saadatabad was almost like a war zone—with the Basij surrounding us and with people chanting slogans at them, occasionally throwing stones, I suddenly realized that some of the protesters were in all probability regime agents, and since I was the oldest person among all these young people, they would finger me as the leader. So, the protests had spread all over the city, and actually were over in my neighborhood within a few days, but I decided I wouldn't go to any other protests, since I felt we had made a point, and it wasn't the right time to challenge the regime this way, anyway.

"But about a week later, I found out that a shopkeeper's assistant down the street from me had been arrested, and I knew he had seen me at the demonstrations on our street, so I sensed a little danger. And a few nights later, actually on the eve of my fiftieth birthday, I heard a knock on my door, and three men were standing there. I let them in, and they looked around at my studio apartment—with no proper furniture anywhere—with obvious surprise. 'You don't have satellite TV?' one asked. No. 'No computer?' No. They were very polite and respectful. 'Sorry,' another said, 'but you have to come with us. If you have any prescription drugs, you should bring them with you.' I changed my clothes and followed them outside, to two Peugeots. I got into the backseat of one, and two men got in next to me, on either side. When we reached Evin, one said apologetically, 'We have to blindfold you now.' Sure, I said. A few minutes later I was walked into a building, and someone came up to me and whispered in my ear, slowly, *"Dahan-et ga'eed-ast!"* ["You are so fucked," but literally "You are fucked in the mouth."] That was the first indication to me that things were really not going to be okay."

He stopped to light another cigarette, took a long drag, and exhaled slowly. I watched him without saying a word. I was getting drunk. But what must have gone through his mind, blindfolded, at Evin, with some thug telling him he's *fucked*? Everybody in Tehran at the time knew about the torture and rape of political prisoners— they were hardly political prisoners, actually, just ordinary people voicing their displeasure at the government, not even at the regime— and in the early days of the post-election unrest, one could only imagine that if arrested, one might very well be subjected to all kinds of torture, too. My friend is the gentlest of artists, a soft-spoken single man who lives simply, without any furniture even, and whom young—much younger than him—Iranian girls find irresistible. Just this evening he had introduced us to his latest girlfriend, a twenty-something who stared at him adoringly, prompting Karri to deem him the Iranian Casanova. He loved Khash and would play with him for hours if we'd let him, or if we had no pity on our friends. *Dahan-et ga'eedast.* For what?

"So they then took me to a room, where they gave me a change of clothes. A white T-shirt and blue pajamas! Who knew that when I changed at home, putting on a white T-shirt and a pair of jeans, that I was matching what I'd be wearing in prison! I was told to sit down on a chair—you know, the old classroom chairs with a desk built in—blindfolded again, and I was in it for an hour or so before I was led to another room and told to sit and raise my blindfold slightly. They wanted me to see the wall I was facing. Some men stood behind me and began the interrogation, which went on for hours, I think. This happened a few times later, too, by the way.

"But after that first interrogation, they took me to another place to give me dinner. Again, someone came up to me and whispered in my ear, gently, 'You're like our brother here.' Wow. That was strange. Dinner was fine, *sangak* bread and tuna, and I ate it all. And then they took me to my cell, solitary confinement. A small cell—I later found out less than two square meters—with a small carpet and some army blankets, that's it. So I spent the night of my fiftieth birthday, which I had once thought was such a big deal, in solitary. It's weird, but you know, I was happy in a way. I thought to myself, what an important man I must be! And the impression that we all had of Evin was that it was a terrifying, horrible place, but I found that it wasn't. The next morning, though, when the interrogation resumed, I realized that this was more serious than I could have imagined. They viewed me as a leader of an insurrection, sedition or whatever, and as someone who planned things—"

"Did you know who had arrested you at this point?" I interrupted him.

"No, I didn't then. I assumed it was the Intelligence Ministry but later found out that I was in Section 2A, the Sepah [Revolutionary Guards] section. And if you were with Intelligence, you were much better off—you had fruit, vegetables, et cetera, since Intelligence is a ministry under the president, at least somewhat accountable, but the Sepah is *velayat-e-faqi*—the Supreme Leadership, and a completely different story. They answer to no one. I was in solitary for about two months, where I thought I was going mad, every day.

"But then one morning they blindfolded me and took me out, I could tell I was outdoors, to a room somewhere. They took my blindfold off, and I was in a room, a big room, with a refrigerator, and all these bearded men were lounging about. I thought to myself, 'The prison must be full, and they've brought me to a room where off-duty guards relax!' But of course I found out it was actually where they incarcerated Sepah guardsmen who were being disciplined for some infraction or another. It was the best section of Evin—where they keep people like the British sailors they had for a few days—and quite a nice place. I was there a few days, with some other people, young people but also other artists, people in the arts. You know, I calculated that half the people were artists of some sort—maybe that tells you that we're politically stupid enough to get caught up in such things! Anyway, it was us and Revolutionary Guards—people who wanted to spill our blood on the outside, and we who wanted to spill theirs—and we were friends in there. We had a good time there; we even had a yard. So I was there for a while, maybe two weeks.

"And then one day they took me back to solitary, which was horrific. Just horrific to go back to that, after being with all these people, playing games and entertaining ourselves. It's unimaginable, what it's like to be out for a while and then to have to endure solitary again. I was in solitary for a while, I don't know how many days, until one day they came and said, 'You're free.' They asked me to sign a piece of paper, a questionnaire, where of course I ticked off boxes saying everything had been great! The food, accommodation, sanitation, that I hadn't been abused, and so on and so on. They gave me back my clothes.

"But of course I wasn't free. I was now in what they called 'quarantine.' You know, Evin only houses political prisoners or perpetrators of financial crimes, debtors and check bouncers. The financial guys get thrown into a quarantine area, a big space with room for thirty or so beds, there's even a phone in there, until they either get released because they've made good on their debts or whatever, or get sent into the general prison population. But now they had given over the quarantine section to political prisoners. There must've been way more of us, I guess. We could get released if we made bail, theoretically, and we found out later that most prisoners from the unrest, the protests, had been in quarantine and had been released between two weeks to a couple of months later. But *we* were still under the Revolutionary Guards' control.

"A few nights later we were taken to yet another building. There was a person there by the name of Heydarifar. Do you know who Pezeshk-ahmadi was?"

"No, I can't say I do," I replied, entranced by my friend's storytelling, as poetic as the language allows, all the more tantalizing for his deep and soothing voice.

"Pezeshk-ahmadi was the state's murderer—by syringe injection—during Reza Shah's era. He had killed people like Teymourtash [Abdolhossein, minister of court], and Sardar Asad Bakhtiari [an early Constitutionalist]. He would go around and execute people by any means, syringe if possible, but even by suffocating them with a pillow if necessary, like with Teymourtash. So this guy Heydarifar was a thirty-something man like Pezeshk-ahmadi, a government murderer who was one of the people ordering torture and killings at Kahrizak before it was closed." Kahrizak was a prison where many detainees in the 2009 Green uprising were sent. A number of them were raped and died under torture, including the son of a prominent conservative with close ties to the Supreme Leader, so Khamenei ordered it shut down and the offending guards and authorities arrested.

"Anyway, in the Green uprising, millions came out into the streets and protested; a few thousand were arrested, and later one hundred of those were determined to be 'leaders of the *fetneh*.' Eighty of those were Intelligence Ministry prisoners, people who were actually politically active. The Revolutionary Guards didn't have any of the so-called leaders of the sedition, so they told this Heydarifar to round up twenty of the street protesters and label them as leaders, too, so they would have their own high-profile prisoners. A case of intergovernmental jealousy, I guess. I became one of those twenty, but I didn't know it at the time.

"A couple of days later we were taken to a hall, where we recognized some faces. You see, in Section 2A at Evin, there are Hajis and Seyeds—the Hajis are the interrogators whose faces you never see, and the Seyeds are the guards, who you sometimes see. When we saw the Seyeds, we realized we were back in the dreaded 2A. This was the hardest part of our entire incarceration. They threw us into a van, some twenty of us, and some of them were just kids. And those kids would hold my hand—me being this older guy—and it made me want to weep. I had strength: I didn't have a wife or kids to worry about, and I don't know, maybe it's my age, the fact that I was in jail for my fiftieth, but I had a strength that these kids, kids who still had a whole life ahead of them, probably didn't. So we were taken back to 2A, turning our own clothes in again, being issued prison garb, back in solitary.

"A few days later, I discovered that we were to be put on trial. The first of the sacrificial lambs! We were taken by bus one morning to the court, the Revolutionary Court. This was the day that Abtahi and Behzad Nabavi were being tried along with us—the big guys!" Mohammad Ali-Abtahi was a vice president under Khatami who had been arrested post-election for allegedly leading the sedition. He confessed, to the shock of his supporters, that he had indeed been agitating to overthrow the regime. Behzad Nabavi was a politician and former MP and an active reformist also charged with sedition.

"There was one other famous guy—do you know who I'm talking about?"

"No," I said. "There were a bunch of very well-known people in the trial, right? That's what astonished everyone—that the regime was going after its own children."

"Yeah, I've never been interested in these people, so I never remember their names," he said, nodding. "Anyway, we appeared that day in court, then again a couple of weeks later, and yet again for the third session. We were the only ones to have three trials! Everyone else only had one, if that. You know, they showed us a film in that last trial, a film about the Basij who had been beaten up by protesters. It was really interesting. I mean, it was so effective that I wanted to attack my fellow prisoners, and even myself, for having been so evil to them! The film was professional, with incredible music—it really tugged at your heart.

"It influenced me, I'm not afraid to admit, which is what great propaganda does. Imagine, it made me hate myself momentarily for deigning to hurt the poor, innocent Basij! Made me think that maybe I had been wrong all along. Anyway, when my turn came to have my verdict announced, it was an incredible sensation. Here I was, a nobody, and there were TV cameras and reporters and photographers with the rapid clicks and flashes of their cameras making a calamitous noise, and I held on to a railing with my hands, tight as I could, so no one could see them shaking.

"Wait!" he suddenly exclaimed. "I forgot to tell you this."

"No problem," I said. "Just carry on."

"Well," he continued, "the night before, I was taken out of my cell and introduced to someone in a room. 'You have your trial tomorrow,' he said, 'and I'm your lawyer.' I said to him, 'How come I'm hearing this now, that my trial is tomorrow and you're my attorney?' He replied that I didn't have to accept him, so I asked him why he took my case. 'Because it will bring me fame,' he replied. So I told him that because he was so honest with me, I'd accept him. He asked me to sign a paper agreeing to have him represent me.

"And then I was taken to yet another room, where two men were standing, wearing sunglasses. At night! So that I wouldn't recognize them, of course, but what a joke! It's funny, really, in the same way that in the darkest human story, there's always humor, isn't there? On the table in front of me there was fresh fruit, and pistachios and almonds, and even potato chips! Chips! I hadn't seen these things in over two months, and I kept staring at them. 'Eat something,' one of them said, adding, 'Your trial is tomorrow, so you might want to think about helping yourself.' I asked him what he meant by helping myself. He said, 'You're a smart guy. You should think about your own skin. You could get five years in prison, unless you help yourself.'

"I didn't eat any of the treats, knowing that he was telling me to basically say something like, 'Yeah, I confess, Mousavi or Karroubi made me do it,' and beg for leniency. So after a short while they took me back to my cell, but not before one of the guys poured some of the almonds, big beautiful ones, into a bag and handed them to me. When I reached my cell, the guard grabbed the bag out of my hand. 'What's this!' he cried, and took it away. So much for the treat!

"So only two of the twenty of us ended up confessing, and blaming Mousavi for their seditious actions, but we who didn't weren't heroes. I remember saying to people who called them traitors that they shouldn't say that—who knew what they had gone through? Maybe we had it easy, which made it easy for us to stand on our principles. Maybe they didn't. We don't know. It's a very strange thing, prison, with torture and confessions. You can't judge someone in prison. Everyone at the trial would start their statement with *Besm'illah*, 'In the name of god,' and end by asking for Islamic mercy and forgiveness, but I didn't. People came to me after, when we were in the prison yard, and said how brave I was, but actually all it was, was that I'd forgotten to say those things! It wasn't out of bravery, quite the opposite—I was scared. I'm not ashamed to say it. Anyway, not to bore you, but after the trial we were sent to the general population, the story of which is in itself a whole book! I've been talking too much, right? Too much detail. I'll make it brief—"

"No, no," I said. "Whatever you want to say, and detail is good. I'm interested."

"The eve of the day the final verdicts were to be announced, for they weren't final in the courtroom after all, I was tense and depressed," he continued. "We'd been there a while. Some of the others, political prisoners all, wondered why, telling me that I was the one who always seemed calm and collected and who gave the younger ones strength. I said I was sorry, but I really was sad that night. We, the twenty Revolutionary Guards' prisoners, had been in jail longer than almost all the other political prisoners—people who had been arrested after us, too. How could that be, we who had been picked up in the first few days—when it wasn't even clear that what we were doing was forbidden yet—that we were in prison while others who were arrested after Rafsanjani's speech, even in the Qods Day unrest, were long gone? I even, for the first time, went to the evening *namaz* in the prayer hall! You can't believe that, can you? *Me* praying?

"Anyway, the next day someone came into the room and starting calling names, one by one. After each name, he'd proclaim, 'Released.' When my turn came, I burst into tears. That was it. I went around the big room saying my goodbyes—to political prisoners I'd become friends with, from senior political figures to even MEK (Mujaheddin-e-Khalq) members whose death sentences had been commuted to eleven years, to monarchists—all good people. I was taken to collect my things, and the guard signed me out. I almost wanted to spend another night at Evin, to say proper goodbyes to my fellow prisoners, to see if there was anything I could do on the outside for them. I mentioned that to the guard and he said I was crazy, that I should hurry up, as my family was waiting outside. I said, 'No one knows I'm being released—there'll be no one waiting for me.' I went out,

and of course there was no one, just a bunch of waiting taxis. Business was good for taxis at Evin those days. I borrowed a cell phone
and called my brother, and then got into a taxi and went to his house,
so he could pay the fare.

"I tried to make it brief, or as brief as I could. Is that all right?"

"Yes, yes," I said. "Your story is fascinating."

"You know," he said, "we had made a pact in Evin, we 'the twenty,'
that we wouldn't celebrate a birthday, Noruz [Persian New Year], or
indeed any other holiday until all twenty of us had been released, and
we stuck to it. I'm proud of that."

He had spoken for over an hour while others—including the
somewhat frustrated host, who needed to check on the food—came
and went from the kitchen, and I could tell he was tired of Evin and
wanted to move on to more pleasant subjects with the other guests. I
shut the tape recorder off, and we got up to return to the party.

Evin has always been on the minds of Iranians, mostly politically
active ones, from the days of the shah, when many in the Islamic
regime's leadership, including the Supreme Leader himself, spent
time in its cells. It had first entered the Western consciousness during the time of SAVAK and allegations of torture behind its walls,
but it was largely forgotten until Westerners were imprisoned there:
British sailors in 2007, and many Iranian American journalists and
intellectuals during the first decade of the twenty-first century. After
2009 it became even better known because of the widespread arrests
of protesters highlighted in the Western media. The American hikers, arrested soon after the elections, probably made Evin as close to a
household word in the United States as it will ever be, despite the fact
that it still houses numerous Iranian political prisoners long after the
Americans were released.

There are a million stories of Evin, and each is different, but I
was taken by this ordinary story of an ordinary man, caught up in
one of the momentous events of the Islamic Revolution—a story
that was not sensational but spoke to what Iran was today, at least for

some of its citizens. I was glad to have heard his story from his own lips, an unembellished and even humble tale, for it reaffirmed to me everything I loved about Iran and more particularly about its people, an affirmation necessary to dampen the cynicism that grows inside you and eats at you with each passing day in the Islamic Republic. Everything, from the thug who said to him, anonymously, "You're so fucked," to the guard who later told him he was a brother; from the camaraderie between Revolutionary Guards in prison themselves and the political prisoners, to the gentle demeanor of one who holds no grudges, wishes for no vengeance—it all was Iran. These were not all things to be proud of. But my friend's poise, his honesty above all, was what I admired and envied. And I knew there were many others like him, there had to be, some probably still in Evin while we drank and partied the night away. I'm not sure if as a child I had met any of my parents' friends who had been in prison, except the one, a Dr. Bazargan, who to this day is still a family friend and who I only remember was as humble about his imprisonment as my contemporary is. Khash won't remember my friend, but I'm glad he met him.

Iran, especially after the 2009 elections and the unrest that followed, is a security state, despite the lack of machine-gun-toting uniformed personnel on the streets or even at the airports. And Evin is the symbol, for Iranians, of that security state. Artists like my friend have always been under suspicion in Iran, even under the shah, and the security state is far more real to them than to many of their fellow citizens. Karri and I witnessed that firsthand one Friday afternoon when we went, Khash in tow, to an art gallery opening, one of many held around the city every Friday. When we entered the modern structure, filled with modern art, there were two uniformed cops and a plainclothesman speaking to the owner. After they left, I asked him what the problem had been. "They wanted to know who was coming to the opening, and if there were any intellectuals, that we should tell them to leave," he replied in an exasperated tone. "They don't want any gathering of 'intellectuals,' which presumably means artists, too. I asked them, 'Isn't everyone who goes to a gallery an intellectual, almost by definition?'"

"Wow. So what did they say?"

"They wanted to shut us down, but I showed them around and said, 'Look, the art isn't un-Islamic.'"

"Shut you down? For what?"

"Who knows anymore? They hate these things, where 'Westernized' Iranians gather."

"But they left, so I guess it's okay," I said.

"Yes, for now. They're probably outside checking to see who shows up!"

I stepped outside to see, but they had left. I went back in, and no one seemed perturbed, not even Karri, by what had transpired. *Karri's getting used to Iran*, I thought. *And so soon.*

At the party where my friend spoke to me about Evin, when we finally left the kitchen to go back upstairs to the rest of the guests and a late dinner, Casanova back to his new girlfriend less than half his age, I wanted to asked him one more Evin question.

"Is there any one aspect of your imprisonment," I said, as we went up the marble stairs, the sound of our shoes announcing our arrival to the others, "that is, if you had to pick only one, that stands out in your memory?"

"I'll never forget any of it," he replied. "But you know, during the first few nights I was in solitary, all we could hear was Koran radio— just verses from the Koran being recited all day. And then one night suddenly the station changed and a song came on briefly, probably only for a minute or two, before being changed back to the Koran. Who knows why it happened. But I remember smiling, probably a more genuine and pleasurable smile, and certainly more of a smile in the heart, than I ever wore the entire time I was there, maybe in my entire life. Strange how something so simple, so ordinary, but so damn beautiful can affect you so deeply. The song was 'The Girl from Ipanema.'"

9

FIGHT FOR THE
RIGHT TO PARTY

—

Almost as soon as we had settled into our own apartment, our daily life in Iran became indistinguishable from that of most Iranians, at least those of a certain social standing, except for the fact that neither Karri nor I had a daily job to go to. But that wasn't so different from our lives in Brooklyn, where I work from home and Karri does too, except for the times she leaves the house to teach yoga. I did some writing, whenever Khash would allow it, and Karri did as much as she could, on the phone and over the Internet, with her business back in New York, which she had left in the hands of her partners.

She had wanted to teach yoga in Iran, but it proved rather difficult, both in terms of finding a space that wouldn't attract the attention of the authorities (obtaining a license to operate a studio, which would have had to be a women-only affair, would be onerous) and in terms of getting people to commit to classes. Friends and family consistently assured her that they would be the first to start practicing, but we realized that the *farda* syndrome was epidemic, and we'd have to live in Iran an awfully long time before *farda* came. Yoga is common enough in Tehran (despite some clerics' rulings that it is un-Islamic), which even boasts a Farsi-language yoga magazine that is sold at every newsstand, and in Tajrish we would often see young women with yoga mats under their arms, making Karri miss it all the more. But to compensate she continued to do her own yoga practice at home.

That meant I took Khash out for an hour or so every morning, for otherwise he would not just mimic her poses, or try to (he is quite good at sun salutations), but would actually try to adjust her as well. We couldn't figure out how he got the idea that yoga instructors (at least Ashtanga yoga instructors) do that, but maybe he's just a natural yogi. I'd take him out to leave Karri in peace, making grocery shopping the one chore I performed every day. We'd sometimes go shopping together in the afternoons, too.

We'd search out stores that carried Western goods—on some days we'd find a product we didn't even know we missed, making it the highlight of the day. One store in our neighborhood that carried canned goods and sparkling water—made in Iran but somehow not common or popular—suddenly started carrying Schweppes tonic water, I discovered one morning, in the little bottles it comes in in Europe. I excitedly grabbed as many as I could, thinking *aragh* and tonic might be a good substitute for gin and tonic, but to my surprise the shopkeeper asked me what tonic water actually was, and what it was for.

I wasn't sure what to say, but I decided to be truthful. "It's used as a mixer for alcoholic drinks," I said. "But of course you don't have to drink it with alcohol," I added, to be safe. "It tastes pretty good on its own."

He shrugged and rang me up, and I rushed home, pushing Khash as fast as I could up the steep hill in his stroller, to show Karri my discovery. On the way I wondered why the shop had started to carry tonic water if the owner didn't know what it was, but I supposed that like many Iranians, he reasoned that if it was European or American, it must be good *and* would have a dedicated clientele among the wealthy Iranians who could afford the ridiculously expensive drink.

Karri was somewhat less excited than I was—neither of us actually drinks gin and tonic ordinarily—but that evening she decided *aragh* and tonic was a cocktail well worth considering when one's choices are limited. Tonic water was also the perfect gift to take to certain kinds of parties, particularly Khosro's, which we now attended every weekend, that is, when we weren't attending a different party.

Iranians love parties. They've always loved them and love any excuse to have one, even if the excuse is simply that it's the weekend, and hey, there's nothing else to do in Tehran. They loved parties during the shah's time, too, and when I was in college, the handful of Iranian students at my school—they started coming over to the United States for college in big numbers in the 1970s—seemed to be the only ones interested in, or actually capable of, throwing a good party with really good non–fast food and proper alcoholic beverages, as opposed to a keg and pizza free-for-all. Which is one reason I gravitated to the small but growing Persian community in my area, the other being their drugs, of which Iranian students were fussy connoisseurs, but that's another story.

I assumed back then that the Iranian students had learned how to throw a party from their parents, for every Iranian girl (and some of the boys) seemed to know how to cook incredibly complicated Persian dishes to serve thirty people or more. There were two drawbacks to accepting an invitation to an Iranian party then: first, all that wonderful food wouldn't be served until the last guest arrived, and since every Iranian thinks they have to be the last to arrive anywhere, that meant ten-thirty p.m. at the earliest for an eight p.m. party, or as late as one a.m. in some cases.

Second, for some inexplicable reason, Iranian parties would start with great music, from the latest hits to good and even esoteric alternative rock, but after dinner would switch to bad Iranian dance music, prompting the women to drag the men out to dance with them, or vice versa. Not being practiced in the art of oriental dance, I would beg off as best I could, but with Iranians no means "yes," an emphatic no means "please beg me some more," and an outright refusal means "please grab my hands and lead me to the dance floor." Every man and woman followed these rules, expert dancers all despite protestations to the contrary, and I think I must have elicited some shocked reactions when, after being dragged off my seat, usually drunk and stoned, people realized I really *couldn't* dance. At least not Iranian style, although I suspect I couldn't and still can't dance any style at all. Nothing has changed in the intervening years, except the music. The Western music, I mean, for Iranians, whether in London, Los Angeles, Dubai, or Tehran, seem to favor the same dreadful Persian pop—with more synthesizers these days, I guess—that they liked when it was still being produced in Tehran and not in California.

Even before we had settled into our own apartment, Karri and I were invited to parties. Friends' parties and family parties. Karri had had only a small taste of Persian partying before we arrived in Tehran, but she understood quickly that without it, life would be tedious in a metropolis that offered almost everything that its Western counterparts did except a place to go out for a drink or a place to listen to noninstrumental music. Before the Islamic Revolution, Tehran had boasted cabarets, nightclubs, and many bars (but few really good restaurants, and no potential Michelin-starred ones). Even then, real partying was mostly done in homes. People did (and still do) go out, particularly young people who still lived with their parents (and Iranian culture meant and to a large degree still means that women live at home until they are married, as do most young men, these days perhaps more for financial reasons than any other). But going out to a cabaret or club was never fully a substitute for entertaining at home, a proposition that Iranians have always considered appealing as it shows off the home decor, cooking skills, good taste, and general graciousness of the host and hostess in a society where showing off and exercising one's *ta'arouf* skills go hand in hand and seem to be the foundations of almost every party.

Partying in Iran is not restricted to the secular or Westernized elite, although the kinds of parties the devoutly Shia—the more affluent ones anyway—throw are radically different, though no less frequent. The first party we went to when we arrived in Tehran was at a cousin's, and since my family in Iran is politically reformist but also mostly devout, no alcohol was served, and the music was a soundtrack of classical Persian music. It also meant no dancing, although the daughters of a couple of my cousins, hijab-less and decidedly lenient in their views on Islamic behavior, did decide at one point to dance.

Karri was stunned more by the sheer amount and diversity of the food that was on offer than by anything else. Every Iranian house that is about to receive guests will have huge bowls of fruit on every coffee and side table, and bowls of nuts—pistachios and almonds—so huge and deep that it would take ages of snacking to get to the bottom, and other bowls of snacks, and often plates of pastries too, enough food to live on basically, before dinner. Dinner means at least two but preferably three or four completely different main courses—always fluffy white rice accompanied by lamb- or chicken-based stews along with other mixed rice dishes—as well as a handful of different salads and soups and other dishes, plus the obligatory *sabzi*, a plate of washed greens—basil, mint, radishes, watercress, or whatever—with cheese, walnuts, and spring onions on the side. Karri quickly adopted *sabzi* into our own menus at home, and I had to purchase it fresh every day from one or another *sabzi* guy whose specialty it was to sell *sabzi*, and only *sabzi*, on a street in our neighborhood. Each bunch of a specific green cost eight cents or so, making our daily *sabzi* intake far and away the least expensive food we consumed in Iran. *Sabzi* also provides many a less fortunate Iranian's—those who cannot afford the far more expensive lettuces and spinach—daily intake of chlorophyll.

What struck me, though, about the parties at my cousins' was the irony that, being known reformists and related to former president Khatami, they were under state surveillance and their comings and goings closely monitored—their homes and telephones were even bugged—and despite their almost complete adherence to Islamic praxis, we guests were undoubtedly a subsection of an entry in a ledger somewhere in the Intelligence Ministry or the competing Revolutionary Guards Intelligence Division or both, whereas the bacchanalian parties we attended at fully Westernized and completely secular Iranian homes seemed to hold no interest whatsoever for the various authorities whose job it is to protect the morals of society and defend the Revolution from decay and disintegration. And we attended many parties like those, too.

Of course not all parties, whether thrown by the elite or by the middle class, religious and otherwise, are as lavish as some we attended, or are blowouts that would put a Brooklyn rave to shame, but they are all a reflection of the culture, of *ta'arouf* and hospitality, of the lightheartedness of Iranians and their inclination to merry-making even in the worst of times. Life might be shameful, but boys and girls just want to have a little fun, too. Intensely religious families throw *rozeh* parties with some regularity on religious holidays—frequent enough in Islam, but even more frequent in Shia Islam, with its imams and various other martyrs to celebrate. At such parties a mullah will melodically bespout an episode from Shia mythology, while men and women in separate rooms weep at the injustice perpetrated on their saints and the unfairness, the *shamefulness,* of their own lives. But in the aftermath of the recitation, these parties are usually as merry as any other, and food and nonalcoholic drinks are served, and laughter and jokes, though appropriate and not bawdy, are heard. And as was not the case in the shah's time, when the wrong word at a party might result in an uncomfortable interview with SAVAK (the secret police that seemed to have informants in every milieu and at every gathering), today's parties are also a place to freely discuss politics, and that's true of parties thrown by religious folk as well as by strict secularists.

Soon after our arrival in Tehran, before we had even settled into our apartment, we were invited to a Thursday-evening party at an estate in North Tehran. Estates are uncommon in Tehran these days, since most were confiscated early in the revolution or split up into many smaller lots and sold by the owners as property values soared in the rapidly growing capital, but this estate was intact. Invisible from the street behind mud walls, the house itself was ordinary: a villa built as a second home, well before the neighborhood, in the foot-hills of the mountains, was even considered part of Tehran proper. But at nearly five acres, the parklike grounds were magnificent, the pool—invisible to prying eyes—a true rarity, and the small gather-ing of guests in their finest a sight to clash with whatever notions a Westerner might have of life in the Islamic Republic.

We had brought Khash, for there are no Iranian parties any-where on the planet where children, from infants to teenagers, are unwelcome, whether the hosts and hostesses are prepared to handle a child in their home or not. This home was most definitely not the place for an infant, from the party setting outdoors by a deep pool, to the baby's sleeping quarters hastily arranged on the living room couch, within earshot of the patio. Smoke from the barbecue set up to grill kebabs, a staple of almost every party regardless of what other main courses would be served, seemed to waft directly into the room where Khash slept, perhaps inconsequential to Tehran residents who breathe smoke every day—the equivalent of half a pack of cigarettes, according to the Tehran health department a few years ago—but alarming to Karri, unaccustomed as she was to Iranians' indifference to all forms of pollution, especially the kind they're responsible for creating.

Karri, to her discomfort, had to obsessively check on Khash—he fell asleep soon after we arrived— whose bed she rearranged on the floor using the cushions from the sofa. But she was rather elated to discover that our hostess, a single woman in her fifties, was serving genuine French wine. Wine is not a popular item for bootleggers or their customers, less popular than even beer, since like beer, it is cum-bersome and expensive to transport relative to its alcohol content.

Besides, not many Iranians have a taste for fine wine, since it has not traditionally been an accompaniment to Persian cuisine, and unlike many Americans and Brits but like the French, they do not consider it an aperitif. It was certainly not going to be on my list of items to order from a dealer.

But this glass of wine was Karri's first taste since flying to Tehran, and she was more than happy to have it. The other enthusiastic wine drinker, aside from the hostess, was a heavily made-up single lady in her forties, dressed in a short dress that didn't become her figure. She had been invited, we discovered, in an attempt at matchmaking with a single friend of mine who had previously shown no interest in her whatsoever. That is not considered an impediment to Iranian would-be matchmakers, a profession almost all Iranians—from the deeply religious to the Westernized secularists—consider their second, if not first, in a culture where meeting potential partners is limited to gatherings at parties and introductions made by family.

This woman, taken with my friend and unconcerned with his obvious indifference, was a staunch monarchist, not unusual among a certain segment of older Tehran society that clings to memories of the lavish parties they or their parents threw, exactly like the one she was attending this night. She launched into a tirade against the ruling mullahs, people she thought were beneath contempt and certainly not worthy heirs to the empire of the shahs. When one guest reminded her that I was a relative of Khatami's, she stared at me and asked, in a friendly enough tone, "Why do they hate the shah so much?"

I replied that I didn't think Khatami or some of the other more enlightened clerics particularly hated anyone, much less someone who had been dead for decades, but I conceded that the Islamic regime was not fond of monarchy, and it (or for that matter any viable successor regime) was unlikely to change its position on that anytime soon. Some Iranians' apparent obsession with the glory of monarchy, rather than the glory of Iran and its culture, I added, is shared neither by the ayatollahs nor by the population at large, and I doubted that too many mullahs thought about the shah, or shahs, very much at all.

This woman was a Francophile, spoke fluent French, and visited France every year, but she was either unaware or unconcerned with what the French had done to their monarchs and aristocracy following their revolution, a far bloodier affair than Iran's. Why, I wondered, given her hatred of Iran as it was, which she willingly expressed, did she not just leave?

"I'm going to," she declared emphatically. "This country is useless for people like me, and I'm moving away permanently, this year or next." *Farda*, again.

Another friend, standing behind me, leaned down and whispered in my ear, "She's been saying that for twenty years."

A few days later we were invited to another party, also at a North Tehran estate, whose grounds were impressive enough but about half the acreage of our last party. This house, once the country home of a friend's father, was situated farther north, surrounded by a dense neighborhood of high-rise apartment buildings: hundreds of apartments enjoyed a direct view of the large swimming pool in the center of the estate's garden, rendering it useless. But the visibility of the entire estate to strangers' apartment windows didn't diminish the enthusiasm of the host and hostess, or their guests, for alcohol-fueled parties—they were regular events on the Tehran social calendar, attended by a who's who of secular Tehran.

Again, and at the insistence of our hosts, we brought Khash, who they assured us would have a nice place to sleep, safe and sound, once he got tired. That place, we discovered, was their own bed, in their bedroom, down the hall from the huge living room. Although Tehran parties don't get going until way past his bedtime, we finally were able to put him to sleep just as the volume on the stereo was turned up to eleven, and the music changed from a mix of Euro lounge to full-on maximum-beats-per-minute electronic dance. Guests danced feverishly on the marble floor of the living room, making listening to the baby monitor we carried with us next to impossible. Between getting refills from the uniformed bartender outside (in full view of the neighbors, incidentally), either Karri or I would walk back to the bedroom every five minutes or so to make sure that Khash had not awakened or fallen off the bed and decided to go for a crawl to get away from the infernal noise, or bad music, as the case might be. But he slept right through it, in fact better than he slept normally, not even stirring the entire evening until we picked him up to go home. Our hostess was pleased that she had been right all along to insist that a dance party at her house was a perfectly appropriate place to bring a baby, but I was a little concerned that if we made this a regular affair, he might grow up to subconsciously favor dance music, and not the good kind.

Although the party was designed to be less formal and more about letting loose on the weekend, the guests still talked plenty of politics, and not just because diplomats were present, including Jane Marriott, the British chargé d'affaires (who, like Karri, is gluten-intolerant and so was thrilled to hear from her that one could buy gluten-free baked goods at a certain midtown branch of a Tehran bakery, as long as one ordered them in advance). One of the first people to approach me, drink in hand, was a woman, probably in her late thirties, who said she lived in London mostly and recognized me from some TV appearance or other and had read my books. "You know," she said, "I voted for Ahmadinejad, but I'm ashamed to say it now."

Why had she voted for him? I asked.

"Because he was the only one standing up for Iran, telling the West where to get off, and not letting them exploit Iran."

But then why be ashamed now? That aspect of Ahmadinejad hadn't changed, had it, even if the election was fraudulent?

"No," she said, "but after what's happened . . ."

I understood what she was trying to say. I had come across Iranians, both inside Iran and abroad, who were completely Westernized, secular, and liberal, and who yet had voted for the conservative and deeply religious Ahmadinejad, in some cases twice. One would imagine that these Iranians would be in favor of reform (if not revolution), of a type that would allow them to enjoy the same lifestyle in Iran that they did in Europe or America. But they were deeply nationalistic, and Ahmadinejad had always, to the dismay of the ruling clerics, emphasized nationalism, even over faith. Of course, wait—Westernized Iranians *did* already enjoy the same lifestyle in Tehran that they enjoyed in their foreign abodes, as evidenced by this very party, which, judging by the parade of exotic cars, the designer clothes, and the well-stocked bar, could have been held in Beverly Hills or the south of France were it not for the ladies' manteaus and shawls hanging conspicuously on the rolling rack by the front door.

Not all Iranians who supported Ahmadinejad through two elections were as apologetic as this lady, but some, in the presence of either reformists or antiregime Iranians, were just a little embarrassed by the security state that Iran had more visibly become under their favored politician—with far more political prisoners than during the previous administration. (A fair argument could be made that this wasn't his sole fault.) Still, the security state didn't seem to care very much about the goings-on at this party, even as the guest list included expat foreigners (the handful that live in Tehran) and senior diplomats from "enemy" countries, such as Great Britain. I wondered if it would harass some of these people on their drives home, say, if the women were *mal*-veiled. Jane Marriott, who left at the same time as we did, drove herself off in a Japanese SUV with diplomatic plates—and with no tail, as far as I could tell.

On another occasion at the same house, the diplomatic guests included representatives from Italy, France, and Germany, as well as the Australian ambassador, a young, beer-swilling, leather-jacket-and-jeans-wearing man, well befitting his country's laid-back reputation, and the Swiss ambassador, Livia Leu Agosti, who also represents U.S. interests in Iran in the absence of an American diplomatic outpost. "I'm keeping an eye out," she said to me in all seriousness, "in case something happens to you."

I expressed surprise that she might be able to do anything for me at all, given that I was in Iran on an Iranian passport and that Iran doesn't recognize dual citizenship.

"Yes," she said, "but they [the government] still care when I make a fuss." Her presence was apt, I suppose, given that probably half the guests were, like us, dual U.S. citizens, but it seems odd that foreign diplomats so easily mingle with Iranians at these kinds of parties and apparently nowhere else. Iranians living in Iran have to be extremely wary of associating with foreigners, especially diplomats, who are often assumed to be spies. Iranians who are completely uninvolved in politics, especially artists, will accept invitations to embassy parties, but no Iranian official, present or former, and no one with any political ambition, would be caught dead speaking to a Western diplomat, least of all while the West was pressuring Iran with sanctions and military threats over its nuclear program. Various acts of sabotage and assassination attempts were also going on in 2011, and the majority of Iranians blamed them entirely on the CIA, the Mossad, Britain's MI6, or all three—intelligence agencies with a presumed presence in foreign embassies allied to the United States.

Certainly none of the Iranians at the funeral service I attended one afternoon in downtown Tehran, on a stiflingly hot July day, would be invited to, let alone attend, an embassy party or one where foreign ambassadors were present. It was the funeral for Hojja-toleslam Mohammad Sadoughi, the cleric from Yazd who was the province's Friday prayer leader and a personal representative of the Supreme Leader. He was the only reform cleric left—after six years of purges—as the *vali-e-faqih*'s representative outside Tehran. As such, his funeral attracted high representatives of the regime, such as the moderate foreign minister, who showed up in a somewhat pedestrian Mazda, texting away in the front passenger seat; arch-conservative politicians; other clerics, moderate and conservative; and senior reform figures, such as the deceased's brother-in-law Mohammad Khatami and his entire family.

Outside the mosque, which was near a busy square, security was tight. A few dozen Basij lounged by their motorcycles parked by the entrance, apparently waiting to heap derision on the former president when he arrived: they and some in the regime considered him a seditionist, even the leader of a path away from true Islamic governance. Khatami's driver and entourage were well aware of this possibility, since it was the norm now wherever he ventured and cameras were present, so they escorted him into and out of the mosque through a back entrance on another street, denying the Basij the satisfaction and him the embarrassment of a rude confrontation.

Later that day I arrived at a party (Karri and Khash were waiting for me), dying for the stiff drink I knew I would find there. Once again I was aware of the incongruity of the state being far more concerned with monitoring, even harassing, its own than with monitoring parties where un-Islamic behavior was rampant. They would be concerned, naturally, if a regime figure attended such a party, and they keep watch on politicians and ministry officials who attend embassy parties, even the formal "national day" parties at embassies where a few invited Foreign Ministry officials do show up as a nod to protocol but leave before any alcohol is served. The almost complete separation of Iranian politics from Westerners on all but the most formal of occasions, in contrast to the citizenry, which relished contact with the outside world, to me spoke to how difficult it would be for Iran and the West to break down the barriers of mistrust that were now in their fourth decade of existence. If you couldn't party together, how on earth could you ever understand each other? The segmented party culture reminded me, also, of the class structure that still existed in Iran, and the growing gap between haves and have-nots—if Iranians didn't mingle with or speak to one another, which they most emphatically did not, how was Iran ever going to realize any of its democratic ambitions?

The expat community in Tehran is minuscule, certainly compared to that in other countries, even repressive China, and some of the neighboring Arab states. Karri, although an Iranian citizen now and someone who had surprisingly quickly adjusted to life in Tehran, was still always going to be an expat no matter how long we lived there, and I knew she would enjoy meeting, and sometimes commiserating with, others like herself. In the absence of clubs and the like for foreigners, which exist in other countries, one cannot just set out to meet other foreign residents in Tehran. So some of these parties we were invited to were a godsend, as far as I was concerned, even if they showed her a side of Iran restricted to the very privileged.

Before we left New York for Tehran, the Polish deputy ambassador in Iran, Piotr Kozlowski, had contacted me by e-mail and had invited us to dinner as soon as we settled in. I accepted eagerly. Our neighborhood in Brooklyn is overwhelmingly Polish—signs on the shops are in Polish—so we actually had more in common with the Poles than would seem apparent, and since the diplomat had a son almost the exact age as Khash, I was optimistic that we might become good friends, and that Karri might have someone other than my Iranian friends to talk to. Once we were in Tehran, I happened to tell a friend of mine, a former senior official of the regime, that I was seeing the Polish deputy ambassador. His first reaction was that Kozlowski was indubitably from the Polish intelligence services and that I should be careful. That didn't dissuade me; their son Aleks, born in Tehran, got on famously with Khash. When Piotr asked me at the end of our dinner if I would be willing to meet the ambassador at the official residence one evening, I happily said yes, despite knowing that it might be another mark against me. An invitation followed shortly thereafter, and again we took Khash with us, for the ambassador, Juliusz Gojlo, insisted that his own young children would enjoy meeting him.

The Polish embassy in Tehran sits on a large plot of land in the northern reaches of the center of town; not quite North Tehran, it was once a neighborhood of fancy shops and large private homes. Today it is dotted with apartments and commercial buildings, although there are still quite a few fancy stores, where Iranians shop for imported party clothes, and restaurants, where younger Westernized Iranians still party, on the main boulevard, whose name was changed from Jordan to Africa (or Afriqa, depending on the sign) after the revolution. This was not because Jordan Street was once named for the country that later sided with Saddam Hussein in the war against Iran, but because the street was named for the American educator Dr. Samuel Jordan, who founded the American College of Tehran, in 1898, later to become Alborz College (high school), the Eton or St. Paul's of Iran, where my father was educated briefly before being expelled for punching the headmaster in the face (for *his* having boxed my uncle 'round the ears for some infraction or other). Jordan may have been an unpopular memory for the revolutionaries, reminding them perhaps of American benevolence rather than imperialism and hegemony, but I have yet to come across an Iranian living in Iran, from the older generations who remember the avenue in its heyday to the younger who have no idea who Dr. Jordan was, who call it Africa and not Jordan. Africa, it seems, sadly, can't get any respect, not even from the citizens of an anti-colonialist, anti-imperialist, and truly revolutionary country.

The Polish government bought the embassy property in 1979, just as the revolution was taking hold, and it houses both the chancery and the ambassador's residence. A striking midcentury modern structure, with beautiful parklike grounds and a swimming pool, it had been owned, apparently, by an Iranian who fled during the Islamic Revolution. To this day the regime refuses to recognize Polish ownership of the land, believing that the former Iranian owner had obtained it through corruption and venality. But as a sign of the government's relative friendliness with Poland—and Iranian-Polish relations have a long and congenial history—it has done nothing legally to reclaim the property and has never made the question of ownership a public issue. (By contrast, it is mired in a dispute with Great Britain over a larger property, a big park really, that the British embassy owns on Shariati Avenue, in the north of the city.) During the shah's time, the house and its grounds were undoubtedly the scene of some fancy parties, certainly wilder if not fancier than the diplomatic dinners that embassies tend to give, but we were happy to have the opportunity to attend a few, and if the political atmosphere had been less oppressive in 2011, other Iranians would have been, too.

We did become friends with the Polish ambassador, his deputy, and their families. They, more than most foreign observers of Iran, seemed to genuinely want to understand Iran, to forge better ties between it and their own country, and to defuse in whatever way possible the crisis between Iran and the West, which always threatens to end in an unnecessary and fruitless war. But they found it almost impossible to do much of anything: no Iranians who mattered, even those no longer allied to the government, could or would meet with them; nor did the higher-ups at the Polish Foreign Ministry follow any advice they might provide. Poland, which at one point during our stay held the rotating presidency of the European Union, could do little that was inconsistent with general European policy on Iran, particularly in light of pressure that the United States brought to bear on its European allies to toe the American line. Policy making on the ground was all but impossible.

Ambassador Gojlo hosted two more dinners for us during our stay, which we very much enjoyed, both in the company of a number of other European ambassadors and diplomats. At one, where I was the guest of honor, an ambassador, recently appointed to Iran, said to me that he and the other diplomats in his embassy had to be careful in their reports back home not to appear to be defending Iran or its policies too much; otherwise they would be accused of having "gone native." Colonialism seemingly lives on, if only in the corridors of the foreign offices of former colonial powers. At the same party, the ambassador cracked open bottles of his finest Polish vodka—bison grass vodka, which had recently become available in Brooklyn, too. That was the most exciting part of the evening for both Karri and me, and for whatever reason it made me feel more at home in my second home than I ever thought a bottle of booze might do.

Karri saw the Polish ambassador's wife on other occasions, and they shared stories of their annoyance at having to ride in the back of buses alone (yes, the ambassador's wife rode the buses, making her and Karri two of the very few expats or even well-off Iranians who did), at wearing the hijab, and generally at life in Tehran. Through the Polish couple, Karri also became friends with the wife of the Canadian envoy to Iran, who, after the downgrading of ties between Ottawa and Tehran, held the title not of ambassador but of chargé d'affaires. She and her husband had served in Iran before, many years earlier, and she knew and loved the place despite the difficulties inherent in representing a country that Iran viewed as little more than a servant of the United States, and an enemy to boot. (Canada's relations with Iran reached their lowest ebb in September 2012, when Canada unilaterally and controversially broke off diplomatic relations, for reasons not fully explained, evacuated its remaining diplomats from Tehran, and expelled the Iranian diplomats in Ottawa.)

Later in our stay we also got acquainted, at yet another party, with the newly appointed British ambassador, Dominick Chilcott. He had previously served as deputy ambassador at the British embassy in Washington, presumably a suitable preparation for one who was to represent the Anglo-American view of affairs to the Iranians firsthand. He had only recently arrived in Tehran, and a few days after we met, he invited us to a dinner party at the British embassy. I had not been overly concerned with our connections to European diplomats while going to their homes and drinking their vodka, although I probably should have been. The British, however, and their embassy were a different story.

At least from the time of the Qajars—the dynasty that preceded the last shah's Pahlavi dynasty, from 1785 to 1925—Iranians of all political stripes have viewed Great Britain with great suspicion. They have not forgotten the British Empire's designs on Iran (or Persia, as the empire called it)—motivated geopolitically when India and parts of the Middle East were in the empire, and motivated economically once oil was discovered. Indeed, at one time Iranians believed that Britain controlled everything in their country, from politics to the mosque, to the benefit of its interests, not theirs. In the early 1950s, Prime Minister Mohammad Mossadeq dared to defy Great Britain by insisting that Iran receive its fair share from its own oil (or at least more than what the Anglo-Iranian Oil Company, later BP, paid in taxes to the British government); in reward he was overthrown by the CIA on the urging and with the assistance of the British.

Today many Iranians, and particularly revolutionary Iranians, hate the British more than any other nation in the world, still consider them to have designs on Persia, and accuse them of interfering in Iran on a daily basis, yet ironically have allowed them to maintain a large embassy in Tehran; the American one, a few blocks away, was long ago ransacked and occupied and remains shuttered to this day, except for the Revolutionary Guard base set up on its grounds. Some Iranian regime haters, both inside and outside Iran, claim that the British in fact still do control Iran—that they brought the mullahs to power and keep them there; others, even high officials, claim that the British deviously block any attempt by either the United States or Iran to mend ties, in an attempt to keep Iran for themselves. It is the only strategically valuable country in the world where they, and not the Americans, have a presence, and where the Americans have to rely on the British for on-the-ground information and intelligence. Whatever one's taste for conspiracy theories, the British embassy in Tehran, at the intersection of two grand boulevards in the heart of the city, is often the scene of protests against Her Majesty's government, and the garden party the embassy throws every year is an occasion not just for protest but for the intelligence and security services to harass Iranian partygoers, and of course to photograph them.

Only a day or two after we received our invitation to the dinner party at the embassy (which we accepted), the British government unilaterally imposed sanctions on Iran's Central Bank. Needless to say, the government viewed it as a hostile act, and Parliament took up the issue of how to retaliate. I was now a little concerned about attending a function at the ambassador's invitation, particularly because the occasion was the anniversary of Churchill's birthday:

The British Ambassador and his wife,
Dominick and Jane Chilcott,

Request the pleasure of the company of

MR HOOMAN MAJD & MRS MAJD

At a dinner to celebrate the 137th birthday of Sir Winston Churchill,

At 8:30pm on Wednesday, 30 November,

At their residence,

Around the same table and in the same room as the
Great Man celebrated his 69th birthday,

In the company of the leaders of our Soviet and American allies,

Marshal Stalin and President Roosevelt,

During the Tehran Conference of November 1943.

After dinner, the Ambassador will propose a toast to
Sir Winston Churchill on his birthday and
deliver a short oration.

Winston Churchill is not viewed sympathetically in Iran, and the authorities could not possibly see a party to celebrate his birthday and the Tehran Conference as an appropriate place for any nationalistic, let alone revolutionary, Iranian to be seen. The fact that Stalin was to be represented by the Russian ambassador and Roosevelt by the Swiss (in the absence of an American envoy) would probably be the icing on the cake of any accusations of antirevolutionary sentiments or, worse, activity. I discussed whether we should cancel with Karri, who at this point didn't feel too threatened living in Iran, despite her run-ins with the Gasht-e Ershad; she left it to me, whom she did worry about, to decide whether going would be too serious a political faux pas. (She was less keen on the menu, which Ambassador Chilcott promised would be exactly the same one that was served in 1943—presumably not vegetarian, and certainly not gluten-free.)

But within a few days, the Iranian parliament, the Majles, passed a law expelling Ambassador Chilcott, who had been in Tehran all of two months and whose party for Churchill would have been his first big event in the country. The order to expel him in two weeks left him free to carry on with his party plans, but I grew increasingly nervous about going, even though the guest list had probably already been scrutinized by Iranian intelligence and I had received no warning phone calls from the authorities, who are always quick to call with "suggestions." So I asked around, getting advice from former officials and from people connected to the Supreme Leader. All of them said that it was a bad idea for me—no, a *very* bad idea—to be seen at the party. I finally e-mailed the ambassador, apologizing for having to cancel at the last minute—for obvious reasons, I wrote—and he replied that he understood. The very next day protesters stormed the British embassy and looted and trashed it. The entire staff, including the ambassador (but not his dog, which was subsequently shuttled around to various friendly embassies before being sent home), was evacuated back to London. Before the party could take place. One day before, in fact.

The Persian year 1390, which had started out horribly for the regime with the big sulk, was going from bad to worse. The storming of the British embassy, reminiscent of the 1979 occupation of the U.S. embassy, was assumed to be the work of the regime, although

THE MINISTRY OF GUIDANCE INVITES YOU TO NOT STAY   179

it hurriedly denied it. The Foreign Ministry even issued a rare apology, or as close to an apology as the Islamic government has ever issued about anything. The police had allowed the protesters, Basij students mostly, to enter the embassy grounds, then arrested a few of them later and cleared the compound within three or four hours, so either it had been planned carefully or some elements of the regime, without approval from the very top, had decided to embarrass both the British *and* the Ahmadinejad government, which had been against intensifying the conflict with Britain and had earlier opposed expelling the ambassador. Even for veteran observers, it was getting hard to follow the machinations of the government, and the regime.

The attack on the embassy was shown live on state TV—itself an indication that state media had advance notice of *something*—and it was the talk of the town for a few days. But the protesters' ignorance of world affairs, and therefore probable lack of high-level state sponsorship, was betrayed by the graffiti they scrawled on the embassy's walls: "Down with *Elizabeth.*" The queen, I have to think, would be flattered that in at least one country in the world she is still viewed as the supreme leader of an empire. Many Iranian politicians (with the glaring exception of the president himself), eager to outdo one another with their revolutionary credentials in advance of parliamentary elections, stopped short of praising the mobs but noted with satisfaction that the Iranian people were sick of Britain and its anti-Iran policies. Even opponents of the regime have very little sympathy for the British, though they might make an exception for the impuissant queen herself. One antiregime Iranian said to me the day after the attack that he thought the British *themselves* were behind the assault—it was obvious to him, he said—because it would validate their actions in sanctioning Iran's Central Bank and show the world what savages the Iranians were. Besides, he said, the British control the mullahs. In any event, few in Tehran, even pro-Western citizens, showed much concern over the loss of a British outpost in the capital, beyond wondering how Iranians would now go about applying for and receiving visas to travel to Great Britain, ironically one of the most coveted destinations for perennially visa-hungry Iranians, Islamist or not.

Karri and I were both unsettled by the British embassy affair, but we were also a little disappointed that we never got a chance to witness a celebration there. Not that there was any shortage of parties. On any given Thursday night, there are parties in parks, in good weather; along the streets, where fast-food and pizza joints give youth who have nowhere else to gather a place to hang out; and even in cars, where kids cruising avenues and boulevards create a party atmosphere with such regularity in some neighborhoods that patrols are set up to block them and in some cases arrest and fine them. Every time we went out on a Thursday night, we would witness these parties in one part of Tehran or another, including our own neighborhood, and Karri was a little annoyed by the fact that traffic, normally run-of-the-mill gridlock, would come to a complete standstill on holidays. Getting out of town was no better, for many Iranians party in the mountain resorts or at the Caspian, making the Long Island Expressway on a Friday afternoon in the summer feel like an empty Indy speedway compared to the highways and roads leading out of Tehran. Three hours for a fifteen-mile trip to a ski resort? Check. Seven, sometimes as many as eleven hours to travel a couple hundred miles to the beach? Check. (At public beaches, incidentally, it is all but forbidden for women to swim, even in full chador, but many jump in anyway.) Party on they do, the Iranians, and nothing—not even the roadblocks, where machine-gun-toting Basij, so young that the fluff on their upper lips signals that their mustaches have yet to grow in, check to see if the women and men in the cars are related and open the trunks to check for booze—will stop them.

We went, *en famille*, to the mountains a number of times, both in the spring and in the summer, when the weather was a pleasant twenty or so degrees cooler and 100 percent cleaner than Tehran's, and in the winter, when snow blankets the area and some of the finest skiing anywhere is to be enjoyed, mostly by Iranians. (Few tourists venture to Iran in the first place, but those who do seem unaware that skiing is a possibility anywhere in the Middle East except in the indoor malls of sweltering Dubai.) We would leave early on Thursday, before the traffic made it impossible to get out of town, and drive along winding mountain roads with hundreds of other cars filled with all kinds of Tehranis: from young people looking to escape their parents for the weekend to families of bearded men and chador-clad women with screaming babies impossibly packed into impossibly small cars. We'd go to spend the night at a cousin's lodge or another cousin's apartment, but not to party.

Entertainment is limited if you're not a skier or aren't throwing or attending a party, but just leaving Tehran for twenty-four hours is a pleasure few will understand until they've spent a good amount of time in the overcrowded, perpetually smoggy, and sprawling metropolis. (Even in my mother's childhood, when Tehran had only a couple hundred thousand residents, her family would pack up their house and move to the mountains, or at least the foothills, for the entire summer. And they would party, although in her religious family's case, without alcohol.) In the warm months, while going for walks in the country, we would encounter religious families picnicking, even camping, by streams and rivers, partying within Islamic norms; they would stare in amazement at the blond, blue-eyed woman with the blond, blue-eyed baby who had just come into view. But we weren't privileged to attend the parties, wild or not, of those Tehranis who had surmounted the roadblock obstacles and were holed up in the villas, lodges, and apartments that many Tehranis, owners and renters alike, use as their weekend getaways.

To leave our apartment for the country, we always had to circle around Tajrish Square, a busy shopping district with its own covered bazaar and stalls that sell some of the best fruits and vegetables in Tehran and which is jammed with shoppers on weekdays but even more so on the eve of the Muslim Sabbath. The only people lounging about are the idle taxi drivers, who stand outside their cabs and in a loud, nasal clamor announce destinations they are willing to serve for three or more customers. But most passersby ignore them, having less business to attend to, on a semiofficial half-day holiday, than shopping to do for the weekend. Unlicensed drivers in personal cars, many of them college graduates with no other job opportunities, drive slowly around the traffic circle, their passenger-side window open, slowing down and leaning slightly toward it whenever they spot someone standing at a corner in the hope that perhaps he or she might be looking for a cheap ride. But on Thursdays business is slow. These taxi entrepreneurs will do good business later, when partygoers head out and then return, sometimes drunk and unable to drive themselves, from their parties.

The sidewalk vendors do brisk business, but the little children who hawk playing cards, chewing gum, batteries, or more often *fal-e-Hafez*, popular fortune-telling cards containing verses and stanzas by the beloved poet Hafez, seem even more forlorn than usual. One child, a small, thin boy of indeterminate age but certainly no older than ten, would sit on the sidewalk on one corner of the square, on his knees with his hands on his thighs, his cards laid out in front of him. I saw him almost every day, passing by with Khash in his stroller as I went to the bazaar for fresh yogurt or farm eggs, or to the vegetable and fruit stands for our daily produce supply. The boy was always silent, never touting his goods. I would give him a little something, which he would wordlessly accept, handing me a card, which I more often than not refused. Unlike some of the other street urchins, he didn't have the energy to argue that he wasn't looking for charity. Maybe his dignity had been crushed, or he simply couldn't be bothered. On rainy and colder days he would sit there getting wet, a dirty piece of plastic covering his goods, shivering as he stoically manned his little corner of the sidewalk, and breaking my heart as he did so.

Khash would stare at the boy, and all I could think was how very different life would always be for the little blue-eyed boy in a fancy stroller, the likes of which the street boy probably had never seen. Islamic Iran has successfully instituted compulsory education for its children, achieving a very high rate of literacy compared to that of any other developing country, but some children are left behind: illegal Afghan immigrants without the papers necessary to register at school, or the children of impecunious parents—some drug addicts and others just plain poor—who are sent out to the streets to make a few rials to help with the family finances. I found it astonishing that in a busy square, with a perpetual police presence, as well as frequent appearances by security forces and surly hijab minders, children like this boy could escape the scrutiny of a state that proclaimed its devotion to Allah and justice. The *mostazafin*, the downtrodden, may not be as numerous as in India, but they exist nonetheless.

On religious holidays, when the mosques in Tajrish hand out free food, the boy would eat, but otherwise I never saw him with a morsel, and as we set off for a party or a night in the country, I wondered what his evening would be like, and what his dinner would consist of. Life is shameful—doubly so, I thought. The revolution had failed him and his family, perhaps just as capitalism has failed too many in the West. What was once unthinkable for the revolution—that little children would beg or sell trinkets by the side of the road while Mercedes and BMWs rolled by, that families would go hungry as others partied the night away, that weekend jaunts to the beach or the ski resorts would become ordinary for a large middle class as others stole rides on overcrowded buses—had, thirty years on, become acceptable.

It is hard to find slums in Tehran—even in South Tehran—of the kind we know in Third World countries, and hard to see very much abject poverty anywhere, which is some credit to the revolution. But the gap between the haves and have-nots is growing, as it did during the shah's time: the 1979 revolution reversed the trend temporarily, partly because many wealthy Iranians emigrated and partly because the revolution provided the less fortunate classes with upward mobil-

ity. Tajrish Square is just one of the places where the gap can be most
obvious. The mephitic odor emanating from fifty-year-old Fiat buses
mixes with the smell of the freshly butchered lamb that fewer and
fewer Iranians can afford. Rickety old Paykan cars navigate the traffic alongside Japanese SUVs and exotic European sports cars, often
driven by young men in dark designer sunglasses and heavily made-up
women in expensive silk scarves. By the concrete walls of the river
gushing down from the mountains just north of the square, we witnessed several homeless families camping all summer. But nothing,
other than the little shivering boy whose phlegmatic countenance is
forever imprinted in my memory, reminded me more of the gap, fiscal
and psychological, between rich and poor than the gathering of the
Tehran Cigar Club, which I attended one late summer evening.

In Iran, Cuban cigars are legal and available; the best and most
expensive are sold at the old Hilton, renamed the Esteghlal Hotel,
near the Parkway intersection with Vali Asr. The Casa del Habano,
a cigar shop that wouldn't be out of place on Madison Avenue or in
St. James's in London, carries a huge selection of fine cigars at prices
to match those in Europe; it is located in the hotel shopping arcade
alongside carpet shops, clothing boutiques, and souvenir boutiques,
none of which hold any interest for the occasional American tourist or journalist who, if he is a smoker, will gravitate to the store at
some point in his stay. The store also keeps a private reserve of cigars,
aged Cubans that are in some cases no longer even manufactured, for
special occasions, such as the Tehran Cigar Club's monthly meetings.

The members of the club are a disparate group of Iranian businessmen and lawyers; expat Iranians who maintain homes in Tehran;
and Europeans drawn from the handful still living in Tehran. They
rotate the duty of hosting club meetings, and the night I was invited
to attend, a young man of about twenty-five was the host at his pent-
house apartment in one of Iran's most luxurious and expensive high-
rise buildings. He was the son of a powerful businessman who had
interests in all kinds of ventures (and was therefore likely to be a

partner of government officials, the Revolutionary Guards, or both) as well as business interests in Dubai, which the son handled to some extent, probably from an equally luxurious sky palace there. A special elevator whisked me up to the top floor, where a second private elevator took me up one more level, opening directly into the apartment.

Huge flat-screen televisions, mounted on two walls in the expansive living room, were tuned to the Persian Music Channel from Dubai, thankfully with the sound on mute. A full wet bar in one corner featured shelves of liquor, stools to perch on, and a bartender in a tuxedo mixing drinks: a welcome sight, but incongruous to say the least. As were the rest of the staff, also in tuxedos, who circulated to take drink orders and distribute canapés and other edible treats. Carrying a generous helping of Johnnie Walker Blue on ice, I stepped out onto the deck, a wraparound terrace with 360-degree views of Tehran unmatched anywhere except at the top of Milad Tower, Tehran's space needle and its tallest structure. Flames from two or three built-in fire pits—of the kind one might see, if lucky, in Malibu backyards—heated the chilly night air, and sofas and lounge chairs were arrayed everywhere.

I lit a cigarette, sat down, and marveled at the view—until I remembered that I could smoke inside. I returned to a comfortable sofa and chatted for a while with a fellow guest, discussing the economy, the political situation in Iran, and, more important, the somewhat unbelievable apartment we were sitting in. The cigar of the night was announced by a Frenchman, who proceeded to give a long speech in English on its provenance—a Bolívar from the year 2000—mostly gibberish to me, since I can barely recognize the different notes in fine wine, let alone the difference between a fair, good, and exquisite Havana. Still, it was delicious, the better of the only two adjectives I'm equipped to use for tobacco of any kind.

Halfway through smoking the monstrously huge cigar, as I was feeling just a little queasy, dinner was served. I had assumed that "cigar night" meant a few appetizers and some booze, but I had misjudged my countrymen's appetite for throwing a good party, which always includes dinner regardless of the occasion. At about this time, our host's girlfriends—yes, plural—arrived. The two young women, both pretty and provocatively dressed (and with six-inch heels) once they removed their scarves and manteaus, fiddled with the stereo until they found a CD of truly execrable dance music that they thought should be listened to at full volume, to accompany the gyrating bodies on the television screens. It was time to go. I looked at my watch, and indeed, it was past eleven, dinnertime for an Iranian party but bedtime for a fifty-plus-year-old father of an infant. The friend who had invited me, also unable to abide the music and the turn the party had taken, offered to drive me home.

We descended to the grand lobby, where the doorman gave us a mischievous look and went outside to my friend's parked car. As we were getting in, a disheveled old man with a horribly deformed face and one arm shuffled by, that arm outstretched for a handout. I pushed some bills into his fist and got in the car, wondering if he was a war veteran, someone who had fought to defend his country against the invading Iraqi hordes to make it safe for the sons of businessmen to have cigar parties, or if he was the victim of a terrible accident, industrial or otherwise. Some thirty floors of a building separated the two extremes of Iranian society: the young, careless men and women who happily displayed their ostentatious wealth and thoroughly Western lifestyles, and the *mostazafin*, for whom Islam was supposed to be their salvation, if not their ticket to a party.

10

ROAD TRIP!

I always knew that Iranians were fond of traveling, not just because of the masses of spectators—apart from welcoming parties—that I saw as a child at the airport in Tehran, who traveled vicariously through those few who could at that time, but also because of the great interest everyone showed then in having me tell them stories of far-off lands and of the journeys themselves. Iranians have always been curious about the world beyond their walls, and have intrepidity built into their genes, but before the advent of cheap air travel very few could afford to venture far beyond the country's borders.

At the turn of the twentieth century, my own grandfather, well before he became an ayatollah, traveled to Paris to study philosophy, crossing the mountainous border with Turkey by donkey and horse, then settling in on a train to Europe, undoubtedly in third-class. Today most Iranians, much as they'd like to travel afar, are once again restricted, less because of the expense involved than because of the visa restrictions that other countries impose on Iranian passport holders. Only a handful of countries allow visa-less entry by Iranians, including Turkey and, more recently, Georgia, and they are popular destinations for holidaymakers and shoppers alike. Malaysia, another friendly country that admits Iranians without a visa, attracts many

Iranian tourists, too, but the long distance means expensive flights. But the charter flights and package tours on offer during the big vacation month of March, the Iranian new year—equivalent to the Western Christmas break and Europe's August—allow many more Iranians than just the upper middle class to travel far beyond the Middle East, to Southeast Asia, for example, and even to countries where visas can be easily obtained through tour operators.

Dubai is another very popular destination, as dozens of flights connect it to various cities in Iran. Traveling there is only slightly more complicated, as the Emirates require a visa, but the process of getting one is handled by travel agents, and few Iranians are ever refused. The distance, a two-hour flight from Tehran, and the many inexpensive package tours mean that many ordinary Iranians can make a quick trip to Dubai, where they can enjoy a brief taste of social freedom: they can swim in the warm waters of the Persian Gulf without a chador or hijab, with their husbands and boyfriends no less; and they can shop in the gargantuan malls to their hearts' content. They can even eat Persian food while they're at it, since the presence of 400,000 or so Iranian expats in Dubai makes the Emirates a Persian-friendly place in more ways than one. Since Dubai is also a hub of international commerce, it serves Iranian businessmen who are in import-export, banking, or any business that requires a substantially less restrictive and sanctions-ridden commercial environment than Tehran to thrive.

Other than our quick excursions to the mountains outside Tehran, we had not traveled far from our apartment by the time the truly oppressive heat of summer arrived, and as friends and family began their summer travels, to Europe or just to the Caspian, we were itching to escape both the weather and the monotony of summer life in the capital. Ramadan was also approaching, the month of fasting for Muslims everywhere—which rotates around the Gregorian calendar due to the discrepancies between the Arab lunar one and the Western solar one—and living in Tehran during Ramadan, especially in the

summer months, can be a miserable experience if one is not a practicing Muslim (and even for some who might be). When I explained
to Karri what Ramadan actually meant, she responded with a look
of terror: no restaurants or cafés open during the day, no eating or
drinking on the streets (or smoking, which for me would be a challenge, as I smoke only outdoors), and very little to do during sunlight
hours, which, it being summer, was more than twelve hours a day. As
a nursing mother, she was exempt from fasting, or rather from being
expected to fast by authorities who might otherwise stop her on the
streets, as was Khash, but I warned her that she might get contemp-
tuous glances from passersby if she chugged down bottles of water
in public in the 105-degree heat, especially if she was alone. She was
a little relieved that she wouldn't get thrown in jail for eating and
drinking in public, but we decided that if there was ever a time to
escape the Islamic Republic, it was during Ramadan, even if for only
a few days.

The Caspian shore is usually a good choice for a few days of
R&R, but with everything closed during the day, it would be no fun
during Ramadan, and since we would be traveling with an infant, a
long flight abroad held little appeal. So we decided on Dubai. The
temperature might be ten degrees hotter than Tehran, with humidity
hovering around 100 percent, but at least you could get a coffee, an
ice cream, or a drink if you're not an Arab Muslim, all day and all
night. At least that's what we thought.

Flights to the Persian Gulf countries are inexpensive, as are
hotels in the off-season, which is when few people—with the exception of German, British, Russian, and Dutch tourists—seem willing
to brave the heat and humidity of the gulf coast. We discovered that
the "warm waters" of the Persian Gulf is a misnomer, at least in the
summer. Think hot, as in bath, no, Jacuzzi water. The pools at the
hotels are filled with water cooled to be at least bearable, but the British and Germans and Russians happily frolic in the sea, leading me
to decide that it isn't only mad dogs and Englishmen but Germans

and Russians, too, who go out in the midday sun. Then again, I'm sure that no dog, if any ever appeared at the dog-phobic Muslim shores, would ever venture into the midday Persian Gulf.

Our flight to Dubai was full of Iranians who had business there (perhaps checking on their dollar bank accounts?), or were on shopping sprees (a number of high-end boutiques in Tehran replenish their inventories by taking empty suitcases to Dubai and returning with them full), or were, like us, looking to get out of town for a few days. And as far as Karri was concerned, being able to safely remove her scarf and undo the top button of her blouse after arriving at the Dubai airport was a good start. Khash was oblivious to the change in environment but happy on the plane for some reason and excited by the airport terminal, which to him probably looked the size of the universe with a million different objects to touch and play with and wide corridors to run down.

At our hotel, Karri hoped to get a cup of tea or a cold drink as she waited for me to check in, but she was dismayed to learn that the lounge didn't serve food or drink during the day. During Ramadan, anyway. Were the restaurants open? she asked. Yes, but only for breakfast, lunch, and dinner. How about a drink? By the pool, but only nonalcoholic during Ramadan. Wine with dinner? Only after sundown. Room service, however, remained twenty-four-hour.

There's not a whole lot to do in Dubai, especially if you're traveling with an infant, besides hanging out by the pool and taking a dip in the heavily salted hot tub called the Persian Gulf. But one thing you can do is go to the malls. We went right away, first because on the Internet Karri had found an organic products store where she wanted to stock up on items unavailable in Tehran, and second because, well, there's not a whole lot to do in Dubai. We thought we'd be able to get a Starbucks Frappuccino at the mall—legalized crack, as one friend calls it; we wouldn't dream of ordering one back home, but a few months with no Starbucks at all had made us oddly nostalgic for it.

So we were hugely disappointed to discover that none of the restaurants, cafés, or bars in the malls were open during Ramadan either, not until sundown, which happened to be close to Khash's bedtime.

The malls did provide a snapshot of Emirati life, perhaps not entirely accurate but one of the only glimpses most foreigners will get: expats prancing about in shorts and revealing T-shirts; Emirati and other Arab women in full black abayas, the Arab equivalent of a chador; and Arab men, mostly in traditional garb and headdresses, usually walking a few paces ahead of their wives if not alone. No one carried a drink in his or her hand, no one had so much as a piece of candy or a stick of gum to chew on.

Outside in the parking lot, I stepped out for a cigarette in the designated smoking area of the Dubai Mall. Suddenly two employees ran toward me at full speed. "Sir," one of them, a South Asian, said breathlessly, "no smoking allowed!"

I pointed to the cigarette sign and the big ashtray in front of me. "No, no," he said, "it's *Ramadan!*"

I protested that I was an American, seeing no point in confusing him with the Iranian thing.

The security guards didn't care. It was Ramadan, and one didn't smoke, eat, or drink during daylight hours, no matter who one was or what one's faith was.

It was quite a contrast to Iranian Ramadan, where smoking on the street was more common than I had expected, especially in the northern parts of the city, even among pious Iranians. And certainly no one, unless they were from the government security forces, would object there if someone visibly smoked or ate or drank. In Tehran, Karri had often witnessed men and women surreptitiously sneaking a pastry or a sandwich in a doorway, slyly smoking a cigarette, or taking a swig from a bottle of water in the park—and to her surprise, no one seemed to care.

One day when I went to pay my fruit seller, who comes from a religious family, I caught him hiding a burning cigarette. "I'm not religious," I said, gesturing at the curling wisp of smoke rising from under the counter. "Go ahead and smoke openly."

"It's the one thing that I can't give up," he replied, bending down behind the counter to take a drag.

Surely he realized his shop smelled of smoke, despite the open doors? It didn't matter, I guessed. I asked why he didn't just go whole hog and eat and drink, too, since he was breaking the fast anyway.

He just smiled, as if I were too ignorant to understand.

Taxi drivers, with pictures of Shia saints hanging from their rear-view mirrors no less, had bottles of water hidden not so well under their seats, I noticed. And as soon as I sat down for a trim before our trip to Dubai, my barber asked me if I was fasting. Actually, he asked it rhetorically, offering me the customary glass of tea, for me to sip in front of a large glass window facing Vali Asr as he cut my hair. I declined.

Iran was fasting, yes, but as with everything else in Iran, rules are viewed as guides and are meant to be broken. The Emirates was different: it had one set of rules for foreigners, whom it is desperate to attract (as long as they don't flout Islamic mores *too* openly outside their hotels and clubs), and another set for Arabs (and actually for all Muslims, although it's rarely enforced on non-Arab Muslims). But in a land where Karri could dress as she pleased, the rules of public behavior—or the Islamic nature of the country, as she pointed out to me—seemed more strict, certainly for the natives, than in Iran, which she felt was far more European in its feel and in the outlook of its citizens, even the outwardly pious Muslims.

Despite the restrictions in Dubai, which were easy to bypass while staying in one of the well-stocked, self-contained, and self-sufficient hotels, we enjoyed the brief break from Tehran. It was nice to be able to go to a bar, albeit only after seven-thirty p.m., and who knew that going to Starbucks—which had an outlet in the small shopping mall connected to our hotel—could become a drug that one might have withdrawal from? Spending time in the Kinokuniya bookstore in the Dubai Mall—where interested Iranians pick up books unavailable in Tehran—was itself worth the trip.

But we were going to spend the rest of Ramadan back at our apartment in Tehran, despite the scarcity of public activities that are permissible in Iran until Eid-e-Fetr, the holiday marking the end of the fast. When we got back, Khash was particularly annoyed by the closed coffee shop at the bottom of the hill from our street, missing his daily dose of love from the girls working there, and he would point to it emphatically as we went on our walks, pleading in his babbling way for me to somehow open it up and take him inside. He was otherwise oblivious to Ramadan, since Karri or I would buy him a drink, coconut water in a Tetrapak usually (which has enthusiastic advocates in Tehran, too). He'd sometimes pour it on his pants, depending on how thirsty or mischievous he felt. And the fruit seller would always give him a banana, which he slowly devoured as we made our rounds of the shops in our neighborhood. The park he liked, which was too hot to visit much before five o'clock, and the nearby House of Cinema (a former Qajar mini-palace) had two rather nice cafés in beautiful grounds—we'd normally go there after Khash was finished playing, sometimes meeting friends; but that was also not an option during Ramadan.

So our life, like the lives of many Iranians, became even more monotonous than it ordinarily was, but we consoled ourselves that it was only two more weeks, not a lifetime. We were invited to a couple of *iftars*, the nightly ritualistic breaking of the fast, but not every other night, as some Iranians are. It's somewhat bad form to go to an *iftar* if one has not actually fasted, and few religious families will invite friends or family who are nonpracticing or won't throw reciprocal *iftar* parties themselves. *Iftar*, falling well after Khash's dinnertime and around the time he would want to go to sleep, was also an inconvenient moment to take him anywhere, although we did manage once or twice. We even had an *iftar* at a cousin's lodge in Darbandsar, in the mountains, where Khash ate before everyone else and missed the mountains of food, beginning with dates, cheese, bread, and tea, that appeared on the dining table just as dusk arrived.

After Ramadan, we finally accepted an invitation to spend a weekend at a friend's house at the Caspian, which Karri had wanted to see and which we thought would be fun for Khash. We left by car, driven by my friend, in the early afternoon on a Wednesday to avoid the traffic jams that would occur later that evening and all day on Thursday. Khash complained most of the way for, unaccustomed to car seats, he couldn't abide being strapped into one. When we arrived, it was too dark to see or do anything, so we bought takeout from one of the numerous restaurants in the area catering to weekend-ers, which was rather delicious Caspian cuisine—different vegetable stews and kebabs than in Tehran, but with the customary fluffy rice. Only in the morning, with perfect weather, did we realize that we were surrounded by hilly forests, lush greenery, and smog-free air such as we hadn't witnessed since our arrival in the dust bowl that is Tehran. Even the mountains outside Tehran are desertlike until one crosses them completely and descends into the Caspian region— which after Tehran and after the torrid Persian Gulf was, to say the least, a delight. A hike in the hills, where my friend owned some property—formerly a tea plantation—was just as delightful, and the view of the sea, placid and inviting, was not something Karri had imagined she'd experience while in Iran. Stranger still, to foreign eyes at least, was what we saw one day at a seaside restaurant. The beach was packed with customers, and while the men with rolled-up pants dipped their feet into the water, the women sat on the sand in their manteaus and scarves, not daring to splash in the surf. Not even the many children went near the water, choosing to play well away from the tide level and seemingly not feeling an urge to jump in. It was probably good training for the girls, who would not, if the Islamic regime survived that long, be able to swim at ease in their adulthood.

A group of women, young and old, sat on some rocks while staring at the sea and chatting to one another. The young ones' faces were heavily and inappropriately slathered with makeup, as usual, rather than sunscreen, and one with bleached-blond hair sticking out from under her scarf, bright orange lipstick, and fluorescent orange nails appeared a little forlorn and removed from the conversation. As ridiculous as she looked, still at that moment what came to mind was what a friend had long ago told me: the Islamic Republic has forbidden *fun*. Khash, of course, was oblivious to this fact, playing as he did with pebbles and sand and enjoying the attention he received from camera-wielding tourists, men and women, who kept asking if it was okay to photograph him. I can't be sure, but I do think that numerous family picture albums and hard drives in Iran include a picture of Khash as a baby, in a Tehran park, on a busy sidewalk, or at the beach.

On the way back to the villa, we drove through a beautiful and heavily forested park—what looked like a nature preserve—with gazebos for picnickers and barbecue pits for kebab grilling. Iranians love nature, and the number of parks and green spaces in Tehran created by successive mayors, and their popularity with the citizens, is a testament to that. But they may love their cars just as much. On the wide sidewalks, right by their cars, families had set out carpets and cushions to sit on and were picnicking within plain sight of gazebos surrounded by ancient trees. A short, *very* short walk would have placed these families right in the middle of nature, away from the fumes of cars and motorcycles and the ugly asphalt, but being next to their cars and still in view of nature probably appealed to them more. On the drive back to Tehran (and I reluctantly drove, since my friend had to leave early, in a different car, to make an appointment in the city), all along the way on the Chalus road, which winds through mountains and valleys, we saw more of these families, parked by verdant spots and relaxing with a thermos of tea or a more elaborate repast on the edge of the road, some even camping, within spitting distance of a far more agreeable spot.

The Caspian, which is, in a way, the Hamptons of Tehran, makes

for a pleasant weekend excursion, but more for relaxation than anything else, and seeing nature is inherently enjoyable for a Tehran
resident. Yet unless one is there for a party, there is nothing to
do. The road that runs along the shore is dotted with the kinds of
shops one sees in every seaside resort town—stores with souvenirs,
gaudy children's toys, and buckets, shovels, and beach toys displayed
outside—and small restaurants and bakeries and ice-cream shops.
But the image is deceptive. Little of the jollity that one might observe
in seaside resorts elsewhere—families enjoying the beach, couples
holding hands on a boardwalk or promenade, people dining at outdoor cafés or drinking at bars—is on display here. Instead, these
things are reserved, one imagines, for the privacy of the villas and the
apartments that Tehranis repair to, and probably never leave, on the
weekend. There is little sightseeing, either, unless one ventures to
the cities farther up the coast, where historic buildings, monuments,
mosques, and churches can be found.

But I knew that Iran offers incredible sightseeing, so once we
were back home, we planned a week's trip south, to the famous city
of Esfahan and, less well known but still impressive, the Silk Road
city of Yazd.

Flying anywhere in Iran is cheap and relatively easy, but it was
not a risk Karri was willing to take, since domestic flights offered
by the national airline and private carriers use outdated equipment.
The airplanes can barely qualify as such—the forty-year-old Boe-
ings and Soviet-era Tupolevs have an unfortunate record of falling
out of the sky, if they ever make it up there, that is. Sanctions on
Iran, both the unilateral U.S. ones and more recently the UN and
European sanctions, have meant that, despite its massive wealth in
both the public and the private sectors, Iran has been largely unable
to upgrade its fleet of civilian aircraft since the revolution—even new
Airbuses are off limits due to the percentage of American parts. And
far too many airplane crashes occur in a country that should have an
impeccable safety record, since its pilots are as accomplished as any in

the West. (Even more stringent sanctions imposed by the West since we departed have virtually cut off Iran's economy from the outside world, which bodes poorly for transportation and much else.) The trains in Iran are a good, if time-consuming, alternative to flying, as are the buses, which are surprisingly luxurious and ridiculously cheap.

But traveling with Khash and all the impedimenta that this involves meant our best alternative was driving. Yazd is a five- or six-hour drive south on a highway that is essentially a straight line through the desert, once one escapes the southernmost reaches of Tehran, and since my family is from Yazd, one or another cousin would inevitably be driving there—in a very nice and safe SUV to boot—in any given month. Ali Khatami, brother of the ex-president and my cousin Maryam's husband, insisted that he take us, as in the late summer and early fall he was driving there almost every week to see his elderly mother, who had suffered illnesses all year, and he would be taking with us my uncle's widow, whom I very much liked and who happened to be his aunt, too. We hadn't decided yet how we would return to Tehran, other than via Esfahan, but it was going to be either by taxi or by train.

The drive to Yazd was easy, and Khash behaved surprisingly well in his car seat, perhaps lulled by the desert landscape, the rush of speeding along at ninety miles an hour, and the constant supply of snacks and drinks. He was a little too curious about the thermos of hot tea that every Iranian family keeps handy for any trip longer than an hour, but it relieved Ali of the duty of stopping for the obligatory tea breaks. Classical Persian music on the stereo also helped, and we arrived at our hotel on the outskirts of the old town a little tired but no worse for wear. The hotel, which I had stayed in alone before, is a converted old mansion, with acres of grounds. The man-made blue-tiled stream running through it gave Khash endless joy and us endless anxiety. But the oddest sight, one that Khash found curious and a little baffling, was that of the dwarf the hotel had hired since my last visit to greet guests; the man was barely taller than Khash and was dressed in traditional ancient Persian finery and shoes and hat, just like the other doormen. He seemed unperturbed that he might be an object of amusement if not mockery by hotel visitors and particularly their children, in a country where political correctness, as it applies to the differently abled (excepting war veterans), has seemingly not arrived. Khash kept his distance, recognizing somehow that the man was an adult but not the kind he was accustomed to seeing, and the dwarf, unlike all the other hotel employees who fawned over this *farangi* child, remained aloof, perhaps because of previous less-than-happy experiences with children his own size.

Yazd, being smack-dab in the middle of the desert, has remarkable weather except in midsummer, when it is unbearably hot. But both Karri and I enjoy the desert air and the vistas, and like most desert towns, this place has a certain languorous quality that is all the more inviting after one has spent time in a metropolis. Clean air, bright sunshine, and incredibly friendly citizens—no hustle and bustle, shoving, and the generally boorish demeanor found in Tehran and other big cities, not even in the ancient Yazd bazaar. Crossing the street is a breeze in Yazd, though probably due less to the courtesy of the drivers than to the fact that there simply isn't as much traffic. After we toured the ancient sites, seeing the old homes, and walking through the alleyways that traders of all nationalities plied centuries ago, we also wanted to see the Zoroastrian temple in Chak Chak, perched on the side of a mountain about a forty-minute drive outside of town, a mecca of sorts for Zoroastrians the world over.

Chak Chak is named for the mountain spring that for centuries has been dripping—*"chak-chak-chak,"* as the Persians, or those with a Yazdi accent, say—through a boulder and nourishing a massive tree. Zoroastrians, followers of the pre-Islamic Persian monotheistic faith, believe it is the spot where the daughter of the last Sassanid king, Yazdegerd III, cornered by invading Arabs, prayed to Ahura Mazda (god) to protect her; in response to her entreaties, the mountain opened up, providing her with a hiding place. The dripping spring, according to legend, represents tears of grief for her, and the ancient tree jutting out of the rock is still believed by some to have grown from the staff that the princess leaned on.

On the drive there through the desert, we passed the village of Ardakan, where my father was born. Our taxi driver, a man my age or slightly older, spent most of the time singing the praises of Ayatollah Khatami (Mohammad Khatami's deceased father and onetime prayer leader of Yazd), not knowing my relationship to the family. He was at pains to describe, especially to Karri, with me translating, how different the ruling mullahs of the past were compared to today. The elder Khatami, he said, was a most compassionate man and never accepted the bodyguards that the revolution insisted he have; he freed drug addicts and even homosexuals sentenced to death by Islamic courts; he was a symbol of what was right and just about the revolution. Our driver was less sanguine about the country's current leadership, especially in Yazd province, and particularly since Friday prayer leader Mohammad Sadoughi, married to Ayatollah Khatami's daughter Maryam, had died.

He also wanted to act as our tour guide, after wondering aloud why on earth an Iranian with an American wife and child would want to bring them to Iran, and to the desert at that. He told us the story of Chak Chak exactly as I knew it, except, nonsensically, he replaced the Persian princess in the legend with a granddaughter of the prophet Mohammad, a Shia escaping the Sunni hordes, who, upon hearing the voice of the angel Gabriel—the same angel who passed Allah's message to Mohammad—tapped her cane on the ground, and the mountain opened before her. The miracle of the spring and the tree and the mountain opening he attributed to Allah's favor for the Shia, erasing the Zoroastrian origin of the site, something he probably learned early in his life from unlearned mullahs who could not abide miracles that were not purely Islamic.

There seemed to be no real Zoroastrians at Chak Chak, other than the guard who charged non-Zoroastrians a fee to climb the steep steps to the holy site, perhaps because most pilgrims, I was told, make their annual pilgrimage there in the spring, a two-week period when non-Zoroastrians are actually forbidden to enter. We encountered many young Iranian couples and families, as one does at any historic site, museum, or tourist attraction in Iran, but Karri mentioned how strange the setting was without the hordes of foreign tourists one sees at comparable European or Asian sites. The large carving above the temple's bronze doors was a Farvahar, the symbol of Zoroastrianism, with the bust of a man atop a winged disk, or sun. That and our driver's attempt to Islamicize the origins of another religion's holy place reminded me of Iranians' internal conflict over their history and their faith.

Iranians are an immensely proud and supremely nationalistic people, men and women who glory in their nation's ancient past and have always been dismissive of, if not downright racist toward, the Bedouin Arabs who brought them their faith. Even the most pious, and even some of the clerics, have been traditionally anti-Arab, which explains to some extent an Islamic Iran's difficulty in maintaining good relations with other Muslim countries in the region. It also creates a contradiction, in revering an Arab prophet and Arab Shia saints whose people Iranians believe to be inferior. Some of the youth of Iran today, who chafe at the restrictions on their lives and disdain the theocracy that places them there, and who dislike Arabs anyway, look to their pre-Islamic past both for assurance that their national-ism is founded and as a symbol of protest against the religion that they feel was forced on them by Mohammad's armies centuries ago and by the ayatollahs today.

There is no greater symbol of Persian glory than the Farvahar, which was even a part of the shah's Pahlavi coat of arms. One sees the winged sun pendants around the necks of young men and women everywhere—every jewelry shop in Iran sells silver and gold versions in all sizes. These young Iranians are not Zoroastrian, of course; nor could they convert even if they wanted to, for the religion does not allow conversion and even excommunicates adherents who marry outside the faith. And they may forget, or be ignorant of the fact, that like almost all state-supported organized religions with a clerical hierarchy, it has a sordid history, particularly in the behavior of its priests, much as Islam does in the behavior of some of its mullahs and sheikhs today.

We had only one social obligation in Yazd, one that we actually looked forward to, and that was to visit the Khatami family: the widow of Mohammad Sadoughi, the late Friday prayer leader; her son, also named Mohammad and who had, since his father's passing, finally donned his forebears' priestly garb; and Khatami's ninety-year-old mother. Ali Khatami, who had driven us down from Tehran, was, of course, going to be present. We took a taxi from the hotel to the old city, where their ancient and beautifully restored house stood behind the main mosque, and the driver had assured me he knew the way to the former prayer leader's house, which was all I told him of our destination. When we arrived, though, I saw that he had brought us to the wrong address.

"That's the house down the alley," he said, "the Friday prayer leader."

I realized that even though Sadoughi had been dead less than a few months, this cabbie had moved on, having brought us to the *new* Friday prayer leader's house. But I recognized the mosque across the street, so we got out anyway and crossed over, passing through the mosque courtyard and to the alley behind, where Ali came out to greet us. The Revolutionary Guard sentry post, which had been occupied twenty-four hours a day by an AK-47-wielding guardsman when I had visited in the past, was gone. The family was gathered in the informal den, including Reza Khatami, another of the former president's brothers who had been arrested in the post-2009 election unrest and was *mamn'ou-khorooj*, forbidden from leaving Iran. We sat down to glasses of tea, some of the famous Yazdi pastries, and bowls of fruit.

Maryam Khatami quickly peeled an orange for Khash, who was happy to have it as he eyed her son suspiciously. He had seen mullahs on the streets, and had already met the former president in his office, but I suspect he was curious about the robes, and particularly the turban, for he always insisted that I take my hat off whenever I wore one. He warmed up soon enough, though, and Mohammad, a bright, genial, and soft-hearted man, even enticed him into his arms. Maryam made some small talk with Karri, in broken English and the Farsi that Karri by now understood, but we mostly chatted about family, and the tone was solemn, as is expected with Iranian families in mourning, which for Yazdis lasts a full year. Reza Khatami was interested in U.S. politics, the presidential election in 2012, and whether I thought President Obama was doing a good job and whether he'd be reelected. Whatever conversation we had about Iranian politics was couched with careful words and accompanied by knowing looks and assenting nods, for we all knew that the house, where the Supreme Leader used to stay when he was in town, was in all probability, no, *definitely*, bugged.

Before we took our leave, we went into a guest bedroom, where the senescent Mrs. Khatami, née Ziaie, was resting. She had recently suffered a stroke and lost almost all her sight, but was nevertheless engaged and very curious about Khash, whom she said she wished she could see. Karri said a few words in Farsi, her accent apparently amusing to the others in the room, and we left, saying our goodbyes to all the Khatamis, me a little sad about the somber mood in the house and the dramatic change in all their lives: not just the death in the family, but the way the once hopeful and ascendant reformists had been brought down by a vengeful regime that couldn't abide even the gentlest of criticism. One didn't feel sorry for the family necessarily, despite the harassment, the calls to Evin prison for hours-long interrogations that Reza—married to the granddaughter of the founder of the republic, no less—had to deal with, and the fall from grace in a regime they had helped create. No, the family would be all right—

better off, in fact, than the vast majority of their countrymen. One simply felt sorry for the country, and Karri, the outsider, concurred. Plus, Mohammad Sadoughi's newfound clerical role meant I had one less friend on Facebook, which, he embarrassingly confessed, glancing at the iPad in his hands, he had now been obliged to abandon.

We left Yazd the next day by taxi, since I discovered that it would cost only about sixty dollars to go to Esfahan, some two hundred miles away. Our driver, a pleasant enough man, had an ample supply of roasted watermelon seeds on the dash and proceeded to plow through the bag, one seed at a time, cracking it between his front teeth and extracting the tiny nut with his tongue, almost all the way to our destination. As such, he was rather laconic, not even expressing interest or irritation when Khash screamed bloody murder. He would only smile, and nod his head. "Kids," he'd say, knowingly.

But when we reached the outskirts of Esfahan, a large city with an industrial base, he grew loquacious, complaining that the Esfahanis were mean people and the world's biggest liars. He didn't know our hotel, even though I told him it was close to the main square and within walking distance of the famous Safavid-era Si-o-sel Pol, or "Thirty-three Bridge" (named for its thirty-three arches over the Zayandeh River), and he insisted he would simply stop and ask for directions, even though we would be intentionally misled. He'd have to ask a number of different people, he said, and would hope that a few wrong directions would cancel one another out and he would eventually be put on the right path. Karri laughed when I translated, assuming it was intercity rivalry speaking. Iranians are as tribal and chauvinistic about their hometowns as, say, New Yorkers are about midwesterners, whose abode some derisively refer to as the "fly-over zone." Or as some Londoners might be about Mancunians—or any northerners, for that matter.

Anyway, we stopped at a traffic circle, and our driver stepped out to ask the driver of another car, parked just in front us. After much waving of hands, our driver returned and proclaimed, "He lied through his teeth. He told me to go back the way we came, which would take us *out* of the city." Karri was unsure whether he had intentionally been given bad directions, or his prejudice didn't allow him to believe what he was told, or the other driver had a different, albeit longer, route in mind. But when we stopped again, and got completely different directions, she began to wonder. By the fourth time we stopped to ask—at which point I recognized the main road leading to the hotel and could guide the driver—she was genuinely tickled. How could it be, she said to me, that our driver was right? Coincidence, I assured her. But the surly receptionists at our hotel, so unlike every other Iranian she had met, made her think that perhaps Esfahanis were indeed a different breed.

The hotel, once called the Shah Abbas Hotel, for the Safavid king who had made the city his capital and built most of it, was at one time a grand Persian structure, an old estate converted to a hotel in the late 1960s and early 1970s. Renamed after the revolution the Abbassi Hotel—the regime seems incapable of even pronouncing the word *shah*—it was virtually unchanged from when I first stayed there, as a visiting student on Christmas holiday from boarding school in London. In 1972. Everything in the hotel, including the furniture in the rooms, seemed to be exactly as it was then, and the only care taken by the owners, a semiprivate insurance company, appeared to be in the gardens, which were as magnificent as ever, their persimmon and quince trees fat with fruit that greeted us when we ventured out for a cup of tea.

It was too late to go out and wander the old city, so after a long sojourn in the fragrant gardens, where Khash delighted in running around, especially on the grass where signs were posted to keep off, we decided to stay in for dinner and put Khash to bed early. Having subsisted on a diet of Persian food for days, delicious as it was, we craved something different, so we went to the cafeteria by the lobby, where I could swear the low furniture and tables were the same ones I had sat on and at forty years ago. The hamburger, a huge but thin concoction in a bun the size of a Frisbee that just had to be custom baked for the hotel, was also exactly as I remembered it, from when my older brother, his American classmate David Smith, and I all ordered the same thing on the first night we arrived in the city by bus from Tehran.

The hotel is a short walk from most tourist attractions, the main one being Naghsh-e Jahan Square, the largest in the world after Tiananmen in Beijing, built by Shah Abbas in the late sixteenth century. In keeping with the schizophrenic naming method of the Islamic revolutionaries, its name was changed from Shah Square to the current "Image of the World" Square, but it is also known, or the regime would like it to be known, as Imam Square. Referring to Imam Khomeini, presumably, and not to one of the imams, or saints, of the Shia faith.

Or perhaps the current Supreme Leader, Ali Khamenei, or his supporters, have designs on the honorific and the immortalization that the name of the square might provide. On the outside walls of the exquisite Ali Qapu palace, on whose columned terrace Abbas once sat and watched the polo games in the square below, are painted two large modern portraits, of a size to be seen from every corner of the vast square, of Ayatollahs Khomeini and Khamenei. Imams both? As Karri pointed out, neither had anything whatsoever to do with Esfahan or the square, and their likenesses were completely out of place in the environment. It was as if Silvio Berlusconi had had his portrait painted on the side of the Duomo in Florence. She was genuinely offended, not because she held any specific antipathy toward mullahs or even the two Supreme Leaders of the revolution, but because their images defaced a beautiful historic monument.

I hadn't thought of that before, on my previous visits to the city, and perhaps as an Iranian one simply gets used to public spots being festooned with portraits of the nation's leaders, even during the time of the shahs. Perhaps journalists and other foreign visitors, expecting an autocratic regime if not an outright dictatorship, don't find it odd either, having seen so many buildings in Tehran and elsewhere with immense portraits painted on the sides, not just of the two Supreme Leaders but of every revolutionary figure, as well as many martyrs of the Iran-Iraq War. I decided it took someone like Karri, neither a visitor nor a true resident, the unlikeliest of tourists in this tourist town, to be offended by the images at the same time she was breathless with wonderment at the sheer beauty of the place. Wonderment also, and a little sadness, at how there could be no other tourists, no one to witness this beauty, other than Iranians themselves.

Much has been written about Esfahan, about the magnificence of the square and the mosques and palaces that surround it, and it has a magical quality that words and images can't quite describe. Nesf-e-Jahan, as Persians still vaingloriously refer to it: "Half the World." At one time—at the height of the Safavids' power and a revived empire—it must have indeed seemed half the world, if not more. The Florence of Persia, Karri proclaimed it, not the first person to recognize it as such, just as we walked past a somewhat faded fresco, painted on the side of one of the Safavid palaces, of a European gentleman of the sixteenth century, with plumed hat and a small dog on a leash. A European ambassador to the court of Abbas, no doubt, at a time when the sight of Europeans in Iran's capital was possibly more common than four hundred years later, even when direct flights connect most European capitals to Iran's.

We put the Esfahani tendency to misdirect visitors to the test only once more, for Karri has an acute sense of direction, and we walked almost everywhere without getting lost. After visiting one museum, however, I felt disoriented and asked a passing man how to get to Imam Square. He pointed straight ahead, but Karri, by now as prejudiced as any Iranian, was sure he had lied, so I asked a young couple strolling toward us, and they pointed in the opposite direction. "Make a left at the next street," the man said.

Karri laughed, saying there was no point asking again and that she would get us back to the hotel. She chose a third way, cutting across a park, where we stopped for Khash to play on the swings in the meticulously clean, rubber-floored playground, that led us straight to the back of the hotel. The surly doorman and receptionists greeted us with barely a smile, but it was almost a relief not to feel obligated to be polite, as one does everywhere else in Iran. Khash was probably a little disappointed that he didn't receive as much attention in Esfahan as he did elsewhere, except for the stares and whispers on the street. Even the waiters in the hotel restaurants, grizzled old types who had probably served me back in 1972, hardly paid any attention to him. One morning I caught one of them trying to conceal a smile as he walked away, just as Khash had thrown a piece of bread on the floor, and laughed heartily, so I knew their demeanor was all show. The hostess, who sat at a small table just outside the breakfast room, finally couldn't resist showing her true colors either: that same morning she leaped out of her chair and hugged him as he ran down the corridor yelling, me hot on his heels and feigning embarrassment at my unruly American child.

I always suspected that Esfahanis, known in Iran for their business acumen and even their cunning, were simply masking their true selves by being standoffish and sometimes even rude. The last time I had been in Naghsh-e Jahan Square, in 2009, I was with Ann Curry and an NBC News crew. We had seen families picnicking on the grass, children playing in the fountains, and overtly religious families—the women in chadors and the men bearded and solemn—lounging about and drinking tea or eating ice cream and *faloudeh,* a uniquely Iranian iced concoction of starch noodles, rose water, and lemon juice, none of them paying us much attention beyond their curious stares. Ann approached one group of black-clad women and quickly fell into conversation with them. They turned out to be as friendly as any other Iranian family, showing her how to wear the chador, complimenting her on her beauty, and telling me, standing by, that she looked better veiled than bareheaded. But of *course* she did.

They also invited us to their home, an invitation we were unable

to accept as we were on a tight NBC-mandated schedule, disappoint-
ing as that was to Ann. It is an experience that many tourists and visitors to Iran share—Iranians, even deeply pious ones, opening up to a
foreigner, treating them as guests of honor in their country no matter
their origin, and displaying the kind of hospitality to strangers that
is unheard of in the West. It goes beyond and is distinct from the
uniquely Persian *ta'arouf* that one also might encounter, although less
frequently as a foreigner. Karri and I enjoyed our brief respite from
that hospitality and didn't engage much with Esfahanis, but we also
recognized, in their veneer of arrogant pride and haughty attitude,
the general demeanor of those who live in what they believe is the
greatest city on earth, indeed, according to them, *half the world*. We live
in New York, after all, and have been to Paris.

We took a taxi back to Tehran, double the price of the taxi from
Yazd for a distance only a little farther, but I knew the driver might
spend hours just driving through Tehran to get to our apartment and
then hours getting out of Tehran on the way back. In fact, he'd probably spend more hours in Tehran than on the highway between the
two cities. We made good time to South Tehran, stopping only for
gas and a quick cappuccino for us and a prayer break for the driver at
a rest area—not unlike those on U.S. highways or the autostradas in
Italy, only cleaner and better stocked.

Khash slept most of the way. When we finally made it home,
after a couple of hours navigating Tehran highways, he shrieked
with delight at seeing our building and ran through the lobby to our
ground-floor apartment door with a big smile on his face. We realized, after we settled in and unpacked, that it wasn't just Khash who
thought of this little apartment as home: we did too. Life in Tehran
had become, finally, normal.

11

POLITRICKS

—

We should listen in earnest to what other cultures offer.

—SEYED MOHAMMAD KHATAMI, PRESIDENT OF

THE ISLAMIC REPUBLIC OF IRAN, 1997–2005

Within a week of our settling down in Tajrish, former president Khatami had invited us to tea at his office in Jamaran, not too far from us, in a compound owned by the Imam Khomeini foundation. Khatami, since stepping down from the presidency in 2005, was slowly being nudged away from relevance to the political culture of the republic. First the Ahmadinejad administration took away the office space in a presidential building (less than a hundred yards from our apartment, coincidentally) that had been granted him by the Supreme Leader. Then, in 2009, when he announced he was seeking the presidency again, he received death (and other) threats. Many Iranians believed that he withdrew from that race because of the threats.

But the truth was that he had always said he wouldn't run if Mousavi did, and he withdrew as soon as Mousavi announced his own candidacy. Subsequent to the elections of 2009, Khatami became something of a persona non grata in Iranian politics—his support for Mousavi, with whom he campaigned, his steadfast support for those imprisoned during the protests against the election results, and his continued insistence that all political prisoners must be freed and the crackdown on civil liberties lifted provoked the ire of the establishment. As a result, he was severely restricted, both physically and in terms of his ability to communicate with the public. The Iranian media were officially banned from even mentioning the names of the two reform candidates, Mousavi and Karroubi, who were languishing under house arrest; mentioning Khatami, therefore, particularly to promote his message, might mean crossing a boundary that few reporters or editors wished to traverse.

I had visited Khatami on the previous occasions I traveled to Iran, even after the elections, when he was under close state surveillance and banned from travel, and I was familiar with the compound, his staff, and even with the Revolutionary Guards in civilian clothes who provided him security. Karri had met him, too, when he visited New York in 2006. But it was going to be the first encounter with a president for Khash, who hadn't yet turned one on the day we headed to Jamaran.

Khatami was genuinely happy to meet Khash, whom he'd asked about when we were still in New York, and to catch up with Karri in his somewhat broken English, and in the hour we spent together, our conversation centered on family and on the Iran he loved. He expressed a certain satisfaction—one that other nationalist Iranians shared—that I had decided to spend a year in Iran, with my family at that, and happiness that Karri, whom he had urged years ago to visit Iran soon, was finally here. But he also referred, a little obliquely, to the state of affairs in Iran—to the "uncomfortable" political climate, as he put it, and the authorities' absolute intolerance of any dissent. When he mentioned these topics, he'd look up at the ceiling, as he had done in meetings with me before, and with a little shake of his head indicate that we were being listened to. I didn't want to say much, for I felt that my recorded words should not cause him more trouble than he already had, and so other than replying to his questions, mainly about what I was interested in writing about, I didn't volunteer much on what I thought had happened to Iran since he left office. By the time we said our goodbyes, his present to Khash of a gold coin in hand (the traditional gift for a newborn family member), I was saddened that the Iranian regime's tolerance of criticism was so low that a former president, who had garnered over 70 percent of the popular vote in two elections, couldn't be trusted, and that he could no longer trust the regime he had served.

Another day, not long before we left Iran, President Khatami told me over tea that to understand Iran, you had to understand the culture. "We have always wanted freedom, democracy, human rights, and so on," he said, "but we have never instituted the culture for them." He continued, somewhat wistfully, "We haven't figured out how to reconcile those concepts with our culture. We can't be completely modern, or reject all modernity. Neither works in our culture, as much as we might try." Khatami, whom people had referred to, either admiringly or disdainfully, as a philosopher-king when he was in office, recognized his political impotence in 2011 and was under no illusions that he might be a factor in reconciling Persian culture with the concepts of democracy and freedom, if that indeed ever happened. It wasn't just that his activity had been restricted by the state; he openly admitted that his time had come and gone, that the youth were hardly aware of him or of his ideas about Iran as a democratic, albeit still Islamic, state anymore, and that a new generation of politicians would have to take on the challenge of reform. He did indicate to me, and I don't think he was being overly optimistic, that he thought he could have some influence on those new leaders—as a philosopher, rather than as a king or even a kingmaker.

The culture he referred to, which he is proud of and wanted Karri to see and experience, is one of beauty, poetry, hospitality, and manners, yet was still very much formed by Shia Islam: mournful, strict, and austere. Islamic culture never fully supplanted an ancient Persian culture that revered power and authority, whether exercised by tribal and village chiefs, priests, or kings and "kings of kings," and that still hides its adherents' true character with its uncompromising rules for public behavior. The political culture of Iran has always been authoritarian, and what Khatami was saying was that reconciling Persian culture with the concept of democracy meant that the political culture had to change, yes, but also that other elements of Persian culture and even of Shia Islam (which unlike Salafist or Wahhabi Islam actually allows for interpretation) had to adapt. Khatami, in his terms of office, had himself been guilty of succumbing to the pull of traditional culture, when it urged him to stand down in the face of higher authority and to "know his place"; and he makes no excuse for his failures to institute long-lasting change. But he believes that his bringing the issue of culture to the fore will at least have an effect on how it is viewed in future political discussions. It was clear to us both, though, that it was the young men and women of Iran who would bring about such change, not the aging theocrats or politicians who ruled over them now. Less clear was exactly who those young people were, in a society where three-quarters of the population was under thirty.

The girl faced me, seated at a small table next to ours in the outdoor café at Hesabi Park, another old mansion in Elahieh, North Tehran, whose gardens have been converted to a public art space. She wore her hair in a beehive, and the Chanel scarf dangling from it did not conceal her bleached-blond hair and matching blond eyebrows. Her perfume was overpowering, so much so that Karri thought we should change tables when another became available, and her tight manteau very much accentuated an hourglass figure. The Sister Sledge song "He's the Greatest Dancer" came to my mind, especially the line, "Halston, Gucci, Fiorucci," except in Tehran today it'd be "Chanel,

Gucci, Louis [Vuitton]," for the men and women, great dancers or not, who are "dressed to kill." The Gucci handbag on the floor by her feet, the fat diamond ring on her slender and perfectly manicured finger, the conspicuously labeled Chanel sunglasses perched above her forehead, the surgically enhanced breasts and altered nose—nose piercing included—were all signs of the new moneyed class; the nouveau riche of Iran are very riche indeed.

Her companion, a dark-skinned chubby man with a shaved head, Bluetooth headset glued to his ear, had his back to me. I could see, though, the gargantuan gold watch on his hairy wrist and his Ray-Bans and iPhone on the table by his side, within easy reach of his stubby, ringless fingers. He seemed bored, fiddling with his iPhone and car keys as the girl carried on speaking, just out of earshot, which annoyed me no end, for I really wanted to hear what she was saying. Khash tried to get her attention—she had to be the first pretty girl who hadn't fawned all over him since we returned to Tehran from our travels, and when he finally succeeded, she gave him a big smile and said something to the man before she lifted her coffee cup, carefully sipping her cappuccino through pursed lips to avoid disturbing her perfectly drawn lipstick. He turned around to look at us and smiled too before returning his attention, or whatever he had of it, to his girlfriend.

Who were these people? They weren't expat Iranians home for a visit to family and friends. They weren't the middle class who shopped for counterfeit designer goods at malls everywhere in Tehran—theirs were the real things. They weren't religious or tradition-minded Iranians, and they weren't quite the secular Westernized Iranians I knew both in Iran and abroad. They were a new breed of Iranians, but ones I felt no connection to whatsoever, and not for any classist or snobbish reasons. Nouveau didn't bother me, and neither did riche; I just couldn't place them in the Iranian culture I knew, or in the political culture that Khatami was talking about. If to Persians life was shameful, as the poet said, these Persians showed no sign of believing it. Whenever I was with Karri in Tehran, I always felt more of an outsider, less Iranian and more American, perhaps because we spoke English and because her presence by my side was a constant reminder of my life as someone other than an Iranian; but I never felt more of an alien than when confronted by Iranians I couldn't identify with.

Even though I had never really lived in Iran, and certainly never until now as an adult with my own family and in my own apartment, it had come to feel completely natural, especially if I was out on my own. Karri, too, now related to ordinary Iranians: to mothers in the park with whom she struck up conversations, whether or not they spoke English well enough; to shopkeepers who patiently counted out change for her, making sure she understood that she wasn't being ripped off; and to cab drivers who did their best to accommodate her and Khash, even taking directions from her, something Iranian men are loath to do, on the best route back to our apartment.

But we couldn't identify with or understand people like the ones in the café at Hesabi Park, or others like them whom we came across, gross caricatures of modern Iranians, even though in their outlook on life, they might resemble, at least superficially, certain Westerners more than, say, the passengers on the crowded buses we rode, or the chador-clad women in the parks we frequented, who smiled and nodded at Karri as their children attempted to play with Khash.

I could relate to the young soldiers I overheard on the bus one day, bemoaning the fact that they were being sent to a far-flung province—the dangerous Sistan va Baluchistan, on the border with Pakistan, which was infested with Sunni separatist rebels and the terrorist Jundullah group; to the street hawker on the same bus who was selling kitchen sponges in the no-man's-land between the women's and men's section, and who, after completing a few sales to the women, turned to the men and shouted, "I guess the gentlemen on *this* bus don't do dishes"; even to the Revolutionary Guards up the street from us who wanted their picture taken with Khash and who asked me, incredulously, if it was true that the U.S. military was afraid of them. Of *them*?

Yes, they were all Iranians to me, even the delivery van driver I got into a screaming match with on the street one day, when he repeatedly honked at me as I pushed Khash up a steep hill, the narrow sidewalk impassable with a stroller.

"Shut the fuck up!" I screamed at him. "Where the fuck do you think I should walk?"

Karri pleaded with me to move on and not get into a fight.

It's my country, I thought, *and I'll fight with whomever I please.*

The driver stopped his car and yelled back at me, "On my head! You can walk on my head, or better yet, on *Khamenei's* head!"

I had to laugh at that, and when I related the exchange to Ali Khatami, he laughed, too. Yes, it is my country, and these are my people. All of them expressed an Iranian character that I knew and was comfortable with and that, to my mild surprise, Karri had come to understand and was comfortable with, too.

Many of the new rich, I knew, were either apolitical or hoped for the political status quo to endure. After all, they benefited from it, and social restrictions didn't seem to crimp their lifestyles. They were unlikely to receive anonymous calls on their iPhone 4S's from the intelligence services, telling them not to speak to this or that person, to be careful about what they said on the phone, or patronizingly, to be a "good boy." One day a young friend—he had just finished his mandatory national service in the army—received a call on his ancient Nokia that threw him into a panic and prevented him from even answering his phone or texts for the following week. "They hear everything," he said to me later, visibly shaken; although a reformist, he was a strict Muslim who had never questioned the regime's legitimacy, not in his twenty-odd years of life under it.

The man and woman in Hesabi Park, and the two young women at the table next to us at Terrace, an upscale continental restaurant, with matching beehives, nose jobs, makeup, and Hermès Kelly bags—authentic ones, I'm sure—who nibbled at salads that were more expensive than the daily grocery bill of most families, were unlikely to do anything controversial. They are unlikely to be part of the change that any person residing in Iran long enough can recognize is bound to come, whether the conservative ayatollahs like it or not; less likely even than the apathetic youth who have lost hope in their country but linger on, politics very much on their minds—it is politics, after all, that has given them their apathy; and less likely than the men and women whose only defiance of the state is in their dress, and who venture into crowded public spaces and are harassed by the morality police. The new rich, for all intents and purposes, live strictly in their self-contained bubbles.

Not all the rich, or even all the new rich, are like them, of course. They are a new breed, I've been told by friends, apart from what many Iranians would recognize as Iranian. One friend, a frustrated businessman who despises the regime even as he continues to deal with it, told me that when the day finally came that the regime fell, he would personally rip them to shreds, these fellow Iranians who prospered under the Islamic regime while remaining immune to its mores, indifferent to the country's corruption and mismanagement, and oblivious to the difficulties ordinary Iranians face. They are complicit, he insisted, in every crime the regime has committed.

A rather severe reaction, I thought. He claimed that they were amoral—which they perhaps were—and un-Iranian. But "un-Iranian" today is "very Iranian" tomorrow, for virtually no one in Iran below the age of thirty would be recognizably Iranian to my parents' generation, especially not to those abroad, just as the Iranian American cast of *Shahs of Sunset* are unrecognizable to most older Iranians who live in Tehran. Khatami had never even heard of the show, while some young Tehranis had. I have friends who are rich, poor, and in between, who are new rich and old money, who are religious and secular, who are regime supporters and antiregime activists—and my inability to relate to that new segment of society was my issue, not theirs, and it was irrelevant to their politics or their future influence on the politics of the country, which is bound toward a more democratic system and which they, the new rich, may or may not adjust to. The Occupy Movement didn't arrive in Tehran while we were there, although the state media reported heavily on it, hypocritically, as an example of the rot in liberal democracies; but it surely will, once, or if, the reform movement is back on its feet, or when the nation finally just gets fed up with its state of affairs, social, economic, and political.

Much like the opposition during the shah's time, whatever movement one day springs from the streets—and youth will be its vanguard, as they were in the shah's time—will rail against an unjust autocratic, as well as economic, system. And any real change may well have to come from those streets. As more than one Iranian said to me, "Iran is a kettle on the boil, and the ayatollahs know it: either they will have to bring it down to a simmer, or it will boil over into the streets." If it does boil over into the streets, others maintained, it will unlikely be a repeat of 2009; it will be more like 1979. But while many of the new rich fled the revolution that overthrew the shah's system, it is unclear what will happen to the new rich in a new revolution. Or if they will even have anywhere to go.

Meanwhile, politics played no small part in our lives in Iran, more in mine than in Karri's, although she was constantly aware of politics throughout our stay. She was angry at Iran for treating its citizens like errant children, angry at her own country for imposing sanctions on Iran that seemed to affect only the people, including her, and angry most of all that anyone would even talk about a war with Iran, much less a war that, some predicted, Israel might launch while we lived there. It is impossible to live in Iran and not be aware of international politics, domestic politics, the nuclear crisis, and talk of war, and not to be anxious about a dangerous future. An American war with Iran, or even just a military strike, would affect Iranians far more than Americans.

The assassination of another nuclear scientist during the summer we were there; a mysterious explosion at a military base, acknowledged as part of the Western and Israeli campaign to prevent Iran from developing nuclear weapons; and the deepening sense that something would have to give in Iran's fight with the West made Tehran a place where, although we were comfortable and reasonably unafraid, we worried. That was even without the "anonymous" or "private number" calls I received on my mobile phone and the ever-present threat that one day those government officials calling might decide that I was actually a spy, like Amir Hekmati, the Iranian American who traveled to Iran in August and was arrested two weeks later. The authorities had refused me permission to work; at what point, Karri continually wondered, would they decide I had to be up to *something* if I continued to stay in Iran?

She was shaken by the news that an Iranian American, simply visiting his elderly grandmother, had been arrested, not when he arrived at the airport but a full two weeks after he set foot in Tehran. "If they knew he was a spy, then why didn't they arrest him at the airport?" she asked me.

I explained that his case was radically different from mine, that he had served in the U.S. Marines, had military identification on him, and had served in Iraq and Afghanistan, where Iranian spies undoubtedly know the name and rank, and probably serial number of every Iranian American in the U.S. military. I found it odd that he had dared come to Iran in the first place, no matter how much he missed his family, at a time when the media was full of reports of CIA and other agencies' clandestine activities inside the country.

Karri agreed that it was odd, but she was not convinced that I was therefore clear of any danger. "They gave him an Iranian passport, they let him in, they let him stay at his grandmother's for two weeks, and then they arrest him?" she said. "Something is wrong with that picture, and it means it can happen to anyone." (Hekmati was subsequently sentenced to death, but in mid-2012 his sentence was overturned. He is, however, as of this writing, still in jail.)

I did receive a call one day in October from someone at the Supreme National Security Council relating to my journalism, asking if I would write an essay refuting an op-ed by John Bolton (former U.S. ambassador to the UN) that appeared in *The Guardian,* on the alleged 2011 Iranian plot to assassinate the Saudi ambassador to Washington.

Fuck you was my first reaction, although I didn't voice it. "I don't have a press pass," I said instead.

That could be arranged, the caller assured me.

"Well," I said, "I can't really do this."

He was unperturbed, and perhaps my tone hadn't reflected the *fuck you* one I wanted it to. "How about placing an anonymous piece in the paper, then?" he asked.

You've got to be kidding me, I thought. After depriving me of work all this time, they now wanted me to be in their service? But I politely extricated myself from the call and from any obligation, insisting that I was in Iran not to work but to spend time with my family. It probably became another mark against me.

On another occasion I received a call from a newspaperman I didn't know who worked for a conservative but anti-Ahmadinejad paper. I have no idea how he got my number. The call concerned Fareed Zakaria, who had just left Tehran after interviewing Ahmadinejad; I had had dinner with the CNN journalist at his hotel the night before his meeting with the president. Ahmadinejad's rivals, in government and in the media, were having a field day, criticizing him for agreeing to the CNN interview and criticizing his administration for allowing Fareed a visa in the first place. Fareed had sympathized with the Green Movement and had been a harsh critic of the regime for its crackdown on protesters, but the conservatives didn't care that much about his views. Rather, his visit and his interview were ammunition that they could use against a president they had come to despise, mostly for his defiance of the Supreme Leader, his big sulk, and his dismissive attitude toward anyone, ayatollahs included, who excoriated him.

The caller seemed to know that I had seen Fareed and, curiously, wanted to know what hotel he had stayed in. "I've called all the major hotels in town where foreigners stay," he said, "and no one has a record of him."

I replied that I couldn't divulge that information, and that if he had any questions, he should ask the Culture Ministry, which had approved the trip, or ask Fareed himself, via e-mail to his Web site.

"I won't quote you," he said, finally getting to the point, "but I want to know if the interview was Zakaria's idea or the president's."

I'd rather not be quoted, even anonymously, I told him, aware that either or both of our phones were being listened to by someone else, pro- or anti-Ahmadinejad, it didn't matter.

As a relative of Khatami, I was already known to be a supporter of reform and of the Green Movement, but the last thing I needed was to get caught up in the conservative infighting that was going on all year, in the politics of divide and conquer that the Supreme Leader seemed to have decided would ensure his supremacy. Ahmadinejad's sulk; the conservatives' attack on him and his allies for that insubordination and for his refusal to share any power with them; the Leader's refusal to let them impeach him but his quiet encouragement of attacks against him—all were elements of a drama that it was best to avoid participating in at all costs. Already too many actors in that drama had ended up in jail, or been harassed by one or another security agency—and these were actors who had supported (or remained silent over) the crackdown on the reformists. The annus horribilis of the political elite that began with a potentially fatal—not only to the protagonists Ahmadinejad and Khamenei but to the system itself—clash between two competing powers was eating away at the core of the revolution: the regime's thirty-year-long unity of purpose. Infighting and palace intrigue had long been a staple of Iran's political culture, all the way back to the ancients, but like everything else Persian, it had mostly been kept private and hidden from the public until now. Perhaps Khatami's hope that the political culture would change was coming true after all, though not through any willful act by the regime.

But I had no intention of becoming an unintended victim of political upheaval, let alone a wholesale change in the culture. The fact was, I did know whose idea the interview was, for Fareed had told me that the president had specifically asked for him, and him personally, to come to Tehran to interview him, in what appeared to be an effort at public relations; he wanted to counter the notion that he was weak and no longer relevant, and he wanted to revel in the spotlight of the international media, something that he had craved from the beginning of his presidency and now sensed he might be in danger of losing. The anti-Ahmadinejad crowd sensed it, too, but I didn't want to be the person who confirmed it for them. Ahmadinejad still had allies in the Intelligence Ministry and in the Revolutionary Guards, and pissing them off was a far bigger risk for me and my family than the other potentially political acts I regularly undertook, such as visiting Khatami, dining with foreign ambassadors, and accompanying reform politicians in their think tanks.

Indeed, while Karri brushed up on her Farsi at the Dehkhoda Institute, I would often head down to the offices of Iranian Diplomacy—assuming our baby-sitter showed up; it was a sort of political think tank, an NGO, and an influential Web site all rolled into one. These were afternoons when both of us would be liberated from the not entirely unpleasant chore of keeping Khash constantly amused, and also from the constant companionship with each other that living in Tehran, both unemployed, had somehow imposed on

us. Karri mostly enjoyed her Farsi lessons at the famous school—
where various foreign diplomats, some Iranophile foreign students,
and a handful of Iranian Americans registered to learn the language
as taught by a stern, unforgiving taskmistresses—particularly once
she became accustomed to the teacher's style. The woman actually
had Karri in tears the first day of class after berating her for unpre-
paredness: it was Karri's fortieth birthday, a difficult enough occasion for anyone, and more so away from friends and family; and she
was taken aback, after witnessing *ta'arouf* and Iranian hospitality so
often, by the style of Persian teaching, which is rather more Victo-
rian than progressive. But after that it was all business; the teacher,
perhaps shocked by Karri's initial reaction, became more courteous,
and Karri looked forward to learning more Farsi.

Meanwhile, I looked forward to spending an uninterrupted
afternoon at one of Iran's only independent political and media orga-
nizations. It's a reform-oriented one, staffed by former government
officials from the Rafsanjani and Khatami administrations who somehow have escaped the ignominy of a prison term while maintaining a
fierce opposition to the Ahmadinejad government, and are even critical of the regime itself at times, albeit in subtle ways. Presided over
by my friend Sadegh Kharrazi, the gregarious former deputy foreign
minister, ambassador, nuclear negotiator, war veteran, and fanatical
nationalist, the center brings together analysts and political figures
(none associated with Ahmadinejad except for a professor at Tehran
University, a classmate and friend of the president) for monthly conferences and the occasional off-the-record briefing. I had no doubt
that among its dozens of employees there were spies or informants,
perhaps unwilling, working with the Intelligence Ministry and probably the Revolutionary Guards, too, and the offices were probably
bugged; harsh criticism of Iranian policy under Ahmadinejad was
voiced, to be sure, but apart from that only a strong defense of the
nation and its rights and even assertions of loyalty to the system. And

THE MINISTRY OF GUIDANCE INVITES YOU TO NOT STAY

no one is more loyal to the nation, to the revolution, and to the ideals it once promised than Kharrazi, who—despite his unwavering support of Khatami, whom he sees as an adviser every week—is also loyal to the Supreme Leader, whose son is married to one of Kharrazi's sisters, and whom he also sees regularly. It makes Kharrazi a rather unique figure in Iranian politics: enormously influential across the political spectrum, a reformist and democrat at heart, but true to the entrenched political culture of the country, a pragmatic operator who believes that the nation, its security, and its interests always trump politics. He is not pragmatic enough, though, to fully conceal his pure contempt for Ahmadinejad and his government.

The conferences at Iranian Diplomacy, which always begin with an invocation from the Koran, played on an iPhone placed in front of a microphone, are mostly concerned with foreign policy, and the invited speakers are experts in the field or former government officials. The views expressed and the debates that follow are summarized and distributed via nicely printed full-color booklets as well as on the Web. Foreigners, particularly diplomats stationed in Iran, are eager to attend or to meet with the staff and their associates, but none are ever invited, indicative of the Iranian paranoia that surrounds contact with anyone the state believes might be hostile to it—essentially, anyone foreign.

What struck me at these gatherings was both the high level of sophistication of Iranian officials and their overreliance on facts and figures, statistics and history—an empirical approach taught and emphasized in Iranian schools and universities—at the expense of more theoretical analysis and imaginative thinking. It explained to me, a little, why Iranian politicians are rarely truly innovative, and why Iranian diplomats, despite their skills, have made very little progress in relations with the outside world in the thirty-plus years since the Islamic Revolution. For instance, at a conference on the Persian Gulf (a favorite topic of xenophobe Iranians), the former commander of the Revolutionary Guards' Navy during Khatami's presidency, Hossein Alaie, displayed impressively thorough knowledge of U.S. warships, their missions in that body of water, and even the first and last names of every commander of every U.S. Navy ship in the region. The information, while impressive, was not particularly revealing or even relevant.

It has always been this way in Iran, since before the time of the ayatollahs and Islamic-approved curricula: know the facts, but don't present opinions that might conflict with any shah- or state-approved message. And since it has also always been impossible for anyone to know exactly what might offend at any given time, leaders have most often kept their opinions to themselves. Ahmadinejad is a glaring exception, and his fall from grace over the year, perhaps even leading to future legal entanglements (as his imprisoned aides have discovered since we left Iran), may serve to deter others.

But it's not just terror that keeps Iranians from expressing their opinions or engaging in creative thought; it's the paradoxical nature of Persian culture. While creative thinking abounds in Iran, it is often kept close to the chest for fear of not just political repercussions but ridicule. Hence a culture that reveres poetry above all tends to disdain artistic endeavors as impractical; the great Persian poets are quoted every day, and their contributions to math, science, and medicine are almost equally heralded, but no consideration is given to the idea that perhaps it was their creative thinking that led to advances in science in the glory years of the Persian empires—advances that Iranians boast of but that have ceased, leaving Iranians at a loss to explain why.

Alaie's Revolutionary Guards do not report to the president. Rather, they report directly to the Supreme Leader and are supposed to be, according to the constitution, removed from politics. But those Guard commanders who served during Khatami's reformist years appear to have been influenced by his philosophy of what an Islamic democracy should look like—a society that allows independent thought and criticism and that sees no conflict in that with Islam. As such, Alaie's more creative thinking, which was not on display at the conference but which he exposed months later in a newspaper article, got him into hot water with the authorities, and his house was besieged by Basij protesters. He crossed a red line, apparently, by seeming to compare the political situation in Iran today with that preceding the fall of the shah, warning the authorities, and therefore the Supreme Leader himself, against making the mistakes that the shah made in creating an oppressive atmosphere that was ripe for revolution.

Alaie was forced to apologize for his impudence, explaining, of course, that he had been misunderstood. Yeah, *right*, just misunderstood. The fact that many Iranians, pro- and antiregime, privately agreed with him (*privately* being the operative word)—a regime stalwart who lived in a secure compound of senior Revolutionary Guard commanders—mattered little to the state.

Alaie's ill treatment made me think back to the time of the shah, and how things have changed and how they have stayed the same. One of my uncles, a deputy prime minister in the 1970s, had once given an interview expressing himself on a matter of foreign policy that the shah didn't like. The problem was not the opinion itself, which was mostly in line with the shah's and the regime's, but the fact that he had dared express an opinion at all. He was summarily fired and declared persona non grata by the regime, but his house wasn't surrounded by thugs, nor was he or his family threatened, as Alaie and his were. *Plus ça change*, in the political culture of Iran.

That said, the range of opinions expressed in Iran under the Islamic regime is much broader than it was under the shah, and there are far more competing political factions today, all state-approved of course, but crossing certain red lines can result in much worse than a "you'll never work in this town again" reaction from the state, as presidential candidates Mousavi and Karroubi sadly discovered after serving their beloved regime for thirty years.

I would sometimes daydream at these political conferences, lulled into a virtual unconsciousness by the stream of facts and statistics that so many of the speakers liked to spew, trying to impress one another and validate their own importance, as Iran's elite are wont to do. I would also stare—again, not considered impolite in Persian society—at the attendees around the big conference table and in the surrounding seats. There sat Ali Jannati, the son of the octogenarian Ayatollah Jannati, that fiercely antireform mullah, one of Khamenei's closest and most loyal advisers, who seemingly hasn't aged a day since well before the revolution—an Iranian Dorian Gray of sorts, and the butt of Iranian jokes. His son looked fit but not young, and I wondered if he was there to report back to his father or the Supreme Leader, and also if, thirty years later, he would look the same as he did on this day. The father was a staunch opponent of Khatami and of any liberal views even before the Green Movement, while the son served in the administration as an ambassador, which only made me realize how different Iran was prior to Ahmadinejad, when the concept of bipartisanship actually existed. Under Khatami, probably for the first time in recent Iranian history, the regime could reasonably argue, despite the human rights abuses that existed, that there was some modicum of democracy in the republic.

In the audience were reporters, too, furiously scribbling notes while they also taped the sessions with their phones or with mp3 recorders. Every newspaper would send one, usually an earnest cub reporter, a far cry from the idle and rich young men and women we saw in the uptown cafés. A fair share of university students were present too; they and the reporters both sometimes approached me at the end of the session to see if they could interview me. I was in their eyes an interesting person: someone who lived abroad and had been critical of the regime, yet still ventured to Iran and even to Iranian Diplomacy conferences. I always had to decline, saying I was not permitted to engage in any journalism, including giving interviews where I might express my views.

One woman reporter, her hijab properly covering every strand of hair but her stylish manteau a sign of less-than-strict piousness, asked me repeatedly, at every conference, when I might be willing to talk to her. When I finally said, "After I return to New York," she said, "Then can you leave soon, please?" She laughed and apologized for her inhospitable statement. But I didn't flatter myself that I was so much in demand: few Iranian American writers, other than the handful strongly supportive of the regime, are willing to talk to the Iranian media or are even accessible to it. Scarcity breeds demand, particularly in the fearful Iran of today.

Standing-room-only gatherings at Iranian Diplomacy and other forums point to Iranians' popular preoccupation with foreign policy, since, as is not the case in the United States and to some extent in Europe, it has a direct impact on ordinary people's lives, even in the absence of conflict or war. Their perceptions are colored not just by the conspiracy theories Iranians are so fond of, but also, in a few cases, by willful ignorance. To my astonishment, nothing of importance—the killing of Osama bin Laden, the nuclear crisis, the Arab Spring, and especially what was going on in Syria, not even the Murdoch hacking scandal—was immune from a grand conspiracy theory or, on occasion, just ignorant appraisal. At a roundtable discussion at *KhabarOnline*, the Larijanis' media outlet, I had difficulty persuading the attendees (university graduates and professors all, and otherwise very bright) that Rupert Murdoch was not Jewish, and I struggled to understand why it would even be relevant to the hacking scandal going on in Britain. Nor could I convince some that the United States and Israel might not have planned the Syrian uprising, or that there might not be a whole lot more to bin Laden's death than met the eye. And yes, I did believe that Osama was indeed dead as a doornail and not hidden in some prison somewhere by team Obama, as some Iranians suspected without being able to give one really good reason why.

But conspiracy, and the concept that there is always something hidden in any news we hear, is not just an obsession of ordinary Iranians; it's part of Iran's political culture. Understandably so, since for Iranians conspiracy theories have often proven, years later, to be true, as most famously with the 1953 coup, which Iranians always believed was a Western conspiracy but which the United States did not fully admit to until well after the fall of the shah.

That most Iranians, and even those in the leadership (of any political persuasion), remain forever suspicious of foreigners and the Western media, and on guard for plots against Iran, has contributed to a paralysis of sorts when it comes to repairing relations not just with America but with perceived rivals and enemies everywhere. The stream of Wikileaks releases while we were in Tehran that revealed the antipathy of Sunni Arab leaders toward Shia Persia were fodder for the political elite, and for many ordinary citizens, too; the revelations were simply confirmation for those who had never believed that Iran could trust even its fellow Muslim states, rather than a sign that perhaps their own mistrust and sense of superiority might be fueling the antipathy.

Later in the year, though, I found myself agreeing with most Iranians, regardless of where they stood politically, that the alleged Iranian plot to assassinate the Saudi ambassador to the United States at a Washington, D.C., restaurant was not based on reality. Everyone was incredulous. It was not that Iranians didn't believe their regime was capable of assassination or that it would hesitate to kill a perceived enemy; rather, they didn't believe the regime was that stupid. Most thought it yet another case of there being more to the story than met the eye. Persian nationalism, which is loath to admit incompetence in the nation's military and security complexes, was at the forefront of the reaction; and nationalism, even extreme nationalism bordering on jingoism, is very much a part of the culture, political and otherwise.

Many journalists in the United States agreed that the plot appeared to be outlandish, and their doubts about the Obama administration's account of it made the rounds in the Iranian media as well as in private conversations. Western governments assigned blame to the Qods Force, the foreign expeditionary division of the Revolutionary Guards headed by General Qassem Soleimani, a shadowy figure dubbed by some (including a senior U.S. official in Iraq) the real-life Keyser Söze, the villain in the 1995 film *The Usual Suspects*; but Iranians, even those who despised the Guards for their role in the 2009 crackdown, defended Soleimani, who was considered one of the brightest and most accomplished men in the leadership. "I'd give my blood for him," Sadegh Kharrazi told me, after speaking to him on the phone about the plot. "He is as incredulous as we are about this, and tells me the Guards don't even have anyone by the name the Americans claim." And Mohammad Khatami, who Soleimani served under, told me he was the most knowledgeable and professional official he had come across during his presidency, while his brother Ali told me that Khatami's administration relied more on Soleimani for expertise on the region than on the Foreign Ministry, or the ambassadors based in Afghanistan or Iraq, where Iran's national interests were critical, regardless of domestic politics. That he would be behind the farcical plot described by Eric Holder, the U.S. attorney general, beggared belief.

It was perhaps a little odd, though, and not a question of "going native," that Karri, an American from the Midwest, would decry the political situation in Iran but defend the country against American and Western accusations. She was initially distressed at the news of the plot, telling me that it concerned her that things between the United States and Iran were getting worse by the day, and that she was feeling less and less confident that the animosity between the two countries wouldn't lead to armed conflict and that we, or more precisely I, mightn't get caught in the middle. She agreed with Iranians, and many Americans back home, who thought the accusation simply an attempt to paint Iran as evil in preparation for a potential war. But this, I realized, was one of the strengths of the regime: as long as it defended Iranian interests, as long as it defined its relationship with the outside world as nationalistic, as one where it was defending the people's interests and not just its own, it would enjoy some measure of support even among those who hated it and even as so many internal factions fought over the urgent questions of what it meant to be an Islamic Republic, and whether Islam should play much of a role in the governing of the country.

Throughout our stay, I vacillated between deep pessimism over the future of Iran, despairing that peaceful change could ever come to my country, and hope. Hope that perhaps I was too old, or too removed from Iran, even as I lived there, to recognize Iranians' determination to bring about a change that would finally realize the hundred-year-old dream of a truly representative government, even if that government or regime would not be to my specific liking. I'd be pessimistic when I saw youth who seemed more preoccupied with leaving Iran than with staying and working to effect change. I'd be optimistic when I spoke to reformers, or to young friends, like the one who had been warned to be a "good boy," who believed they would outlast any dark period in Iranian politics. For personal reasons, I was saddened that Khatami might not be a significant agent of change, and that he might not outlast the ayatollahs who had turned on him; and in a strange way I admired his nemesis, President Ahmadinejad, not for his views or his policies, but for his courage and his determination to be a part of whatever changes would come to Iran.

Ahmadinejad was indeed determined to be a participant in the cultural evolution, political and otherwise. To the delight of the media and conversationalists all over Iran, he continued to battle other conservatives who were less socially liberal than he (whatever his motives), like a boxer almost down for the count who nevertheless always seems to have the energy to get back up, bloodied perhaps but still sure on his feet, for one more round. Neither Ahmadinejad nor even the Persian annus horribilis were going to go away quietly for the leadership of the republic, not if he had anything to do with it. At one meeting between the Supreme Leader and the "three powers"—

the executive, the judiciary, and the legislative—Ahmadinejad showed up with a file under his arm, according to someone who was present. He was under continual fierce attack, his aides were threatened with arrest (some were subsequently imprisoned), and his political capital had sunk to an all-time low; he had already pronounced, obliquely, that he had his own "red lines" that the regime must not cross, including going after his cabinet members and closest allies.

And now he told the Larijani brothers, who represented the other branches of government, that should he or his top aides find themselves out of a job or in prison, then the files he was holding, containing information about foreign bank accounts, details of children living in the West, real estate holdings inside and outside Iran, and the like, would be made public. The first file, he said, looking straight at Ali Larijani, the speaker of Parliament, who had the power to impeach him, is *yours.* Yes, to understand political Iran, you have to understand the culture: the traditional culture—unquestioning of authority, distrustful of strangers and foreigners, unwavering in loyalty to the state's interests—that determines the elite's behavior, and the culture of the Tehran street, which Ahmadinejad so perfectly represented. And street culture, more of a constant in Iran than any other, is always going to be a part of Persian culture, no matter how it evolves.

Shaban Jaafari, known as Shaban Beemokh or Shaban "the Brainless," was a street tough, a *laat,* who had been instrumental in gathering other *laats* to demonstrate in the streets, with clubs and other weapons, for the return of the shah after his flight to Italy in 1953, when Mossadeq was at the height of his democratically elected power. As much as the generals and politicians who conspired with the CIA and MI6—which provided the cash needed to pay the *laats*—he was responsible for the success of the coup that brought the shah back to his Peacock Throne. Later, after the Islamic Revolution forced Jaafari into exile to California, he is said to have remarked, "We *laats* made a coup and handed power over to the intellectuals, while you intellectuals made a revolution and handed power to the *laats*." He wasn't entirely wrong, if one considers the political culture surrounding the presidency of the street tough named Mahmoud Ahmadinejad. But the *laats* of 1979 are today really the elite *apart* from Ahmadinejad, the ruling class who seem to have bought into the unquestioning political culture that Khatami insists must change. It is ironic, then, if not yet another paradox, that Ahmadinejad, the figure who sparked a searing conflict within the regime, may one day be also thought of as the person who sparked the change, when it properly comes, in the political culture of the Islamic Republic.

12

HOME

"What are we going to do about fruit when we go back to New York?" Karri and I wondered. We certainly didn't mean the fruit for guests, the pretty, imported fruit that is set out in bowls in every Iranian living room, next to small plates and cutlery. No, we meant the sometimes bruised local fruit, the only kind we bought and that our greengrocer would pick out for us, in our rhetorical question, which we wondered aloud more often the closer we got to the end of our stay in Tehran. Tasty as the fruit was, I suspect we asked the question as a way of expressing sadness that our adventure was coming to an end, and that we would actually miss Iran, despite all the things we didn't enjoy about life in Tehran and the oppressive political atmosphere that affected us probably more than the average citizen. I would miss Iran more than Karri, naturally, but we also wondered if Khash would miss it, or miss the attention he received from strangers, the hugs and sweet talk he experienced every day, and yes, even the fruit, which he loved and which, as we expected, he is now much less fond of back in Brooklyn.

I reflected on how the way my son started his life in some ways mirrored how I'd started mine. I was born in Tehran but left at eight months of age for the English-speaking world; he was born in New

York and left at eight months of age for the Persian-speaking world. My awareness of language, Farsi at home and English outside, was the opposite of his experience—English at home and Farsi everywhere else, some of which he understood by the time we were ready to leave. *Dast-bedeh*, "Let's shake hands," and *Beeya*, "Come here," the refrain of our doormen every day, would have him running to them. He spoke his first words, *baba* (Persian for "dad") and *mama*, which he first pronounced as "ba" and "ma," in Tehran, and he took his first steps in an apartment in Tajrish; mine too had been spoken and taken abroad.

He was fascinated by the cats that roamed the streets, alleys, and *joobs* of Tehran and occasionally took up residence in apartment building courtyards like ours, or in the gardens of houses where residents fed them. That fascination wouldn't remain with him long, but it was a part of Iran—for most Iranians, the concept of animals as pets is alien—and I was glad of it. My own first pet of sorts was a stray kitten that had wandered into my grandfather's garden one summer when we were vacationing in Iran. My brother and I quickly adopted it, naming it Doody (for its color, gray), feeding it and playing with it, until the day it decided it would move on to greener, or more enticing, pastures, exactly as the cats in Iran do today.

I also reflected on whether, after leaving this time, I would ever be able to return to the country of my birth, and whether Khash would ever come back, with or without me. A close friend said to me that he was shocked that I had come to Iran to stay this long, and that I had been foolhardy; our stay had, as he said, *be kheyr gozasht*, "passed mercifully," but I shouldn't think of returning for a very long time. While we were there, my father in London talked to us on Skype every day, and if he couldn't reach us, sometimes because the Internet or the VPN or both weren't working, he would call on the cell to make sure we were still okay. At least under a strict dictatorship, he later told me, you know where you stand, but in the Iran of today, you never know who'll come after you. He was right, of course, but I couldn't worry too much about it, even though I knew people who had spent time in prison for lesser offenses than my writing and my commentary in the U.S. and British media.

I felt a little guilty, actually, for abiding by the law, for not speaking out while in Iran, since unlike many of my compatriots I had a platform, if I chose to avail myself of it, from which I could rail against injustices. Injustices like the imprisonment of Nasrin Sotoudeh, the lawyer separated from her young children for no apparent reason other than her defense of civil rights activists. Or the unjust fate of Haleh Sahab, a democracy activist exactly my age who had been furloughed from Evin to attend her father Ezatollah's funeral, where she was beaten by Basij forces and died on the spot. My cousin Ali had driven to the funeral but had been surrounded by the Basij as he drew near. "Do you want us to smash your car right here?" they asked him, rather less politely than it sounds. "No thanks" was his reply, and he turned around and left. He drove a brand-new Lexus, after all. And I needed to stay out of jail for selfish reasons, too, if only to ensure that my short time with Khash—short because of my age—would not be cut down further.

Still, I wondered about my self-preserving silence in the face of injustice. There were countless such stories of injustice, but none of them seemed to matter to ordinary Iranians. Was I like them now? We had a life in Iran, and we were mostly concerned about the same things others were: what to eat every day, the health and welfare of our child, where to find a little respite from the daily routine, how much money was in our bank account, and how we'd replenish it. We lived better than the vast majority of Iranians, yes, but if this was my home, then shouldn't I be playing a part in making it better? No, I was surely more of an intruder in my country, no matter how much I felt at home, with my American wife and American child, one who might learn some Farsi but would grow up American. Even my pen was of no use here.

Yet I continued to feel that I was home. If anything, Iran is a land of contradictions, and Iranian-ness a mess of contradictory emotions. During our trip to Dubai, even on our sightseeing excursion to Yazd and Esfahan, I had felt twinges of guilt for embarking on pleasure journeys, not so much for having the luxury of being able to take them, but for taking them *at this time*. I felt a little guilty, too, when I'd see a war veteran, someone who had defended his country—I hadn't even done my national service, having been exempted from it a couple of decades later due to my advanced age; or when I'd see soldiers in uniform, nothing like the security forces, who would stand in line at the bakery to take a *sangak* or two and were unfailingly polite and respectful of their civilian counterparts, some soldiers even offering me, their elder, a seat on the bus. If war ever came, I reflected, it was these boys, mostly conscripts, who would fight and die, while I would be safe in New York, pontificating on the injustice of it all. Life is shameful indeed.

If I was ashamed of myself, though, I was proud of Iran. Proud of my fellow Iranians for accepting my family as their own, proud that Karri had found my country to be so very ordinary in so many ways, and proud that despite the difficulties of life in the Islamic Republic, a life that so many, especially young people, seemed to dream of escaping, it was hard to find suffering on a scale that both Karri and I had witnessed in other countries. When we had returned from our short sojourn in Dubai, walking through the airport in Tehran felt not all that different from how I feel landing at JFK or La Guardia. Throughout my adult life, I had always felt myself to be Iranian and American in equal measures, but I had never really felt that Iran, the country itself, was my *home*. As a child visiting for summer or Christmas holidays, I'd felt it was my parents', really my *grand*parents', home and not mine—my home was a rented apartment in some foreign country or an embassy-owned dwelling in Washington or Tokyo. To live in Iran, with an apartment of my own, and to share it with my wife and son, was a little disorienting at first, for I had never imagined that I would even visit, let alone live in Tehran, for many years after the Islamic Revolution.

But the nagging sense of belonging somewhere else remained with me all along. I would have dreams in which I somehow arrived in Tehran but couldn't figure out how to leave, waking up in a panic sometimes at the thought of being stuck in a country that I desperately wanted to be part of but also wanted to be able to escape. My status as a dual citizen today gives me that advantage over the vast majority of my fellow countrymen who live in Iran: I can leave anytime, subject to the fancy of various intelligence agencies, of course, but a comforting thought nonetheless. But it was different now. This time, walking through the corridors with other Iranian travelers, even though I worried a little about passport control and the ever-changing lists of undesirable Iranians it maintained, I felt like I belonged.

The flight from Dubai that day had been full, and we dutifully stood in the line snaking around passport control, me holding Khash in my arms. Unusually, the line for foreigners was long, too, although only a quarter as long as that for Iranian nationals. As we got close to the inspection booth, the officer working the foreigners' line left his post, probably for only a few minutes. A German man standing next to us, frustrated by his slow-moving line began to complain loudly, telling the Iranian officials off, saying how incompetent they were. In English. The officer manning our booth finally yelled back, telling him to shut up. In Farsi.

It was presently our turn to approach him, and as I handed over our passports, he grumbled, "He can get lost, shouting in a foreign language. Who does he think he is? He can wait, or he can get lost." He scanned our passports, paused a moment after mine was swiped, and looked up. "So you're Hooman Majd!" he said with a slightly malicious smile, lips curling downward. Again, the signal, given to all Iranians under scrutiny of the Intelligence Ministry, that I was being monitored, was designed to make me feel a little less welcome in my home. The same treatment is doled out to other members of my family, especially the Khatamis, at least those who are still allowed to leave the country, the difference being that they have only the one home.

But accustomed to this act by now, I just nodded, and he handed back our passports. "Tell me," he said, before we walked off, "how do they treat Iranians in foreign airports? Not well, I imagine. The foreigner can wait until he goes blind." Or "blue in the face," as an English speaker might say.

My concern that my comings and goings were being carefully noted by the authorities—and that they wanted me to know that they were—was offset by my empathy for the immigration officer's irritation at the boorish foreigner. Would the German man have screamed at immigration in JFK, for example, where the wait for foreign visitors to enter the United States can be excruciatingly long? Or would an American scream at Heathrow, where Karri and I have both had to endure waits of over an hour to get through passport control? I actually felt like slapping the foreigner, telling him to respect my country—my home.

Getting into a taxi and giving the address of our own apartment, not a hotel or a friend's house, and telling the driver the best way to get there only added to my sense of being home. Karri, who had automatically whipped out her scarf and manteau and put them on in the plane, seemed placid even as she struggled with Khash, who decided, as he always did in Tehran cars, to stand on the seat and look out the back window. Karri wondered out loud if I had instructed the driver to take the best route, something she inevitably did when we got into a taxi in New York. Yes, in a strange way that I would never have imagined, she was home, too.

Beyond her struggles with the restrictions on dress and behavior, I was struck, and delighted, by how well Karri adjusted to Iran. I was truly shocked at how very much at ease she had become with life in

Iran when one day at a restaurant she ordered a salad for lunch and was told that by law they couldn't serve salads anymore, due to a cholera outbreak. *Cholera?* That would have sent her into a wild panic in New York, but here it seemed not to affect her much at all. She had the fish. The fact that restaurants were forbidden to serve greens of any kind due to a handful of cholera cases—which had come from Afghanistan, the government assured its citizens—was reassuring in a way, and it bolstered her belief that the government, awful in some other ways, was as health conscious as she was. (The smoke-free restaurants, cafés, and public spaces helped, too.) And that was saying a lot. What, she wondered, were we supposed to do with the *sabzi*, the greens that we bought from sidewalk vendors and produce stands? If we could even find any, for a lot of sellers, the *sabzi-foroush*, would stop selling greens, I told her. But then we would just have to wash them more thoroughly than before. Or cook them, as the government recommended. The cholera scare—and it was more of a scare than anything else—lasted a few weeks. But before it was officially over, *sabzi* was again available in the markets and on the street, and slowly the restaurants started serving salads again. What was more surprising to me than her initial reaction was her asking, every time we ate out, if the salads were back on the menu, without knowing for sure if the danger had passed. I guess she had her amulet with her, and in Iran, of all places, she was at ease.

The concept of home has always been amorphous and indistinct for me. As a child, I knew home only to be where we lived, which changed every few years because of my father's career; I also knew that Iran was the real home of my family, albeit one I didn't know. As an adult, the question "Where are you from?" has always confounded me a little, since the answer implies having real roots somewhere, which despite my strong attraction to the country of my birth, I'm not sure I have. Anywhere. The struggle for me—feeling like an interloper in a society, Iran's, that I have no right to intrude upon while also feeling a strong emotional connection to it—actually makes me feel more at home there, not less. Mainly because the emotional connection is largely, if not entirely, due to Iranians' attitude toward any other Iranian: whether you (or they) like it or not, you are one of them.

That is something I've never completely felt anywhere else, except at times in America. Years ago, when I was in the music business, somehow the subject of Iran came up in a conversation with some colleagues. I warmed to the subject, and one person asked me how I knew so much. "Because I'm from Iran, of course!" I replied. "Where did you think I was from, with a name like Hooman?"

His response: "California?"

I was amused of course, by his thinking that a strange name had to have been bestowed by Californian hippie parents, but it did make me feel one with America.

Still, walking the streets of Tehran, pushing my son in his stroller, also somehow feels right and not just exciting and an adventure; the smells of the city, the air in the parks, the interactions with shopkeepers, even the yelling matches with drivers, especially those who like to drive backward at high speed down alleys, ignoring pedestrians in their way, all feel wonted and part of who I am.

On my first visit to Iran in 2004, after a thirty-two-year absence, and after the nightmares of not being able to leave had finally disappeared, I tried to find the street my grandfather's house had been on, the house where we spent some summers, the house where my mother was born over eighty years ago. I knew it had been torn down very soon after the revolution; my mother had made one quick trip to Tehran to sell it when her mother died, and I expected that an apartment block would stand where it once stood, on a corner of a street and a tree-lined alley with a deep *joob* running along one side (the bane of drivers, including my father, who I remember cursing after dropping the front wheel of his used powder-blue 1961 Renault Dauphine car into it one day). I thought the little deli might still be there, as so many delis from yesteryear still are in Tehran, which sold everything a little boy would want, from *adams-e khorous-neshan*, "Rooster" brand chewing gum, to sodas, nuts, chocolate, and little plastic toys. I hoped that finding the street would jog my memory, that I'd feel a stronger connection than ever to the soil, to the mud walls, and to the air of the city.

My family in Iran naturally all remembered the house well, but no one had any idea how to get there. Highways crisscrossed the city that didn't exist when anybody I knew had last gone there; the names of the streets had all changed, mostly to the names of martyrs of the Iran-Iraq War, and sometimes more than once, presumably because a more important young man had been martyred; and the neighborhood, which had been chic enough when my grandfather bought the house before my mother was born there, was now deep in the heart of downtown, not quite South Tehran but pretty close, a neighborhood where no one ventured anymore unless they had specific business there.

Nevertheless, I went with a friend to investigate, taking a taxi to the closest major street that still did exist, then walking around hoping to stumble onto something familiar. Apartment buildings were everywhere, four- and five-story blocks that were as ugly as they were poorly constructed, but the alleys and the *joobs* were there, too. Turning corner after corner, something would ring a bell, and a few times I was sure I was on the right street, but couldn't verify it.

We stepped into a shop and asked. Ayatollah Assar? Yes, one old man remembered my grandfather but couldn't place the house. Was I his son, the one who was in government once? No, I told him, that's my uncle, who escaped Iran in 1979 and has never come back, as much as it is his strongest desire.

We continued to explore the neighborhood, and my friend Kaveh, who has lived in England most of his life, actually found *his* grandmother's house, still intact, or at least he thought it was her house, on a street that he declared recognizable the minute we stepped into it. The smell of the neighborhood, though, the smell of the remaining mud walls that hadn't been torn down, the *joob*, the trees—it was familiar. I was saddened that I couldn't find the street where I had had such happy memories, but I consoled myself that maybe I had walked on it without knowing it, and when I returned to my hotel uptown, I thought maybe it was better that the house and even the street weren't there. Reality could not possibly rival a childhood memory, and my memory was intact, if rose-colored. That memory was one of the things that had kept me connected to Iran, and if it was disturbed, who knew how I would feel? Not finding the house also kept me somewhat rootless—now there truly was nothing for me to directly claim as mine.

And in a strange way I felt relieved. The house my father grew up in in Yazd, which I saw on that same trip, meant little to me, as I had never been there before, although I did rather enjoy imagining my father, the stern but loving man who had forced me to get on a horse at age three, himself playing as a child in the unchanged garden. But those were my father's roots, in Yazd and Ardakan, not mine. And when I had Khash with me in Iran, as much as I wanted to walk down the alley of my childhood with him, go to the deli I once frequented, ask for a Cooka, as Coke was called, and buy him a toy whistle or a bag of balloons, I knew it would mean something only to me, and never to him, not even if I showed him photographs when he grew to adulthood. The only meaningful thing to him then would be that his father had had this inexplicable connection to, and love for, this far-off land, and that he had once dragged his wife and infant son to live there for a year.

My sense of being home was barely colored by the security state we lived in, although I was reminded of it every time I met a friend or relative who was in any way politically active. I tried to imagine how the security state, much more tangible now than on previous visits, compared to the one at the time of the shah, when SAVAK agents were presumed to be lurking in every corner ready to inform on you, even in one's own home. People still speak up, complain, and even curse the authorities in public, in a way that would have been unimaginable forty years ago.

And not that it would strictly qualify as vocal political dissent, but in a state where Islamic values *are* political, a neighbor on our street, populated with religious families, had a dog that yapped away all day, oblivious to the fact that the state frowns on dog ownership. Signs at park entrances inform the public that dogs are not allowed, and while we were in Iran, Parliament even threatened to propose a bill outlawing dogs altogether. Of course Parliament did no such thing, predisposed as it is to bombast and bluster, and the veterinary clinic at Parkway and Vali Asr, where the Basij and security forces like to gather under a bridge to harass and sometimes leer at female drivers, was able to keep its conspicuous billboard, a large photograph of a pet dog, visible to millions a day.

A dog-owning acquaintance in Tehran, disgusted with the way they are treated in Iran—if they're not the pets of the upper class, that is—once said to me, "Churchill said you can judge a civilization by the way it treats its animals," condemning not just the regime but his own people, too.

My *ghoroor*, or pride, got the better of me. Yes, I told him, but Churchill would have done better to worry less about the treatment of dogs by wogs and more about the treatment of those wogs by his empire. We Persians are not perfect, not even close by any stretch of the imagination, but I couldn't bear for my culture to be criticized, least of all by an Iranian anglophile, and in Tehran of all places, the city of my birth. Yes, this was home, and Iranians were my people, too.

Before the revolution, the shah had dogs himself, Doberman pinschers actually, befitting his personality, and in that time there was no personal behavior, especially un-Islamic, that would get one into trouble with the state—other than political activity not in line with the one-party (Rastakhiz) system, instituted by the shah at the same time that he changed the Iranian calendar from its Islamic origin to reflect 2,500 years of rule by kings of kings. Iran didn't feel like a security state to me then, or to anyone who just visited, because it wouldn't have crossed anyone's mind, except for some of the clerics and other revolutionaries, mostly communists and leftists, to even think of engaging in political activity, let alone talk about it.

Today, everyone engages in political talk, and many in activity, even if it is online or only anonymous. The state cannot arrest them all, but it can intimidate in a way the shah didn't need to. The Green Movement is a perfect example: two years after the movement erupted on the streets, the regime was still pressuring its subjects to disassociate from it. "Don't be fooled by this," a friend told me many times, waving his hand in a circular motion, as we drove from our apartment in his car around Tajrish Square to some destination or another. He meant the bright sunshine, but also the busy shoppers, hawkers, kids running behind their mothers, the packed cafés, and the complete sense of normality one felt. "It's really quite dark," he said, "and we're very much in a security state." It didn't really affect us on a daily basis, just as it didn't affect the millions of Tehranis like us who ventured out every day, to work, to shop for necessities, or to play, and it affected other cities and rural areas even less. But it was there, and we knew it.

The security state had virtually no effect on visiting Americans, despite the lingering, even intensifying, conflict between the United States and Iran about everything from the nuclear issue to Iran's support for Hamas and Hezbollah, to its overt support of Bashar al-Assad of Syria, and to its actions in Iraq and Afghanistan, all of which the Iranian leadership interpreted to mean that the United States was hell-bent on changing the regime. But no state authority ever batted an eye at the fact that we were dual citizens, and Americans in Iran rarely felt threatened; not journalists like Ann Curry and Fareed Zakaria, who visited while we were there, and not my friends the writer Alan Weisman and his artist wife Beckie Kravetz, who also traveled around Iran unmolested while we were there. We had breakfast with them at a lovely outdoor café while their interpreter and guide, a young man who may have been an informant, willing or unwilling, for the Intelligence Ministry nevertheless kept his distance—a good two blocks away. And not Karri, who would surprise people when she told them she was American, not German as they assumed, and would elicit great empathy and admiration from almost everyone she met, including chador-clad women on the bus who wanted to strike up a conversation with the unlikely foreigner in their midst.

Toward the end of our stay in Tehran, as friends and some in officialdom were hinting that staying much longer could get uncomfortable with the tensions rising between Western countries and Iran, Christmas approached. We had planned to go to the United States for the holidays and then come back to Tehran after the New Year, but were now thinking that it might be best if we didn't. The assassination of the scientist and the more recent explosions at a military base, a comprehensive report in *The New Yorker* on U.S. covert activity by agents on the ground (which was widely read by regime insiders), Britain's sanctioning of Iran's Central Bank and the British embassy episode, and the accelerated pace of currency devaluation all contributed to a growing sense that as things got progressively worse, any suspicions that I might be an agent of the West could harden, with unpredictable consequences. (After arriving back in the States, a friend with close ties to U.S. intelligence told me that a very recent Iranian intelligence file, handed to the United States by Omani intelligence—Oman has close ties to both Iran and the United States—specifically named me as a U.S. intelligence operative. "They don't know which agency you work for, CIA or the Department of Defense, but I saw the file," he said, "and it's your name." A year in Tehran must've finally convinced the Iranians that I could be nothing but a spook.)

As a December chill descended on Tehran, with forecasters predicting another early snow, our neighborhood of Tajrish was busy with shoppers; most avoided the exposed alleyway stalls and instead strolled inside the attached mini-malls, as overheated here as they are anywhere in the United States. There were Christmas decorations in some windows—and a Christmas shop in one mall drew kids to its windows full of tree ornaments and plastic Santas—and no security forces dissuaded shopkeepers or their customers from celebrating or even recognizing a non-Islamic holiday.

The scene sharply contrasted with the Shiite passion plays going on inside and outside the bazaar, and with the thousands of black-and-green Ya Hossein flags fluttering outside virtually every street-side shop, signifying a devotion to the beloved Shia saint Imam Hossein, the justice-seeking grandson of the prophet who was martyred by the ruling and tyrannical caliph's Sunni army in Karbala. It was also now the Arabic month of Moharram and the season of Ashura, a commemoration of Hossein's martyrdom and the most solemn period in the Iranian calendar, which, being lunar like the Arabic, varies from the Western by a few days a year.

As ordinary Iranians, including me and Karri, went about our business, shopping for food in the bazaar or for clothes and household goods in the malls, the more pious attending mosques for mourning ceremonies, there was little indication that Iran was now facing a much deeper international crisis, with Western moves to tighten the screws on the regime. But outside any of the many *sarafi*, foreign exchange bureaus, people gathered on the street to watch flat-screen televisions displaying the almost minute-by-minute slide in the rial, which had held its value for most of the time we lived in Iran; and men and women gathered at the kiosks to buy dollars as a hedge against crippling inflation or just because they thought the government might soon run out of them due to new international sanctions against Iranian banks. I was there to change much coveted dollars into rials, about as rare a transaction as can be, for almost all exchanges were the other way around. But along with me and whatever tourists were present in Iran, the government was routinely pumping hundred-dollar bills into the economy in an effort to keep the rial stable. Still, in late 2011, confidence that the regime could withstand international financial pressure, particularly after the British government cut all financial ties with Iran, was at an all-time low.

To me, the slide in the rial (which subsequently accelerated in January and February) merely capped the Iranian leadership's annus horribilis (the Iranian annus ends in March), certainly for the Supreme Leader and President Ahmadinejad, but also for every politician in between. All had been at odds with one another in 2011 over seemingly every possible matter of state; no one had come out on top, and the Leader himself was still supreme but demoted in the eyes of many citizens. It had been an awful year for the Iranian people as well, and more anni horribiles were undoubtedly on the way. Toward the end of the year, the increased talk of war or military strikes on Iran raised anxiety in Tehran to levels I had never before witnessed: war over the nuclear program had always been the subject of chatter in Iran, but few people had taken the notion very seriously, and in fact in ordinary conversation with Iranians, war would often be referred to jokingly. In December, however, my optician, who has a wry sense of humor and who hosts a salon of sorts with locals—from wealthy to poor—every evening in his shop, captured the mood of the city when he said, after I asked him what he thought of all the talk of war, "*Boosh meeyad. Een daf-e boosh meeyad.*" "You can smell it. *This* time you can smell it."

It didn't matter if war came or didn't—and some people even said to me that they hoped it would and then be over with, so they could get on with their lives. What mattered was the anxiety, which I couldn't see abating anytime soon. It was weighing more and more

on Karri, too, convincing her that combined with all other fac-
tors, returning to Tehran after the New Year made little sense, even
though she found it hard to believe that there might actually be a
war. "The anxiety is enough," she agreed. After I reconfirmed our
flights back to New York, she was relieved when I told her that KLM,
which flew direct to Tehran but had to make a stop in Athens to
refuel on the way back to Amsterdam, had now started flying bigger
planes that could make the round-trip without refueling. (Iran had
stopped refueling European airlines in a tit for tat when European
countries stopped refueling Iran Air flights, turning a five-hour flight
into an eight- or nine-hour one, and with an infant, that was more
of a nightmare than it had to be. It was incomprehensible to many
Iranians how refusing to refuel a passenger jet that probably carried
Iranians less enamored of their regime than most would do anything
to pressure the government to change its ways.) At this stage in our
Iran adventure, Karri said, she was simply thankful that in this case
we would not be personally affected by the Iran-West conflict. Iran
was in some ways great, yes, and perhaps even a second home of sorts
where she had grown comfortable with the culture, but she was, I
knew, really looking forward to going home.

On Ashura itself, the black-uniformed security forces were out in
force in Tehran, swarming Vanak Square, Tajrish, and other major
intersections. Mourning processions continued there as they did every
year, predating the Islamic Revolution, with slowly marching self-
flagellating men, their chains falling on their backs to the rhythm
of drums and *noheh*, lamenting anthems. Scores of spectators par-
ticipated by beating their own chests or simply watched, as we did
near our apartment, Khash transfixed in his stroller. It was difficult
to say exactly why the security forces had been called out, for this
was what Ashura always was, and what it would always be, no matter
the regime in Iran. Was it because this year the authorities feared, in
light of the Arab Spring—or the "Islamic Awakening," as the Iranian regime preferred to call it—another spontaneous outbreak of

protest against the regime? There had always been a security presence at Ashura, but never like this, so that must have been the reason, but they needn't have worried.

Exile groups had once again called for protest via social media and various foreign-based Web sites, but on the days leading up to Ashura, no one I knew inside Iran, not even regime haters, seemed to pay any heed. "We're sick of those exiles telling us what to do," one person said to me. "Let them come here and do it themselves." I sympathized with the sentiment, and having finally lived as an Iranian among Iranians inside Iran, I realized that no matter how sincere, how genuinely concerned about the future of the country Iranians abroad might be, they could have little say in how, when, or even why the Islamic Republic would reform, change, or collapse under its own oppressive weight.

A couple of weeks earlier, in a driving rainstorm, I met my friend Jalal for afternoon coffee at the House of Cinema coffee shop, a place where intellectuals, pseudo-intellectuals, students, and ladies (and gentlemen) who lunch often gather. The billboard outside advertised Julian Schnabel's by-now-four-year-old *The Diving Bell and the Butterfly*, with Farsi subtitles; another, larger billboard across the alley advertised Masoud Dehnamaki's *The Outcasts 3*, a pro-regime comedy that skewered the opposition, the Green Movement and its supporters, and was a surprisingly huge hit in Iran. Asghar Farhadi's *Jodaeiye Nader az Simin* (*A Separation*) had also been a huge hit in the summer (and later won an Oscar), though presumably not with the same audience. That was Iran, or at least Tehran, I thought; two societies with conflicting social mores and political leanings living together, sometimes in the same families, the tension almost imperceptible but bubbling nonetheless—just as Farhadi showed in his film. (A Facebook campaign against *The Outcasts*, urging moviegoers to boycott it and see Farhadi's film instead, had no effect, except on those who were already Green.)

Another friend, a man who left Iran after the revolution, raised two sons in the United States, but returns often to Tehran alone, sometimes for months at a time, joined us. Jalal, the son of an ex-diplomat like myself but, unlike me, from an aristocratic family, had lived his childhood abroad and had been educated in England—he still has a perfect British accent—and at Georgetown Law, but he had returned to Iran years earlier and set up a law practice, married, and had two sons who went to Iranian public schools, learning their perfect English at home. We spoke about the political situation, about war, about sanctions that affected everything, including Jalal's practice, and about the United States and its presidential election coming up in 2012.

As we switched between Farsi and English, almost without realizing that we did, I wondered why Jalal, despite all the difficulties, despite his obvious secular outlook, and despite the fact that he could live anywhere he wanted, chose to remain in Iran, when so many people less fortunate than he yearned to emigrate. I asked him.

"Well," he said, pausing for a moment and then leaning slightly forward, "it's our country after all, isn't it?" Indeed, it is, a heart-breaking one, and one that I was about to abandon again, at that.

* TAMAM SHOD *

—

On October 25, 2012, my father, Nasser Majd, né Nasser Majd-Ardekani, passed away in London. In the last two weeks of his life, in hospital, he wasn't interested in much, other than tying up loose ends before his permanent departure from the world. He did, however, still show a keen interest in news of Iran, asking my opinion on a number of issues, including the ongoing internal political battles and what the intensified sanctions were doing to his country and to his people. It was a little ironic, but fitting and gratifying, I thought, that the man who had been my bridge to another world, the half that was a part of me but that I didn't know growing up, was now looking to me to be *his* bridge to that world that was always his.

Before his cremation, I received a handwritten letter of condolence from former president Khatami, who represents a regime my father sulked at, from exile, for thirty-three years, and who arranged a memorial service in Tehran that was attended by former ambassadors, reform politicians, and family and friends. I also received a condolence phone call from former ambassador and foreign minister of the shah Ardeshir Zahedi; the person who was the cause of my father's first sulk told me he had never known a more honorable or patriotic Iranian, that Nasser Majd was like a brother to him, and that I should think of him as my uncle. Perhaps his big sulks worked, after all, but my father probably knew that before he took his last breath.

ACKNOWLEDGMENTS

Special thanks to my entire family, naturally, but with thanks also to the following people: my agent Andrew Wylie and his associates at the Wylie Agency, Rebecca Nagel in New York and Luke Ingram in London; my editor Kristine Puopolo and her colleagues at Doubleday/Random House, Sonny Mehta, Bill Thomas, Daniel Meyer, Janet Biehl, and Michael Windsor; and my UK editor, Helen Conford, and her colleagues at Penguin. And to the Iranians and Americans without whom this book would not be possible (in no particular order): Ali Khatami, Seyed Mohammad Khatami, Amir Khosro Etemadi, Iman Mirabzadeh Ardakani, Sadegh Kharrazi, Mohammad Sadoughi, Mehrdad Khajenouri, Karan Vafadari, M.M., Afarin Neyssari, Ali Ziaie, Ali Attaran, Ken Browar, K.J., Majid Ravanchi, Davitt Sigerson, Ali Akrami, E.A.H., Glenn O'Brien, Kaveh Bazargan, Jalal Tavallali, and Michael Zilkha.